I Will Restore You
In Faith, In Hope, In Love

Volume II

I Will Restore You
In Faith, In Hope, In Love

Volume II

Queenship
PUBLISHING COMPANY
P.O. Box 42028 Santa Barbara, CA 93140-2028
(800) 647-9882 • (805) 957-4893 • Fax: (805) 957-1631

Library of Congress #: 97-65315

Published by:
    Queenship Publishing
    P.O. Box 42028
    Santa Barbara, CA 93140-2028
    (800) 647-9882 • (805) 957-4893 • Fax: (805) 957-1631

Printed in the United States of America

ISBN: 1-57918-072-8

Declaration

The decree of the Congregation for the Propagation of the Faith, A.A.S.58, 1186 (approved by Pope Paul VI on October 14, 1966), states that the **Nihil Obstat** and **Imprimatur** are no longer required on publications that deal with private revelations, provided they contain nothing contrary to faith and morals.

The author wishes to manifest unconditional submission to the final and official judgement of the Magisterium of the Church.

His Holiness, Pope Urban VII states:

"In cases which concern private revelations, it is better to believe than to not believe, for if you believe, and it is proven true, you will be happy that you have believed, because our Holy Mother asked it. If you believe, and it should be proven false, you will receive all blessings as if it had been true, because you believed it to be true." (Pope Urban III, 1623-44)

The Catechism of the Catholic Church **states:**

Pg.23, #67: "Throughout the ages, there has been so-called "private revelations," some of which have been recognized by the authority of the Church. They do not belong, however, to the deposit of faith. It is not their role to improve or complete Christ's definitive Revelation, but to *help live more fully* by it in a certain period of history. Guided by the Magisterium of the Church, the sensus fidelium knows how to discern and welcome in these revelations whatever constitutes an authentic call of Christ or His saints to the Church."

Acknowledgements

A debt of gratitude is owed to family and friends who support this work and dedicate themselves to bringing it to fruition through much sacrifice and prayer.

Without the guidance of the priest who is my spiritual director, this work would not be available to others. It would have remained a secret in my prayer journals. It was through him that the Holy Spirit moved to make these writings available for the broader Church. This is the fruit of your labor, Father. You have engaged in serious spiritual warfare to make it possible. I am most grateful for your spiritual guidance, example of prayer and service, teaching, priestly intercession and discernment. You have supported my family every step of the way. Your own life is a prayer in and for the Church and I thank you, kind shepherd.

I acknowledge with deep gratitude the support and prayerful intercession of the United Hearts of Jesus and Mary Prayer Group. Through everything, you have supported this work and helped me to keep going. So many of the messages were given in your presence. Thank you.

A special acknowledgement to M.H. for your time, talents, and sacrifice in typing this manuscript. You have a servant's heart and I am most appreciative.

Again, I acknowledge gratefully, Mr. Neal Hughes, for the execution and donation of the cover image. It is a blessing to behold and each time that I do, I realize what a gift you have given to us, to the Church by so beautifully portraying our greatest gift, the Blessed Sacrament.

To Queenship Publishing, a debt of gratitude is due your ministry, which touches the spiritual lives of countless souls. Thank you for believing and supporting this work from the beginning. Bob and Claire, your guidance and friendship are pure gift. Thank you and may God reward you.

Finally, I thank my husband, sons, father, mother, brothers, and mother-in-law. In my mother and mother-in-law, I have examples of women of faith who have suffered valiantly for the sake of the family. Through the joys and sorrows, your love and support means so much to me. Unto eternity, we will be a family. God has made it so.

Praise be to God from whom all good things come, through Mary, Mother of all families.

Dedication

To Saint Joseph
Guardian of the Universal Church and Families

Dictated by Our Lord, Jesus and Mother Mary

On February 18, 1998, at 6:15AM, quite suddenly, I felt the presence of Jesus and Mary right before me. They appeared standing beside one another. Jesus began to speak while Mary remained silent but nodding her head slightly in agreement and indicating, *"Do whatever He tells you."*

Jesus said: **Little one, dedicate this volume of locutions and reflections to St. Joseph, guardian of the Universal Church and families.**

It is to be a sign of the depth of prayer and spirituality desired by God within families. I am augmenting My Mystical Body by bestowing many divine graces upon the lay faithful. I am calling husbands, wives, mothers and fathers, brothers and sisters, children, to profound holiness through daily prayer and the sacraments.

I have chosen many victim lambs within the lay faithful whose sacrifice is an offering for the sake of families. It is necessary to build marriage and the family again upon that pure and gratuitous love that is dedicated to sacrifice.

Families are under terrible attack. I wish to support them by means of these messages. I will bless families who use these as a means of meditation and prayer. I wish to restore families because they are a community called to reveal, protect, and communicate love.

St. Joseph and Mother Mary are the special guardian intercessors for all the families of My Mystical Body. Holy families are needed for the restoration of the Church and the salvation of the world.

I am glorified by this work. Many graces flow from it. Thank you for your sacrifice. I love you. I am your Jesus.

Later, in the evening, Our Lady became present to me again and said: *The first volume of messages given through you were an invitation from God for conversion; a call to "**Come and See**," an invitation to intimacy.*

*The second volume of messages are an invitation to "**Come and Be**," a call to transformation in Christ; an invitation to embrace the cross and its purifying love, beckoning all to the unifying love of Calvary. It is the necessary step toward restoration and the resurrection. Peace. I am your Mother.*

Contents

Foreword

By Fr. Ignatius, S.T.L., S.S.L., Spiritual Director

I highly recommend this second volume of messages to priests and lay people alike. As a priest of thirty-five years, I have been enriched by witnessing and sharing in the spiritual journey reflected in these messages. The warmth and intimacy of Jesus and Mary's love radiates from them. Although the Church does not require us to believe in private revelation that would in some way "improve or complete Christ's definitive revelation" she does say that it may "help us live more fully by it in a certain period of history." (*Catechism of the Catholic Church*, pg. 67) Certainly in my priestly vocation, these messages have been of tremendous help in living more fully Christ's revelation of God as Love. In our period of history, love has lost its meaning. In the messages, we discover True Divine Love working in the life of a modern wife and mother.

Today, more than ever, we see the institution of marriage and the family being attacked on all sides. In the life of this victim lamb of the Lord, who has been given the name of "Grace" to protect her vocation, I have been amazed at the graces I have witnessed and the depths of suffering that she has been called to accept. Daily Mass and Holy Hour before the Tabernacle, Rosary, weekly confession, prayer group meetings, have enabled her to carry a daily cross of hidden suffering over a period of years. Constant personal prayer permeates her life: her heart and mind are ever turned towards the Lord.

The fact that she bears the cross without sinking into bitterness, hostility, anger, or revenge reveals the genuineness of her spiritual life and in someway seals the authenticity of her messages. Only God's grace and love enable her to live such a life of faith, hope, and love. An ever greater depth of spiritual courage and discernment, the fruit of the cross, have enabled her to meet the many and varied attacks of the evil one against her and the family. To study the contents of this book reveals the tactics of the enemy and how Satan attacks our spiritual life and our families.

The intercession, protection and support of a weekly prayer group has been very necessary to her spiritual journey. As a member of this prayer group, I have witnessed her gather strength through these prayer meetings to carry the cross. They are a protection from Satan and enrich her spiritual life. Mary's maternal love pleads for cenacles to be formed.

The immediacy of the messages given to fit the problems of today and the intense personal love expressed in them are a help to all the faithful but especially to any priest who is open to them. Scandals abound today and any priest who supplements his breviary and Mass with this book is truly being given grace for his mind and heart to be the pastor, the shepherd of souls. If the shepherd loses his way, woe to the sheep. He can do no better than add and use this book in his priestly vocation. Through this lay woman the dignity and value of intercessory prayer for the priesthood is emphasized. The sacrifices and prayerful intercession of the lay people for the priest of today is of inestimable value.

From the restoration of the family will come the restoration of the Church and through the Church, the world. The health of the domestic Church brings health to the universal Church and the world. May St. Joseph, the Guardian of the Church, to whom this work is dedicated, bless this work and all those who read and meditate over its content. May Mary, the Mother of the Church who suffers, nurtures, and pleads for us, unite us in the battle where her Immaculate Heart will triumph. In the Holy Spirit, she will lead us to the Eucharistic Reign of Jesus where all will be restored in faith, hope, and love.

I leave you with the words of St. Paul to the Ephesians (6:10-17) **"Finally, draw your strength from the Lord and from His mighty power. Put on the Armor of God so that you may be able to stand firm against the tactics of the devil. For our struggle is not with flesh and blood but with the principalities, with the** powers, with the world rulers of this present darkness, with the evil spirits in the heavens. Therefore, put on the Armor of God that you may be able to resist on the evil day and having done everything to hold your ground. So stand fast with your loins girded in truth, clothed with righteousness as a breastplate, and your feet shod in readiness for the gospel of peace. In all circumstances, hold faith as a shield to quench all the flaming arrows of the evil one. And take the helmet of salvation and the sword of the spirit, which is the word of God. With all prayer and supplication, pray at every opportunity in the Spirit."

Explanation of the Cover of the Book

On October 9, 1996, while praying the Rosary with my spiritual director, the following vision was received and Jesus asked that an image be drawn depicting the vision. Jesus also led me to the artist who would draw the image for the cover in fulfillment of His request.

During Father's meditation of the Resurrection decade of the Rosary, suddenly, I received a vision of St. Peter's Basilica in Rome. It was being raised up toward the heavens for all on earth to see. It had been thoroughly purified and made radiantly beautiful becoming a treasury attracting the whole world. The Light of the Holy Spirit overflowed the Mystical Bride of Christ and radiated outward through the windows and doors, which were wide open. From within, the Holy Spirit radiated out to the entire world, all people, and all nations.

Then the scene changed to the interior main altar of St. Peter's Basilica. The Dove of the Holy Spirit had wrapped His wings around a beautiful Gold Monstrance containing the Eucharistic Jesus. This was a gesture signifying the Spirit's protection of the True Presence of Jesus upon the altar. When the time arrived ordained by The Father, the Holy Spirit opened His Wings fully to reveal the glory of The Eucharistic Jesus present upon the altar. Brilliant light rays burst forth from the Blessed Sacrament and the Holy Spirit and all of creation received the grace of restoration in Faith, Hope, and Love.

On October 14, 1996, in prayer, Jesus indicated that the cover image should depict the Immaculate Heart of Mary, her pierced heart, near the Blessed Sacrament and within the altar area of St. Peter's signifying her maternal mediation.

Holy cards of the cover image are available from the publisher.

Introduction

I Will Restore You In Faith, In Hope, In Love, Volume II

Dictated by Mother Mary

On March 19, 1998, the Feast of St. Joseph

In the church after morning Mass and Holy Hour, I knelt down before the statue of St. Joseph and said a few prayers, mostly about my family. As I was walking away to leave the church, I heard St. Joseph say, "Child, return to your home and write. The Blessed Virgin, St. Mary, will speak to you. I, Joseph, bless you."

On the drive home I was tempted by the devil who presented many other things which needed my attention, suggesting that I do these first and write later. He is always tempting me to disobedience, trying to distract me with other things of the world. I rebuked him and went home to my prayer room and began to pray the Five Joyful Mysteries of the Rosary. I admit that I was very close to giving into the strong temptation to take care of other things first and pray and write later having a natural tendency to procrastination. The power of St. Joseph's words helped to overcome the temptation.

After praying the Five Joyful Mysteries, I entered into a prayer state for about one hour. When I awoke from this state, Our Lady dictated this message.

Dear child,

On this important feast in honor of my most chaste spouse, Joseph, I bless you, and through you, I wish to bless many, many souls.

Please write for all those who will take up and read these messages. So led by the Holy Spirit, there will be many hearts moved to open this book which is a treasury of grace to be distributed throughout the Mystical Body of Christ.

Dear children of God,

May the Peace of My Son, Savior of the world, be with you now and forever. Dear little children, I who am your Mother by the order of God's grace, have many graces to bestow upon you. But first, you must open your hearts.

Do not be afraid of prophecy. Authentic prophecy is a gift of the Holy Spirit and comes from God through a human vessel but does not originate from the human vessel. God is truly speaking to you through the Church, through Christ's Vicar, through the sacraments, through the faithful, humble and obedient cardinals, bishops, and priests and through the lay faithful. Throughout history, God has chosen simple but pure souls through whom He can give His timeless message of Love. Do not be surprised that the Most Holy Trinity speaks through an ordinary wife and mother today. This is God's way. He uses the simple and ordinary to confound those who think they are wise.

The messages that are coming to you are pure grace from heaven. If there are many messengers, it is because it is necessary. Heaven is trying to pierce through the darkness and chaos of your present age. Since this age is bombarded with evil, since many souls are falling into sin, since many are on the path to perdition, heaven is opening the floodgates of grace and through My Immaculate and Maternal Heart, mankind is being showered in abundance with every kind of help!

These messages are a reflection and witness of the continuing revelation of God's Love as revealed once and for all in the Gospels. They are a grace worthy of respect because they are both a catalyst and support for conversion.

Dear children, you have not yet understood that you are loved by God; that He is in your midst seeking complete union of heart. If you understood, you would not hunger for love in your heart and peace in your soul. If you had responded to God's Love, His thirst would be alleviated. Some have responded, most have not. There-

fore, God has sent many to speak to you of His Love and Mercy. It is urgent that you listen. The hour is late! If you continue as you are living now, few will see heaven.

You must learn to pray. These messages will help you to pray from the heart. You must convert daily. That is, you must grow in faith, hope, and love every day. You must not sin. The world is failing to acknowledge its sins. If you do not acknowledge sin, you cannot repent. Few ever say to God, "I am sorry for offending you." Yes, dear children, God is being offended at every moment of every day.

But there are generous souls on earth among the Mystical Body who appease the Father's justice. And the Presence of My Son Jesus in the Holy Eucharist preserves the world, which would otherwise self-destruct! The faithful souls who pray and sacrifice carry the cross in intercession of the salvation of the world.

Dear children, the Father, Son, and Holy Spirit are merciful unto every generation. And to your generation special graces have been given. These are meant to guide you through the decisive battle between good and evil. You are chosen to live in these decisive times of terrible spiritual darkness pierced by supernatural light. With this comes responsibility. You are the apostles of Divine Light meant to spread more Light. Please do not shun the Light and all that the Holy Spirit is doing in the world today. He must work through imperfect vessels because everyone is imperfect except God who is perfect.

Do not be afraid to take up and read a message book, which has passed through the test and discernment of a priest representing the Church. Pray to the Holy Spirit first. Ask Him to teach and guide you as you meditate on the messages. I will assist you to live the messages, if your heart is open to me.

You are free dear children. You can open or close your heart to God's grace. But I urge you to open your hearts now! This book will bring special graces to your spiritual life. As God has guided this ordinary messenger, He seeks to guide and bless you.

*The Father, Son, and Holy Spirit, the community of saints, and holy angels, are calling you to **"Come and See," then "Come and Be!"***

The earth will be restored in faith, hope, and love. This is God's Covenant. But you must decide to partake. Many things on earth must change first, and they will by the power of the Holy Spirit.

Therefore, in union of hearts, let us prostrate before God, our Father, and together let us cry out: "Come Holy Spirit! Restore creation that we may live as one family faithful to Your law of Love. Come Holy Spirit! Restore creation! Let the Eucharistic Reign of Jesus come through the Triumph of the Immaculate Heart. Come Holy Spirit! Restore creation! Live in my heart. Change my life. Then I will not be afraid. And I will live in the Truth. Amen."

*Dear children, Jesus has requested that this messenger remain anonymous to protect her vocation as wife and mother and to permit her to work in the Church as an ordinary lay woman. On this feast day, Jesus and I, Mary, together with St. Joseph, confer upon her the name of **Grace**. This will serve to help identify this work meant to bless many with heavenly graces.*

Thank you, beloved children, for opening your hearts to me. Allow me to bless you; to walk the journey with you.

*Dear child, I have thus dictated the **"Introduction"** for the second volume of messages. Thank you for your sacrifices. You suffer but heaven is with you. Persevere. Thank you for making the messages available to prepare hearts to receive Divine Love. It is by the power of Divine Love that restoration will come. I bless you, together with St. Joseph, in the name of the Most Holy Trinity. Be at peace. I love you. Your Mother*

The following day, Our Lady confirmed what was received at the prayer meeting when she said: *Please make this work available and affordable to as many as possible. And what proceeds from it should go to a non-profit charity or ministry within the Roman Catholic Church to assist more people to receive spiritual nourishment. Thank you for doing as I request. I am your Mother who loves you all.*

The Eternal Father

Asks that We Meditate on These Scriptures

On Sunday, March 22, 1998, at Holy Communion, I received an image of the heavens opening up. From the heavens I saw the

Eternal Father extend two arms outward. They were opened wide in a gesture of a welcoming embrace from a Most Loving Father.

Then He directed a most powerful outpouring of heavenly Divine Grace to draw the earth, all of creation, back toward His loving embrace. I saw that the globe of the earth began to draw closer to the embrace of The Father.

Then I heard the following interiorly: **Blessings and peace, My child. I, who am your Eternal Father, beckon all back into My loving embrace.**

I invite all to meditate upon the reading from the letter of St. Paul and the Gospel according to St. Luke regarding the Prodigal Son. Through these I will bless people with deeper knowledge and understanding of My Paternal Love and Mercy.

Come back to Me, My children. Your Eternal Father is calling you. Come back to Me. I love you.

Reading: 2Cor.5:17-21

"If anyone is in Christ, he is a new creation. The old order has passed away; now all is new! All this has been done by God, who has reconciled us to Himself through Christ and has given us the ministry of reconciliation. I mean that God, in Christ, was reconciling the world to Himself, not counting men's transgressions against them, and that He has entrusted the message of reconciliation to us. This makes us ambassadors for Christ, God as it were appealing through us. We implore you, in Christ's name: be reconciled to God! For our sakes God made Him who did not know sin to be sin, so that in Him we might become the very holiness of God."

Gospel: Luke 15:1-3, 11-32

"The tax collectors and the sinners were all gathering around Jesus to hear Him, at which the Pharisees and the scribes murmured, 'This man welcomes sinners and eats with them.' Then He addressed this parable to them: "A man had two sons. The younger of them said to his father, 'Father, give me the share of the estate that is coming to me.' So the father divided up the property. Some days later this younger son collected all his belongings and went off to a distant land, where he squandered

his money on dissolute living. After he had spent everything, a great famine broke out in that country and he was in dire need. So he attached himself to one of the propertied class of the place, who sent him to his farm to take care of the pigs. He longed to fill his belly with the husks that were fodder for the pigs, but no one made a move to give him anything. Coming to his senses at last, he said: 'How many hired hands at my father's place have more than enough to eat, while here I am starving! I will break away and return to my father, and say to him, "Father, I have sinned against God and against you; I no longer deserve to be called your son. Treat me like one of your hired hands."' With that he set off for his father's house. While he was still a long way off, his father caught sight of him and was deeply moved. He ran out to meet him, threw his arms around his neck, and kissed him. The son said to him, 'Father, I have sinned against God and against you; I no longer deserve to be called your son.' The father said to his servants: 'Quick! Bring out the finest robe and put it on him; put a ring on his finger and shoes on his feet. Take the fatted calf and kill it. Let us eat and celebrate because this son of mine was dead and has come back to life. He was lost and is found.' Then the celebration began.

Meanwhile, the elder son was out on the land. As he neared the house on his way home, he heard the sound of music and dancing. He called one of the servants and asked him the reason for the dancing and the music. The servant answered, 'Your brother is home, and your father has killed the fatted calf because he has him back in good health.' The son grew angry at this and would not go in; but his father came out and began to plead with him.

He said in reply to his father: 'For years now I have slaved for you. I never disobeyed one of your orders, yet you never gave me so much as a kid goat to celebrate with my friends. Then, when this son of yours returns after having gone through your property with loose women, you kill the fatted calf for him.'

'My son', replied the father, 'you are with Me always, and everything I have is yours. But we had to celebrate and rejoice! This brother of yours was dead, and has come back to life. He was lost, and is found."'

Messages

1. **8-4-95** Prayer Group Rosary
Blooming in Unity in the Immaculate Heart.

As we began to pray, Our Lady showed me a single rosebud of rare and exquisite beauty. The bud was closed, each petal folding perfectly together. Each one of us was represented as a petal on the rosebud. We were close together, one folding into the next. Then the rose began to open little by little, each one of us growing individually and collectively. The rose continued to grow more open, spreading its petals, its fragrance, and its beauty. The rose was exquisitely beautiful as it opened up completely. It spread much perfume, holy fragrance. All the while, this rose has existed within the garden of the Immaculate Heart of Mary. We were firmly rooted within the garden of her heart, by means of our consecration to Mary, and by means of the grace of God, which has nurtured us. We have been raised for God's glory and for a very special mission for the good of souls. Then Our Lady exposed her Immaculate Heart to us. There was so much grace and power that I could only observe her heart for a moment. It was almost overpowering. She said: *The power you experienced is the power of pure, unconditional, maternal love!*
Then she spoke:

My *dear little children,*
I have nurtured you for a long time. You have bloomed within the garden of my heart. In you, I rejoice. My joy is full when my children permit me to assist them. My joy is complete when my little ones respond to God's grace, seeking only His Divine Will. I implore you to go forward in faith, in love, with much trust, much courage, to carry out the work God has requested of you. I will

send my broken ones into your path. Like the rose that is in full bloom, completely open, please receive my broken children into your hearts, into your embrace. I will send them to you so you can assist them to bloom through love and prayer. God's grace is upon you so you can minister to the hungry and thirsty little ones. The gifts of the Holy Spirit shall be with you so you can be instruments of God's pure love. Each one of you shall stand secure as you embrace my children, teaching them as I have taught you. Each one of you is a vital part of the whole. The rose is beautiful when all the petals are together, in their proper place, in their proper function, each giving glory to God according to the way chosen by God. Each of you is a beautiful rose petal, and together you shall remain, forming one exquisite rose in my garden of love.

Dear ones, walk with me along the path of faith. The Church, and indeed the entire world, shall be restored to beauty. There will be peace, according to the Father's divine plan when love reigns in the hearts of His people. I have embraced you, nursed you, and raised you to be His willing instruments for the good of many souls. Do not worry that you will lose your unity or love for one another as you go forward to embrace other souls who are called to assist you in fulfilling God's plan. God has chosen souls according to His perfect Will. He will bring them into your path. Each has his unique role to fulfill. Many souls will come to know of God's Love and Mercy through your endeavors because they are born of the Divine Will. I will never leave you. You are beloved children of my Immaculate Heart. You are the fragrant rose of rare beauty, in full bloom in the garden of love, my heart. Please permit God to work through you. The work set before you is very vital for my peace plan and for the kingdom of the Divine Will. I bless you tonight and always. Peace, peace, peace. Love, love, love and pray, pray, pray. Your Mother

2. **8-4-95** Rosary, my home
Each Heart Should be a House of Prayer

Peace be with you my little ones.

I am pleased to be in your midst; pleased that you answered my call; pleased to gather you under my mantle, and most pleased to assist you to fulfill the Will of the Father. You cannot compre-hend the pain and suffering existing in the hearts of my children. Again, I implore you to assist me. Tend to the hearts of God's chil-dren. Each heart should be a house of prayer, a holy temple where God dwells, reigning in love and peace. I have taught each one of you, through the graces of prayer. Responding to grace, you have been transfigured into willing instruments of God's love and peace. I implore you, dear little ones, open your hearts to all God's chil-dren. Teach them as I have taught you, in love, through the graces of prayer. It is important that you remain pure of heart. Always acknowledge your poverty, so God may use your weakness to re-veal His greatness.

Little ones, building a house of prayer, a refuge for the faithful, is truly opening yourselves to receive God's children, your broth-ers and sisters. Love them. Pray with them, permit the Holy Spirit to flow through you. The Holy Spirit is truly in you, with you, guid-ing, teaching, raising you, in love and wisdom. Be attentive and responsive to His voice in your heart. Again, I remind you of the difficult time to come, a time of great trial for the Church, and a time of a true crisis of faith for all souls. God's children will turn to you. You have been prepared by grace. You have been formed by God to assist His people in their hour of great need. The Church will be restored, one soul at a time. Each soul shall be transformed by love. Then God's house will be restored to a holy house of love. Do not concern yourselves so much with the materials of a house of prayer. You are the "materials"; you are the foundation; you are the instruments. People will come to you for prayer, for healing, for comfort, for love. If you remain as the littlest, the poorest, God will work great miracles through you. The greatest miracle is con-version of heart; a soul transfigured into the image and likeness of the Most Holy Trinity.

Follow only the voice of the Holy Spirit. All is unfolding ac-cording to God's timing. Do not run ahead of the Holy Spirit. Do not worry. Do not doubt. The Holy Spirit goes before you to ready the way. Wait. Pray. Move only according to the Holy Spirit. Trust. God Himself will accomplish the work according to His perfect plan. The Father's Providence is over you. His Love and His Father's embrace is for all. Be at peace. Rejoice! God is using you to help restore His people to a holy people, to restore His Church to her radiant beauty and to restore the world to peace. His Majesty will prevail. His reign is at hand. Love transfigures, and His Love is everlasting. I bless you. I love you. Your Mother

3. **8-5-95** 7:30 PM Mass, Vigil of the Transfiguration
The Transfiguration

Following Mass, Jesus spoke. **It was My desire to fortify My disciples, Peter, James, and John, upon the Mount of Tabor. Transfigured, I revealed My glory. I wanted them to behold My victory. The truth of My glory was imprinted upon their hearts. It would mark them. It would sustain them. My Transfiguration fortified their faith. It foretold of My glory, the resurrection, the victory. It was a foretaste of their own victory in and through Me. The Father confirmed for them: "This is My Beloved Son in whom I am well pleased. Listen to Him!" This would sustain them when the Son of man and Son of God would lay down His life for the salvation of all.**

Today also, I am fortifying My chosen disciples. Today also, I reveal My glory in the souls I am transfiguring into My image and likeness. Like Peter, James, and John, your faith will be tested. I have forewarned you. It has been revealed to you. Signs, wonders and prophets have proclaimed to the world the great and terrible day of the Lord, the separation of the goats from the sheep. The Father confirms, "This is My Beloved Son in whom I am well pleased. Listen to Him." Today many prophets, apostles of these latter days, are proclaiming one message: Prepare, Repent, and Convert. I am today transfiguring the whole of My creation. My dominion is over all things!

On Tabor, My face shone like the sun; My garments became white as light. The face of the earth will shine like the sun, radiantly beautiful. Souls will mirror My image, becoming radiant as pure light. Divine Love is the light, which transfigures. Faith is the light that sustains. Truth is the unshakable foundation. The Word is life eternal. The Spirit is the trumpet blowing to the four corners of the earth. He is wisdom in depth; counse-

lor to the little ones. The Blessed Virgin Mary is the gateway to the transfigured world. I have thus foretold you. Prepare. My victory, your resurrection, is soon to come. Your groaning resounds to the heavens. Your groanings will be transfigured into love: love for God, love for one another. Then Creator and creation will melt into one united heart. As if you were on Mount Tabor with Peter, James, and John, you shall see My glory on earth and live. Those who live will repeat the words of Peter, saying: "Lord, it is good that we are here." I love you, the whole of My creation, with a tender, merciful love that is everlasting. Be transfigured into My image for your good and My glory. Your Jesus

4. **8-7-95** Tabernacle, 8:30 AM Mass
St. Martha

*Soul, you are before Me as Martha. There are many thoughts racing through your mind. You are concerned about many things. *Soul, I know each minute detail of your existence. It is good that you come before Me. Give to Me all your concerns. Please do not doubt. *Soul, My beloved one, you are today but standing on the rim of My Sacred Heart. Come My beloved, dive into the fathomless sea of My Love, My tender Sacred Heart.

I did as Jesus asked. Peace enveloped me. Love penetrated me. I sensed myself motionless as if simply floating effortlessly in the sea of His vast love, until I seemingly dissolved. I could no longer perceive where I ended and He began. When I awoke, I entered silence. I implored Jesus to help me to fulfill my duties with clarity and strength. I asked Him to increase my capacity to love everyone and to sacrifice for souls. I asked for the grace to integrate these graces into my daily life. My secular duties are more and more a penance.

Jesus said: *Soul, you are impatient. You are relying too much on yourself. Rely on Me only. Draw from Me everything.

Say to Me, "Jesus, please help take care of this - please help take care of that." I will do it for you. Do not analyze. Trust. I will never leave you. *Soul, I will not withdraw My voice from you. You will hear precisely when I give you to hear. I will not leave you deaf and blind. Nor will I withdraw My tender, loving grace from you. If you fall, I will bend to pick you up. Do not fear. Everything depends on Me, not you.

*Soul of My Cross, I alone know of your suffering. Thank you for your sacrifice. You have much difficulty and responsibility, yet you have much grace to carry your Cross. I uphold you. *Soul, we are one united heart of love. I breathe in your fragrance. I am pleased. I will give to you My unlimited riches. You are being adorned in white. Your hand is in Mine. We walk together in My garden of grace and beauty. Live in Me as I in you. Take My peace. I love you, *Soul. Jesus

5. **8-8-95** Rosary with Father, My home
The Pope, the Holy Spirit, and Jesus to His Priest

When Father "invited" Our Lady and the saints to pray with us, Our Lady was very joyful. When Father mentioned the saints, I immediately sensed the presence of St. Francis of Assisi and Blessed Faustina, with us as special intercessors.

When Father prayed for the Holy Father, I saw the following. The Pope was standing. There were religious (priests and nuns) with their hands around the Pope's feet and lower legs. They were trying very hard to "pull him down." The Pope's eyes remained fixed on Our Lady who stood before and above Him. She sustained him in this trial. From her issued forth rays of grace that poured into the Holy Father. From the Holy Father, I saw grace emitting like waves out to the entire world. Our Lady said: My *beloved son is my echo.*

As Father was praying, Our Lady was beckoning him to come with her. One hand of hers was held to her Immaculate Heart. One hand was outstretched to Father. She was calling him to "Come." She appeared joyful.

Then she spoke these words: *My beloved son and priest, it is very important that you dispose yourself to me and to the move-*

ments of the Holy Spirit. Pray always in union with my Immaculate Heart. I am truly with you, watching over you. I love you. Your Mother
Then I saw the following:
First, the globe of the earth.
Second, heavy clouds above the earth.
Third, I saw the heavens above the entire universe.
Fourth, I saw Our Lady standing between the heavens and the earth.
Fifth, I saw the heavens pour out "water" like sheets of water. I understood the water to be the Holy Spirit. The water fell to the earth only in the areas where there were no clouds to block the water. Wherever the water touched the earth, there were beautiful gardens in bloom. Where the water could not reach, it remained as dry wasteland. The clouds represented our sin, our rejection of God, our division and all those things which prevent the present grace of the Holy Spirit to penetrate, to bring to life our earth, our souls.

At the Finding of Jesus in the Temple decade, Father prayed that all would find Jesus and never let go of Him. I saw Jesus, as the Good Shepherd, embrace Father. Father returned the embrace and wrapped his arms around Jesus. Jesus said: My **beloved priest and brother, I love you. I uphold you in My tender, yet strong, embrace. When you are weary, when your arms feel as though you are going to "let go," know that I am there to uphold you. In Me, it shall be accomplished. I am with you always, even when My embrace cannot be perceived. Like Peter who walked on the water as long as his eyes remained fixed on Me, you will fulfill the Will of the Father as long as your eyes are fixed on Me. Peace I give to you. Know the source of peace in your soul. My beloved, I am blessing you. Your Jesus**

6. **8-11-95** Feast of St. Clare of Assisi
St. Clare and the Blessed Sacrament

Dear child,
    On this day of remembrance of St. Clare, I remind you of the gift God seeks most; the gift of yourself, in totality! St. Clare is a beautiful example of complete surrender to God, Most High. St.

Clare saw clearly through all the things of the world, onto a higher good, a more sublime and everlasting reality, the beauty of Jesus, the love of the Spirit, the Kingship of the Father. All these coalesced for St. Clare in her love of the Blessed Sacrament. Her love of poverty, material and spiritual, enabled her to remain in holy humility, as one completely dependent upon her Lord and Savior. Her charism is light for your soul.

Look to the saints, the holy ones of God. Ponder their life, their sacrifice, their faithfulness, and their love. Ponder and imitate their virtues. Strive to walk the journey to God as one of the family of the saints. These holy souls are presently interceding on behalf of all souls, including yours. It is fitting, it is good that you recall the lives of the saints. Theirs is a legacy of holy example and teaching. God chooses many, but the response is varied. The saints responded to the full. Their gift was total surrender of self to grace. O how the Most High God blesses the soul who puts none before Him; those to whom He is foremost. God is pleased to give such a soul the treasury of His riches. He does not withhold, but gives generously. Little one, imitate the saints. I love you. Your Mother

7. **8-12-95** In Church
Abortion and Apostasy Pierce Her Heart

I prayed alone before the tabernacle. Then I got up and knelt before a beautiful statue of Our Lady. Gazing up at her face, I had a sense of her pierced heart. Suddenly I heard: *My child, my heart is pierced. There are two swords, which today are piercing my heart, causing my sorrow. The first sword is abortion. The second sword is apostasy. Abortion is an assault on my maternal heart of love. It is the killing of innocents. It is the negation of life. God intends life, not death.*

Apostasy is widespread. Faith is being abandoned. There is, everywhere, an exodus from the Church. Man has turned away from God to pursue the path laden with carnal passions and falsehoods of every sort. These are leading souls toward perdition. When faith dies in a soul, the higher reality is denied in that soul, leaving only the carnal (natural) *man, because the soul himself denies the su-*

pernatural reality. These are the swords piercing your Mother's heart. There are more, but these are most painful.

Pray with me child. You alleviate my suffering when you gaze upon your Mother with such tenderness, openness and love. I return your gaze and see before me one of my littlest ones coming to open herself to me. Yes, child, approach me and permit me to be your Mother. My heart is touched by your openness to me. I know your burdens. You know I will intercede for you. I am joyful to know your strong desire to love my Son and I will always help you to do this. Seek the Will of God above all else, then you will be more accepting of whatever He is doing in your soul, especially if He is permitting you to suffer. Learn to appreciate all that He is doing even if you are suffering. Know it is His hand that is fashioning you. When He tries you in the crucible of suffering, offer no resistance. He is loving you and seeks only love in return. I rejoice to see the Creator work so intimately with His creature.

Thank you for coming before me today. Thank you for sharing everything with your Mother. Thank you for sharing my sorrow also. In the mercy of Our Triune God, our suffering will not be everlasting. His love, however, is everlasting. He is our hope. I bless you in the Name of the Father, the Son, and the Holy Spirit. You are in my heart. I love you. Your Mother

Today I suffer interiorly very much. My Mother comforts me. Normally I can name my interior suffering. Today, it is too comprehensive to speak of. It is "everything," supernatural and natural. It is intense and painful. I struggle to maintain a "normal" countenance and carry out my duties as best I can.

8. **8-15-95** In a church, out of town. Feast of the Assumption
   of the Blessed Virgin Mary
   Imitate Saints Peter and Paul

My dear children,
On this feast day of my Assumption into heaven you find yourselves in prayer in the Church of Saints Peter and Paul. Like Peter and Paul, you have been called into discipleship. My little ones, your discipleship is an anointing from God. You have been chosen

by God, called by God. He has anointed you with His holy grace to be a disciple of these latter days, this momentous time of transition. Contemplate the discipleship of Saints Peter and Paul, and follow.

Like Peter, let faith in Christ be grounded in you so that you are as unshakable as the truth within you. Like Peter, when you fall, throw yourself on God's infinite mercy; repent and persevere. As Peter was enabled to walk on water when he focused on Jesus, so too Jesus will work miracles through you when you focus on Him alone, in and through your discipleship. Look to Peter of today and follow him as your guiding Light. He is God's voice for the world. Look to Paul and permit his zeal for Jesus and the Church to ignite your own heart, so that you are full of zeal for God and His house. Matthew, Mark, Luke, and John hold before you the Gospel message. I am today holding before you that same Gospel message. What is to be done, my little ones? As disciples of the Lord, we are called to proclaim the Gospel message to all the world, in spite of difficulty and persecution. Lay your lives down for the spreading of the Gospel message of love: Faith, Hope, and Charity. May all come to know, to believe, to love. We are dedicated to the work of the Lord, just as the first disciples were dedicated to that end.

Today, the name of Jesus is known but not loved. The Church is wounded and bleeding due to division, apostasy, and rebellion. God in His infinite mercy, has chosen His disciples of these latter days to do as the first disciples did - prepare the way for the reign of God. In the cenacles, wherever my children have responded to the call to prayer, I am with you as in the upper room with the disciples. A new Pentecost is soon upon you, my littlest ones. Empowered by the Holy Spirit, the wonders of God will be made evident. You are the living flames, which will ignite the world with love, who will restore the Church to love. Let your fiat resound to the heavens.

On this day (Feast of the Assumption), *let us give all thanksgiving, honor and glory to God Most High. His mercy endures for all ages. He who is Mighty has done great things for all souls. My Assumption is a perfect example of God's love and mercy. Let this feast day bring you hope. The Word of God is filled with the promise of eternal life in paradise, in one union of love. Therefore, always have hope! Do not be discouraged or grow impatient. Wait in anticipation and hope of the promise of the Eucharist reign of Jesus, through the triumph of my Immaculate Heart, peace on earth, and a world transfigured in and through love. In heaven and on earth, I am with you. I love you. Your Mother*

9. **8-16-95** Traveling in my car
His Living Flame of Love

While I was driving, Our Lady began to speak. A friend wrote as I dictated Our Lady's words.

My dear little ones,
My Son desires to transfigure you into His living flame of love. As His living flame of love, you will be His light, which illumines the path for many. You will be the warmth of love, melting hearts and souls. The fire within you will burn brightly for the good of many. Draw ever closer to me, your Mother, so I can assist you always to carry out the Will of the Father. My Son is increasing your capacity to love. He is also increasing your capacity to suffer. This is preparation for the difficult time which will soon be upon you. I implore you to trust completely in His grace. His grace is always sufficient. Love alone will triumph. You must learn to love as Jesus has loved you. To love is to lay down your life for others. Jesus calls you to love. I call you to service. You are in my army of little souls. In and through this army of littleness, love will triumph.
There is, today, too little love in the hearts of God's people. Your mission, therefore, is to cause God, who is Love, to be loved. The hand of God is upon you. Through His hand you will touch many. Permit God to use you always and everywhere. In this manner, wherever you are, Jesus will be present. Just as my Son was persecuted, you will be persecuted for your faith. Love your persecutors, pray for them. They have not come to believe because they have not opened their hearts. They suffer much in their blindness. I suffer much to observe so many unbelievers who do not know God and, therefore, do not know love. I long to take each and every soul into the garden of my Immaculate Heart. I suffer because so many refuse my maternal assistance.

You who are consecrated to my Immaculate Heart alleviate my suffering. I share my suffering with you. Together we can pray, interceding on behalf of all unbelievers. My spouse, the Holy Spirit, is in your soul. He will lead you along the path of sanctification. He is today transfiguring one soul after another. Together we are preparing the way of my Son. His reign is at hand, the reign of peace on earth. My little ones, you cannot comprehend the graces from heaven that are upon you. Through your acceptance of the graces, you shall give glory to the Triune God. Thank you for your obedience. Thank you for responding to my call. Thank you for sacrificing for souls. Though you will suffer, your blessings will be many. It is through the suffering that you will be made one with my Beloved Son, our Lord and Savior, Jesus Christ. I bless you in the Name of the Father, Son, and Holy Spirit. I love you. Your Mother

10. **8-18-95** Feast of St. Jane de Chantal
You Will Judge Yourself in the Truth

Following Mass, I entered contemplation for over an hour. When I came out of this prayer state, peace permeated me. Jesus spoke in a very firm tone. **Soul! You are to return home, tend to your duties as mother and wife; write in obedience to your spiritual director (I had not been writing); accept your suffering. You are with Me in the Garden of Gethsemane. You will pass these hours of suffering with Me in the garden. I am loving you and you are loving Me in these sufferings. The night of suffering will pass. Drink from the chalice with Me. My Mother is the angel who I send to comfort you as you wait in prayer with Me in the garden. It will pass. It will benefit the salvation of the world. You will glorify your Lord. We are one living sacrifice of love for the good of all souls. Focus on the resurrection, the joy, the hope, the transfiguration of all.**

Soul! Isn't it enough that we are one heart? You, My beloved, take on My suffering and I take on yours. As one heart, we share everything! This is love. I am holding you to My Heart, pressing you to its depths. This Heart of Mine is pierced and

suffering. Why? Because, from My creation, I hear: "God has forsaken His people and His Church. Where is Our God? He has broken His Covenant." Soon I will come again in your midst to reveal the truth. The Covenant was broken by you, My creation. You turned from Me. You abandoned My law and followed your own lawlessness. Now you find yourself in misery. I will come to heal your misery with the oil of My love. I will shine My light into your darkness, and you will see yourselves as you truly are. The truth will not judge you; rather, you will judge yourself in the truth. There will be no lying then, no self-deception, only truth before Me.

Soul, I will heal My creation as I healed you. Now pray and drink of the chalice with Me, in the garden, where love, humility, and obedience overcame all darkness and death. Soul, such is the immensity of My love for you, to share My Heart with you. Beloved, you are Mine. I love you. Jesus

11. **8-19-95** My home, 10 PM
Aversion to Prayer

For the past ten days I have experienced aversion to prayer. This began as a slight aversion, but it increased each passing day. The spiritual life daily became more distasteful, until tonight, when it escalated to a most strong aversion to everything having to do with the spiritual life. I forced myself to pray the Liturgy of the Hours. As I did so, my mind wandered. My thought: "I hate this!" Looking to my prayer desk with all the statues and holy pictures, I was violently tempted to push all of them off to the floor, to be rid of them. I refrained and reached for my journal instead. I hoped that I would become recollected and able to pray if I read Jesus' words to me. Instead, I was absolutely repulsed by the writing, repulsed by the messages. I had a strong desire to destroy the journal and never write again. Because of the violence of this attack, I recognized the devil's work. I left the door open for him due to my own negativity and incapacity to suffer the extreme darkness, which has come upon my soul.

My intellect knows the darkness is a gift from God. The interior suffering is greater than ever. The darkness grew daily. All prayer and spiritual exercises grew absolutely tasteless, even repulsive. Only my deepest will hangs on. My heart is as if dead! Love has turned into a dark void of nothingness, utter and complete nothingness. Jesus is causing me to die again and again. I resist and am frustrated. I feel myself regress back to the "beginning." My weakness and poverty are so evident! I am repulsed at myself, who I am before God, where I stand naked and vulnerable. There are degrees of nakedness and vulnerability. This is too much nakedness and too much vulnerability. I struggle. Why? Because I am sick, and wounded. I suffer and die. Somehow I know, there will be more sickness, more suffering, more death and it will continue to increase. Love has seemingly abandoned me. I am wounded with His darts in my heart and left only with pain and suffering that grows.

Because my memory is imprinted with His Love, and the Master's fingerprints are all over the memory, I cling to the truth. This is love. This is grace. This is the cross. This is union. He is loving Me. I will not refuse this cup of suffering, though everything in me recoils. If it be the Will of God that I walk in total darkness, in distaste of Him and the spiritual life, I "will" do so for one reason. I love my Lord and Savior boundlessly. He is my goal. None is above Him. He is my reason for living and my reason for dying.

Father advised that I not share this suffering with others or it will be "externalized" and I will have a release of it. I must suffer and endure it in my deepest secret center for love of God, and for my good, so that this trial, which God permits, will be fruitful in due time. This is how my soul's capacity is increased. Capacity to love seemingly grows in proportion to capacity to suffer silently and in secret, sometimes hidden like the broom in the closet. (Cf. St. Bernadette)

12. **8-21-95** Feast of Pius X My home, 10 PM
Each Soul Represents a Facet of My Divine Love

In prayer I was asking Jesus for direction regarding so many private revelations that I hear about. I was confused by the fact that He seems to be speaking to so many people today. Jesus taught me.

Soul, My Love for each individual soul, from the beginning of all ages, is unique for each particular soul. Each soul represents a facet of My Divine Love. As My Divine Love is infinite, without beginning or end, then each individual soul can radiate a most unique ray of My Divine Light. Each revelation from heaven contains the same Living Word, the same Gospel message. However, the Word alive in the individual soul is distinctly individual, some richer, some poorer, some full, some fuller. Each soul is uniquely Mine. Each soul is loved by Me in a particular manner which is perfect for that individual soul. Therefore, today you are witnessing My Light radiating through many different vessels. Like a multi-faceted diamond of many strategic cuts, each vessel is a reflection of a portion of My Divine Light. This Light originates in Me and ends in Me. Each soul's illumination is My design. My Love cannot be contained, even in all the souls who have ever been created or ever will be created. Such is the immensity of My Love, a love you will never comprehend to the fullest, even in heaven.

It is My Will to raise as many holy souls as there are stars in the heavens. These souls, who are poor and humble, who pray with pure hearts, shall become as bright and full of light as the stars that illumine the sky. These will shine like diamonds before the throne of My Father. These are a sign of My Love and Mercy for this age. Therefore, dear soul, do not limit My works, My revelations in these times. Though your comprehension and capacity is so very limited and small, My comprehension is infinite and My capacity is unending. Though you perceive so many "revelations," I tell you, that amongst all the darkness, there are relatively few "lights" illuminating the path to heaven. Oh, how merciful I am to you, My creation! Because I am Love, and I do love you endlessly. How little you love Me in return! Your Jesus

13. **8-25-95** Prayer Group Rosary. Glorious Mysteries. **Do Not Lose Hope!**

My dear children,

I bless you as you reflect on the Glorious Mystery of the Resurrection of my Son. Ponder this mystery in your heart. Know it is your inheritance. It is your hope. My little ones, do not lose hope. Even in the midst of much suffering in the world, you are called to be the light of hope for all. Each of you is being formed by the divine hand of the Father. He knows precisely what is good, that which is necessary for your soul that you may partake of the resurrection to the full.

Trust in your heavenly Father as a little child trusts in his father. He loves you infinitely more than you can comprehend. Never doubt that your Father is overseeing every aspect of your life. He who created you has designed the perfect journey for you. Some of you have been sent out into the desert. You are thirsty for God as you walk in the darkness. Your longing is an act of love, which glorifies God. Some of you are enjoying an abundance of sweetness from heaven. Your willingness to accept these graces is an act of love, which also glorifies God. Each must walk his particular journey with a singular goal: the glory of God. There are many burdens upon your heart tonight. Many are worried about your families. I have taught you that your intercession is extremely powerful. Your families are indeed inside my Immaculate Heart. Your perseverance and faithfulness in prayer brings grace upon many. Within these cenacles, where there is faith and purity of heart, my maternal grace abounds. My peace plan will be brought about through the intercession of the cenacles throughout the world.

My dear ones, many are faltering in their journey because their faith is weak. Let the sacraments be your strength. These will fortify your faith. In faith, you can walk in much hope, hope of the resurrection, hope in the salvation of the world, hope in the glory of God. Thank you for gathering to pray the Rosary with so much love in your hearts. Be at peace. I love you. Your Mother

14. **8-29-95** Tabernacle
Pride: No One is Immune

*Soul, it hurts Me when your pride enters into your thoughts and deeds. I seek a pure heart, without stain of pride. Pride is so very dangerous, dear soul. Almost secretly and silently it creeps into a soul. What begins in purity can slowly deteriorate in pride. Pride offends Me, *Soul. Always subject yourself to obedience. There can be no contest of wills in love. My Will I feed to you, both through these messages and graces, but equally through My chosen director for your soul. Do not hesitate or analyze his direction. I am speaking through him for you. If he is outside My Will, I will take that up with his soul. In that case, your soul is not accountable if you are in obedience. Pride can mask itself in so many ways, *Soul. It can appear innocent. It can appear as good, when it hides behind accomplishing "a good," such as in ministry in the Church. But whatever pride touches, it becomes stained. It can be clever, delivering itself in small doses so that even its victim cannot detect it. Every human soul is susceptible to pride. Beware, *Soul. Obedience is a great protection against pride. It is a very special grace I give to you in putting you under the authority of My beloved priest. I will always direct you through him.

*Soul, do not confuse zeal for My work with impatience. Zeal is pleasing in My sight when accompanied with purity of heart and conformity to My Will. Impatience is born of your own will. Do not confuse prudence with procrastination. These works require much prudence. But procrastination is not pleasing in My sight, as it usually is born of a lack of self-discipline. *Soul, I want your heart to be simple and pure. Subject yourself and every step you take for Me to the priest I have chosen for you. I want you to entrust yourself so thoroughly into his hands, as if they were My Hands - because they are. Then pride will not stain your soul, and your will shall bow to Mine. Then you will have peace in all situations and circumstances. Surrender everything unto Me. Put yourself under My authority in every thought and deed.

Now please write for My priest.

You, also, must be aware of your own pride. You are not immune. You also are to subject yourself to My Way and My Will. Seek first My counsel and wisdom. Pray, My son, for the grace to accept the words I speak through this messenger. As you discern these words, My Light will come upon you. You will "know" by My Light in your soul. My works are a blessing for you and My messenger. In the proper time many will be blessed by these words. I will call you to enrich these words with your own. Come to Me in prayer and I will give you "light." I love you with My tender and merciful Heart. I am truly with you. Peace. Your Jesus

15. **8-29-95** Feast: Beheading of John the Baptist.
Rosary with Father, my home.

Preparation is Prayer, Sacrifice, and Repentance

On this day of remembrance of St. John the Baptizer, I am with you again to pray and teach you. St. John preceded my Son to prepare the way for His coming. I am today preceding my Son to prepare the world for the reign of His love and peace. I am calling for conversion of heart. Preparation is prayer, sacrifice, and repentance. Preparation requires sacrifice.

In this age, many vessels of election are being called into a crucifixion of self, with a resurrection of a new self. The new self is a purified vessel of God's love, a surrendered soul, willing to sacrifice for the good of God's plan. You are in the midst of this process. It is difficult at times. I know your difficulties. There is an abundance of grace which is with you, enabling you to say, "Yes, my Lord," even if with tears in your eyes. I know your heart, little ones. They are open and turned toward heaven. Daily, be willing to surrender to God's plan for you. Permit the divine hand of God to fashion you. He alone creates His beauty in you. You are radiant with His love. You are a sign for others when you radiate His peace.

Peace is rare in the world today. Peace, therefore, stands out. Strive to let nothing of this world rob you of your peace of soul.

My son and my daughter, thank you for your efforts regarding the doctrine defining my role as Co-Redemptrix, Mediatrix, and Advocate. The proclamation of this doctrine is God's Will. It is a vital part of the triumph of my Immaculate Heart. The Church will receive many graces through this proclamation. This Pope is chosen to be the Pope who proclaims this doctrine. He will accomplish this at much cost to himself. Your prayers for him and for the proclamation of the doctrine are necessary. Never underestimate the power of your intercession. Your intercessory prayer has power because you are uniting yourself to Jesus, who is infinitely powerful, as mediator between man and God the Father. Share everything with Jesus in love and dependence on Him. Jesus so loves intimacy. Seek His Heart. Ask His counsel. He will feed you His wisdom. Few are the souls who are humble enough to declare dependency upon God.

*I present the crucifix to you, my little ones. Look. Pray before the crucifix. Be thankful to God for His love and His suffering. He who loves you wishes to share His Cross with you. The crucifix is proof of God's love for sinners, for you. Who can love as He can? Strive to love more each time you pray. I will help you. I love you. Your Mother

*In the very beginning of the Rosary I saw Our Lady holding the crucifix in her arms. It struck me the way she so lovingly caressed it. She esteemed the crucifix as the most precious of gifts.

16. **8-31-95** My home 11 PM
Co-Redemptrix, Mediatrix, Advocate

I heard Our Lady's voice. There was no salutation. She simply began the first sentence. *The Father's greatest gift of love is His Only Begotten Son, the Word Incarnate. Within my being, the Word became flesh. The formation of His flesh in my womb took place over nine months, but for all ages the essence of the Word, Divine Love, remains with me, for I am the chosen vessel of God's love for all creation. The Heart of the Redeemer, Son of Man and Son of God, is eternally united to my maternal heart through the order of divine grace. Our hearts are as one and cannot be separated. Chosen vessel of God's love for all creation, I am, in all ages, the Co-Redemptrix through my cooperation with the redemptive act, an act of union with my Son.*

The proclamation of the doctrine defining my role as Co-Redemptrix, through my cooperation with God's divine plan of salvation; whereby I wholly accept the immolation of my Son as salvific; defining my role as Mediatrix of all grace, the one through whom the eternal fountain of divine grace pours Himself out upon all creation; defining my perpetual maternal intercession as advocate for all souls; will bring to the Church a vitality of grace. When man obeys the Father, his obedience calls forth the power of Divine Love in graces incomprehensible to man. In clearly defining the theology of my maternal role, the Church will be laying the proper foundation for generations to come. The foundation is necessary for the reign of peace, the era foretold in Fatima. When my son proclaims this doctrine, the floodgates of heaven will open and the Church will receive renewal in love. A new vitality will be born through the power and wisdom of the Holy Spirit.

Blessed are the hearts, the hands, the voices uplifted in supplication to Almighty God, interceding and toiling for this proclamation. These hearts, these hands, these voices who are in union with my son will, together with His consecrated hand, place this jewel into the center of my maternal crown. All of heaven intercedes and joyfully waits. All who intercede for this work do so by the power of the Holy Spirit; for it is not by your own wisdom that you take up this work, but by the wisdom of God, which is upon you through the Holy Spirit, who is the author of this work. My maternal heart called you. The Holy Spirit came upon you. You responded. Thank you for your fiat. Persevere. It is near. I am with you. Pray for my son, the Pope. Those who are not in union with him bring much suffering upon him and the Church. I love you. Your Mother

17. **9-3-95** At a Convention
Inexpressible Holiness of God

At Adoration something happened to me that I cannot describe. It is too sublime! After about one minute in the presence of the Blessed

Sacrament, I sensed my spirit seemingly fly into the Blessed Sacrament. It was almost a violent separation, but I had only peace. I believe this happened in an instant. I was taken somewhere and given knowledge directly in my soul.

I saw Holiness identifying His absolute Perfection in love and purity. I was seemingly taken to a place (not necessarily a "place"), where God the Father sat in the center. Jesus sat at the right hand of the Father. And to the left of the Father was the Holy Spirit. I was like an ant before the throne of the Most Sovereign, Majestic, Holy of Holies, and the Blessed Trinity. I beheld myriads of angelic spirits singing the praises of our Most High God.

This experience was to teach me of His True Presence and to "honor" and "adore" Him in the Blessed Sacrament. His Holiness is present to the world in the Blessed Sacrament. But there is little "reverence" for His True Presence and His absolute holiness. This experience was almost shocking. I say this because the holiness I was permitted to experience so far exceeded my concept of God's holiness. The Superiority of God is incomprehensible. It is shocking that sinners refuse to bow to Him, to submit to His sovereign authority. When we see God in His absolute Holiness, we will be shocked and humbled. I do not mean that He is unapproachable. He invites us to approach, but with humility and poverty of spirit, with reverence and awe! The power of His True Presence is Love, divine, infinite, unconditional, incomprehensible love. His Love marks the soul, and the soul yearns for His touch. All of us are marked with His love. It is our reality, our destiny. His Love is perfect and holy. It pains me that I cannot express the "holiness" that I saw.

I prayed: "My God, a lifetime is not enough to exalt You. My God, Your holiness is utterly unspeakable. How mercifully You bend to us, yet we spurn Your love and Your sovereignty. O my God, how base have we become? What do we hold as sacred now? What is holiness to us? Thank you, all you choirs of angels and holy saints who never cease to exalt our Holy God. Sing His praise for us. Intercede for us, O Holy Mother of God, that one day, after our purification, we too, will sing with you to His honor and glory forever. O Most Holy Trinity, be adored. Come, O purification, and make us holy! Amen."

At the closing convention Mass, following Holy Communion, I was in a deeply recollected state of prayer. I was thanking the Most Holy Trinity for all the blessings and graces of the conference.

Jesus spoke: **My dear ones,**
It is My nature to lavish souls with divine love. Blessed are you who gather in expectant faith. You come to My altar in poverty. You leave My altar rich. I give Myself to each soul, that you would come to understand once and for all that I am love. And love seeks love in return. It is My nature to be generous, for My riches abound forever. I do not condemn you, My people. Your lawlessness brings suffering and condemnation upon yourselves. Only love can heal you. I seek to restore your lawlessness to order. If you love Me, keep My commandments. Blessed are you who humbly serve Me and My Church, for you are appointed guardians of faith, hope and love. Your hearts are adorned with charity. Your fragrance is joy, joy that comes from knowledge that you are lavishly loved and infinitely valuable in the eyes of your God. Peace be with you. I love you. Jesus

18. **9-8-95** Feast of the Birth of Our Lady. Prayer Group Meeting
Blessing from Mary: Grace from Jesus

During the First Joyful Mystery, Our Lady prayed for a moment over each one of us, putting her hand gently upon our heart. She was planting the seed of a new grace, which Jesus speaks about later. She prayed: *Let it be done to you according to the Word of God.*
At the First Glorious Mystery, Jesus spoke.

Blessed are you, My little ones, for I have placed My Mother in your midst. Blessed are you who embrace her in obedience to My Word. On this day of remembrance of her birth, all of heaven rejoices; hymns are sung in her honor because she is a chosen vessel of God's Divine Love for all creation. Blessed are you who entrust your hearts to her maternal care. She will guide your journey along the path of holiness. She will embrace your

heart into her own maternal and pure heart and teach you the way of the Divine Will.

On this special day, I have a gift for each one of you. I have planted a new seed into your heart. This new seed is to be cultivated by My grace so that it will grow into a beautiful offering. This offering will be presented to The Father in due season. I, Myself, will cause this new seed to grow in you. This is My gift, given in honor of My Mother. This new grace will assist you to bloom into the person I have called you to be. Trust that this will come to fruition in you. Pray always and the light of the Holy Spirit will shine to guide your every step. The gift I give you is for your personal sanctification, but also for the sanctification of the world.

I love you, My little ones. Thank you for your love, service, and your prayer from the heart. I see how open your hearts are to Me. I am pleased to bless you abundantly. I will never forsake you. Be at peace. Love one another as I have loved you. In My Holy Spirit, you will grow in patience and wisdom. My love, Jesus

19. **9-8-95** Feast of the Birth of Our Lady, my home
True Wisdom and 1 Cor. 2

Early in the day, I sat in prayer before my Fatima statue. I was praying that I might always walk in truth regarding the graces in my soul. I was contemplating the work before me in organizing the messages in response to Our Lady's request to "prepare" the writings. I prayed for light, wisdom, and truth. I said to Our Lady that this would require much time and effort and take away time from prayer. I was negative about the messages. Our Lady became very present to me, as if she was standing right before me. She was very consoling. She said: *My daughter, please read 1Cor.2 It will help you. You are truly a doubting Thomas. Your faith is so very little. Be at peace. I am with you. Your Mother*

I read 1 Cor. 2. Light entered my soul and peace came upon me. I was led to ponder this Scripture over the next couple of days. At night, I would awaken with it on my mind. When Our Lord or

Lady want to impress something like this on a soul, to teach and guide, the soul is frequently reminded of it.

1 Cor. 2: "When I came to you, brothers, proclaiming the mystery of God, I did not come with sublimity of words or of wisdom. For I resolved to know nothing while I was with you except Jesus Christ and Him crucified. I came to you in weakness and fear and much trembling, and My message and My proclamation were not with persuasive words of wisdom, but with a demonstration of spirit and power, so that your faith might rest not on human wisdom but on the power of God. Similarly, no one knows what pertains to God except the Spirit of God. We have not received the spirit of the world but the Spirit that is from God, so that we may understand the things freely given us from God. And we speak about them not with words taught by human wisdom, but with words taught by the Spirit, describing spiritual realities in spiritual terms. Now the natural person does not accept what pertains to the Spirit of God, for to him it is foolishness, and he cannot understand it, because it is judged spiritually. The spiritual person, however, can judge everything but is not subject to judgment by anyone. For "who has known the Mind of the Lord, so as to counsel Him?" But we have the mind of Christ."

This passage taught me to judge messages with the mind of the Spirit of God. Their Wisdom is not of the spirit of the world. Also, their value is not in the written style or sublimity of words. Their value is according to what the Spirit of God can and will do with them. This is true for all the messages of this time.

20. **9-10-95** Written in midst of a restaurant waiting
    for my husband and friends.
Intimacy Requires a Decision

My *Soul, the elation in your soul is My love and My joy in you. In serving Me, you are blessed. My very life of love is in your soul. Nothing of the world could cause the elation I give to you. You are living in accordance with My plan for you. In doing so, I bless your life in every way. *Soul, you are My beloved because I chose you to be Mine. I set you apart for My-

self. Your response is a decision you have made for Me. Having made Me the center of your life, you are partaking already of the bounty of My banquet of Love. As long as your heart is open, as long as your intentions are My intentions, I will continue to pour Myself into you, knowing you will not spurn My Love. Humble yourself so that I can draw you ever closer. How I love humility! Few are humble souls! Blessed are you for permitting Me to love you. As I love you perfectly, according to your individuality, I love each soul in a perfect manner according to their individuality. Few return My Love. My Love is constant for all. But intimacy is an invitation which requires a decision according to your free will. My Sacred Heart suffers with longing to transfigure souls into the image of My love. You will bless My Church with your life of prayer, sacrifice, and service. As I draw you to Me, many will follow, seeking the intimacy which radiates through you because you love. As I rest in your soul, let there always be peace within. I am your peace. I love you, *Soul.
Your Jesus

21. **9-12-95** 11:30 PM, my home
Only in Prayer

Dear children,
    The constant flow of my messages and my visitations in this age is unprecedented in the history of the Church. Let this be a sign to you. You are living in the time of great struggle foretold in the Scriptures; a time of darkness preceding the Light; a time of spiritual warfare preceding the time of peace. Just as the Holy Spirit came at Pentecost, He is permeating the present darkness with His light of love; raising apostles of these latter days. The Church is being purified in these times by the grace and power of the Holy Spirit. The Holy Spirit is the very heart of the Church.
    My children, what does this mean to you? It means that the Spirit of the Living God is knocking on the door of your heart to awaken you from your unconsciousness. Many of you are already sleeping the sleep of the dead. Many of you suffer because of your

compromises. *You are caring only for your mortal self without regard for your eternal self (soul). Awaken, my little ones! Turn back to God! Live the abundant life God intends for you; a life of love and peace.*

In all my messages I implore you to pray. Why? Because only in prayer can you return to God. When you want to "know" someone, you must spend time with them. When you spend time with God, this is prayer. Only in prayer can you come to realize that God loves you unconditionally; infinitely more than any human lover can. Only in prayer can you become your true self before God. Only in prayer can you discover His plan for your particular journey and only in prayer can you embrace it. If you do not pray, you will suffer because you are outside God's perfect plan for you. The world is strong. The struggle against evil cannot be won on your own. Especially in America, there is too much isolation and self-sufficiency; too little relationship. Cold stone hearts cannot love. You have forgotten to take care of one another because there is too little love in your heart.

You are roaming in the desert, children, when God seeks to lead you into the Promised Land. I implore you, do not delay. Decide for God today. You cannot say you have decided for God if you do not pray; if you do not keep His commandments. Please permit the Holy Spirit to set your heart on fire with love. Please permit the Holy Spirit to teach you God's ways of love, mercy, charity, hope, and joy. My children, heaven is bending to earth to fortify you for a time of a true crisis of faith. There will be more saints, more victim souls, and more martyrs from this era than any other. If you would stop, listen, and pray, you would walk in the wisdom of God, which is surrounding you.

I remind you of the power of the Rosary. So strong is the power of the Rosary that it is Satan's most despised prayer next to the Holy Sacrifice of the Mass. If you pray the Rosary as I ask continuously, there will be less suffering in the world; in your families.

Please, dear children, do not take for granted my messages and visitations. The day will come when you will walk in dark faith and these will be the little lights that will fortify you through the purification. Only in the Holy Spirit can you understand my words. Only in the Holy Spirit can you live the messages. Persevere. Be faithful unto God. He will never forsake you. Love is calling you. Let there be Peace. Respond. I love you. Your Mother

22. **9-13-95** Rosary with Father, my home
The Blood of the Two Hearts

Chaplet of Divine Mercy: Almost immediately, in a swift, intense way, I saw the Church, represented by St. Peter's Basilica in Rome, being covered in the blood of the Lamb. The blood dripped from above, where the United Sacred and Immaculate Hearts were bleeding onto the Church. The Church was engulfed by a whirlwind tornado, which was strong enough to toss the Church about. Then I observed the Church going through a scourging like Our Lord's. I then observed the Church crowned with thorns and being mocked as Jesus was mocked and ridiculed. Then I observed the Church hanging upon the cross at the intersection of the crossbeams. All the while the United Hearts of Jesus and Mary continuously bled over the Church, which was now covered in blood. Then the earth shook like a quake with lightening and thunder. The Church on the cross began to illuminate and send forth brilliant rays of white and gold light all over the earth. Both the cross and the Church were illuminated in brilliant beautiful light. The blood of the Two Hearts flowed through the Church for the restoration of the world.

Following the Rosary, Father gave me the Eucharist because I could not get to Mass today. Jesus said: ***Soul, you could not come to Me so I came to you. I Myself have blessed you through the consecrated hands of My priest. I, Myself, have rendered you perfectly still because you are My target. The arrow of Divine Love has landed in you. I rendered you silent so that in the silence, only My Divine Love would resound in you. I love you. Jesus**

23. **9-14-95** Feast of Triumph of the Cross
Triumph of the Cross

*Soul of My Cross,

Rejoice in the Triumph of the Cross. It is My victory and My glory; a sign for you. For by the cross, you also are victorious. Evil and death have no power over you. I have overcome these for you. The cross is a sign of contradiction; the Father's infinite love for creation; His omnipotence displayed in a wisdom He gave to the world, but the world could not comprehend. The wisdom of God can be accepted only in the Light of the Holy Spirit. Never before has God's ways and man's ways been more contradictory. Man has turned from Me; abandoned My commandments and turned "love" into nothing more than selfish idolatry.

I will make of you, a sign of contradiction for this age. You will bear the burden of sin in union with Me. You will carry the cross with Me. You will save souls with Me. The sin of the world has never been greater. The weight of this sin will be borne by many souls who have offered themselves as living sacrifices of love. Though the victory is Mine, it is still being completed in each age until the end of time. It is completed through souls, united to My Heart of Love; who dedicate themselves to cooperate in My sufferings to bring about victory for all souls. My suffering continues as long as souls reject My Love and My victory for them. I desire to heal, to unite all souls that the whole of creation would partake in My victory. But I will never violate your free will. I love whether your decision is for Me or against Me, I love!

If only you knew what the cross has won for you, My creation, you would exalt the cross day and night. The Triumph of the Cross would resound in your heart and your hearts would be full, having permitted My Divine Love to penetrate you. You would live as I intended; your hearts full of peace and love. Soul, take up the cross with love. Offer all suffering for the good of souls in union with Me on the cross. Be a living sacrifice for Me. Above all, love. Love Me, love souls, love joy, and love suffering, because suffering embraced by love is a sacrifice which makes us one; therein is your joy. Peace. I love you. Jesus

24. **9-15-95** Feast of Our Lady of Sorrows
A Mother's Sorrow

My children,
I weep as any earthly mother weeps for her children. I observe so little love among you. When there is so little love, there is so much suffering. You are walking in waywardness, my little ones. I am sorrowful for you. Many of you never think beyond your earthly pilgrimage. Many believe only what you see, feel, touch. Yet all these will pass away. The gift of life itself has less value in the world. Families are broken. The Church is divided. Your hearts are like deserts. These are the swords which today pierce my maternal heart.

All of you are God's family. I am your Mother. In my heart is a treasury of love and assistance for you. I can attend to each one of you individually. I can intercede for all your needs. Yet only if you permit me to do this for you. Many deny me the privilege of being their mother. Here is my sorrow! Your greatest need is to turn back to God as little children so He can restore your life; so you can know the truth of His Love for you; so you can learn to love your Creator, Father, as He loves you.

My children, you are insecure, but the security you seek is within you. You are starving for love, but the love you seek is within you. When you look inside yourself, you will find you have spent a lifetime giving into worldly values, which are false and transitory, while you have rejected the priceless treasure of God's love and holiness which is within you. Your soul is the essence of who you are; the center; the part of you which will exist into eternity. Yet, this is the part of you which you have neglected. Your soul is created to be radiantly alive with divine love and goodness; full of beauty and purity. Instead, I observe souls which are empty; lacking knowledge, and love for God; darkened by sin; without radiance or life. This is my sorrow!

My children, you are offending God. You are suffering because you have forsaken God and goodness; you have forsaken Love,

Himself. How long little ones, will you forsake the remedy for the world, for your soul? If you desire restoration, acknowledge God. Humble yourself. Convert your heart to love. Reconcile with God through repentance. Pray, pray, pray. Then you will know God's infinite love for you and the world will be restored to peace. The peace only God can give. Then my sorrow will cease. My tears will be for joy! I love you so very much my little, little ones. Your Mother

25. **9-20-95** 3:20 AM Hotel Atlantico, Rome, Italy -
    Pilgrimage with Prayer Group
Pilgrimages Deepen Faith and the Call to Intercession

At 3:20 AM, my room is absolutely black. I am awakened by "light" which seems to illumine my room. Seeing only darkness exteriorly, my interior sees tremendous "light" filling my room. There is a strong presence of angelic beings, many of them, as "light." Jesus seems to be sitting on the edge of my bed. He begins to gently speak to me about the prayer group and Our Lady. When He spoke of Our Lady, the illumination grew much brighter. Jesus is most joyful when He speaks to me of Our Lady. I listened to Jesus, enjoying His company and His words. After approximately twenty minutes of being in His presence and listening He said gently, **Now, will you please write My words?** I turned on the light and began to write.

Jesus said: **Please write My words for the group.**
   Blessed are you, My littlest ones who heard My Holy Spirit calling you and responded in faith. Blessed are you, My littlest ones, for seeking My Divine Will and accepting My invitation to come away from your routine to be with Me in love and in expectation of My blessings.
   Your expectation is your hope in Me.
   Your acceptance is your trust in Me.
   Your response is your surrender in Me.
   Each of you has responded at a cost to you; a sacrifice, a step of faith. Your sacrifice is a pleasing offering in the sight of the Most Holy Trinity. Indeed, The Father, the Holy Spirit, and

I, your Lord Jesus, shall accompany you throughout your pilgrimage. Great are the blessings which await you. Let your hearts be docile. Be attentive and recollected so the Holy Spirit can teach, guide, and bless you in the silence of your heart. I have called you to come apart from your work, your ministry, your vocation, for a while, that you would grow in the knowledge of My love for you. I call you to intimacy with Me. Only in the profound knowledge of My infinite love for your particular soul, will you be able to serve Me in the capacity I am calling you "to serve."

This journey will serve to deepen your faith in Me and in My works. It will serve to enkindle your hearts to greater love, faith, and hope. It will serve to increase your confidence in My call to each one of you. Indeed, I am calling each one of you to serve in the hour of great need, in My Church, and in the world. If My Divine Will is indeed the desire of your heart, then I say to you, "Take up your cross with great love and follow Me in total abandonment of your way for My way." Abandonment does not require understanding of My way, rather it requires trust which is your faith in action. I seek from you a childlike acceptance of the Father's perfect plan for you. He is over you. Be little. Be pure of heart. Be simple. These are My ways, gentle and kind. They are the opposite of the ways of the world. As I have called you each by name, put aside the spirit of the world. Put on the Spirit of God, which is love. Unconditional love seeks the good of other souls. Become a servant of Mine through your service to souls.

I have called you into intercession. Intercession is a high calling; a cooperation with the redemption of the world. I will fix your heart on Me so that I can give you My Heart, so that you can love as I love, so that My thirst for souls will be your thirst for souls, so that together, as one heart, we will gather souls for the eternal kingdom. Rejoice. You have been chosen by God. Place all your trust in My merciful Heart. I accompany you always. My peace I give you. It is a great gift. Be joyful in it. I love you. Your Jesus

Jesus continued to dictate the message that follows.

26. **9-20-95** 3:40 AM Hotel Atlantico, Rome, Italy
Mary, the Treasury of the Most Holy Trinity

*Soul, it is beyond your human comprehension to know the singular role bestowed upon the Blessed Virgin Mary as Mother of God, Mother of All!

From the beginning to the end; in heaven and on earth, no other vessel so completely radiates the love and grace of the Most Holy Trinity as she does. She is radiantly alive with love of God. The fullness of God cannot be contained, but no other being can contain as much fullness as she does. Though she is not infinite love, the one Who is infinite love, so thoroughly permeates her being, that He is her treasury! She is the treasure of the Most Holy Trinity through whom We bestow the inexhaustible treasury of Our love and grace to the entire world.

I cannot express to you, the love the Most Holy Trinity has for the Blessed Virgin Mary because you could not take it in, but I say to you - this is her hour! It is her army that will lead into the era of peace. It is her army that works for the triumph of the United Sacred and Immaculate Hearts. It is her army that will crush Satan's army. It is her hour! Blessed are you to be part of her army. Her humility will overcome the pride of the world. Her obedience will overcome the rebellion of the world.

She will restore the Church by the power of maternal love. Her spouse is the Holy Spirit. The Holy Spirit is the heart of the Church. No other being is so endowed by the Holy Spirit as Mary. Therefore, the Church is to be as the very heart of Mary, the storehouse of the Holy Spirit; the treasury of God's riches for all humanity. Mary will lead souls back to the Church just as she leads souls back to God. She has a singular understanding of what the Church is to be. She has a singular role to restore the Church in the light of that understanding. There is a great apostasy now, but she will lead souls back to the Church by restoring it so the Church is a mirror of the garden of her Immaculate Heart. Bless you for loving the Immaculate Heart of Mary. She is the treasure of the Most Holy Trinity. Peace. Jesus

27. **9-22-95** On Bus from Cascia (St. Rita) to Assisi, Italy
Enjoy the Beauty of My Creation

Observing so much beauty traveling through Italy, the land-scape, hills, clouds, sky, trees, all of nature seemed radiantly beautiful. My heart became inflamed with love. I saw God's hand in all of nature and the presence of the Most Holy Trinity seemed to envelop me like a blanket enfolding me. I was full of Jesus, the Holy Spirit, and the Father! My soul cried out "Abba, Father" and I was a child in the arms of the Most Loving Father. My soul cried out "Jesus" and I was walking hand in hand with my beloved Lord. My soul cried out "Holy Spirit" and my being was seemingly filled with divine love. The presence of the Trinity was overwhelming. I found myself thinking of Peter's words, "depart from me, a sinner." Then, the Trinity enveloped my soul all the more.

Jesus spoke after a period of sublime silence.

*Soul, feast your eyes on the beauty of My creation. (Referring to the beautiful Italian countryside I was traveling through. Jesus' disposition was one of happiness and pleasure with His creation.) **Do not be afraid to enjoy My created beauty. It is for you. Delight in My work. Out of nothingness it was created by Me. Do not be afraid to enjoy the company of good people, good food, wine and music. None of these can steal your heart from Me, *Soul. I alone have possession of your heart. Do not feel guilty to enjoy these other things. I have not called you to limit you but to the fullness of love. I give to you good things. These things are but a moment's pleasure, which leave your heart hungry for the one eternal good. Do not fear. You are Mine. You belong to Me. Nothing will steal you from Me. I am with you always. What is Mine is under My constant protection. *Soul, I am with you. I love you. Jesus**

28. **9-23-95** Assisi, Italy - Group Pilgrimage
Serve the Church Humbly and Obediently

I have called each by name. I have bound you together by My love. My own hand has fashioned you so that in loving Me,

you will serve My Church. The Church will be purified and restored. Restored to love! The charisms of Francis are your example. Lead My people by them. Only in humility, obedience and purity can My Church be restored to love. My people are starving for love. My people are wandering in parched desertlands. Lead My people back to Me; back to My Church. The Church is meant to draw people to her. Her sanctuary shall be holy; her beauty, pure and inviting; love shall be her radiance; the Living Word, her foundation; the truth, her pillar; the Holy Spirit, her heart. Out of the parched desertlands I will lead My people to My house and feed them the food of holiness. I will make of you, partners in My household. Prepare to serve My people; prepare to feed My sheep. I will show you the way, for the harvest is close at hand. Walk as Francis walked. In His lowliness, I raised him up. In His poverty, I made him rich. In His obedience, I made him bow to My authority on earth (Church) and in heaven. My Divine Will was his life. In it he received the royal crown of love. Acknowledge your own poverty. Seek only My Divine Will. Walk in simplicity like a child. Be joyful, I have chosen you. Accept your daily crosses with patience, courage, love, and perseverance. Offer your joys and sufferings for the good of souls. United with My passion, you shall save souls. Live a life of prayer. Only then will your harvest be plentiful. Strive to love all souls at all times as I love you - unconditionally. Radiate My peace, My love. My sheep will make their way to you seeking nourishment. Give souls what I give you; the gift of prayer which leads to union with Me. Serve My Church in her hour of need. Like Francis, make yourselves an offering to Me. Be united in My Love. You are rooted in My Heart. I love you. Jesus

29. **9-24-95** 1:20 AM (Perugia) Assisi Hotel – Group Pilgrimage
St. Francis Foretells of Rejection

Suddenly I was awakened out of a deep sleep and in the presence of St. Francis.

He said: "Little dove, do not resist me. Do not be afraid. It is I, the little poor man of Assisi. You are in my home and I am with you. Little dove, you have been chosen by the Most High God to be united to Our Lord and Savior, in the sufferings of His passion. Your heart will bear the wounds of the crucified Jesus and your soul will be elevated on the cross of the Beloved.

His Majesty has plucked you from the world. You, His little flower, have been chosen to be the Bride of Christ. The wedding cup is the cup of suffering; suffering that co-redeems. You are His little portion, impoverished, but out of your desolation He will create an abundant garden yielding a bountiful variety of fruits (good works with love) and fragrant flowers (sacrificial offerings). You will know the company and have assistance from many Saints and angels. You are but a little, little seedling now. Your faith has yet to be tested, little seedling. But you have been found worthy because of your love for the Most Holy Trinity. The Father delights in one thing above all — love! Though you are afraid of many things, you are not afraid of love. Therefore, His love burns feverishly inside you. Thus, He smiles upon you. The Most Holy Trinity has formed your heart into a radiant furnace of love which will fuel all that is required of you, causing you to fulfill His Will for you, procuring for you His paternal affection, enduring forever."

Here I was so full of grace, yet doubtful. I prayed to St. Michael. I began to weep. I desired to push this aside and go back to sleep, rejecting this. His presence brought peace, but his words pierced my heart. I was afraid. Fear was on the surface. Deep inside I felt only utter unworthiness. I turned off the light and tried to go to sleep. For twenty minutes I pushed this aside. Francis was silent, patient and kind. I was very much awake. I said to Mary: "Please dear Lady, help me to know if this is truly St. Francis." She said: "*I am with him.*" That is all she said. It was enough because her words brought peace. I turned on the light and asked Francis directly: "Why Francis, do I resist you?"

St. Francis tenderly said: "Little one, you are afraid the Most High God will seek from you all that He sought from me. You are uncertain as to whether you could abandon your life of comfort; detach yourself from love of creatures for the sake of Love Himself; bear the marks of Christ crucified for love of souls; become a beggar in the eyes of man; suffer rejection and thorough examination like the slave of all. Do not worry, my little dove. You can do none of these. Christ alone will procure these for you by divine grace, all the while caressing you in His Almighty hand. The Most High God will feed you the wisdom of His cross a little piece at a time; for a seedling is handled with much gentleness and patience.

I am your brother, little dove, and I say to you, - already you are a beggar, utterly impoverished. You will know the love of saints and angels because you will know the rejection of friends and family. We will be your family. We will raise you up, little one. (I wept as these words pierced me and St. Francis waited.) One thorn at a time will enter you little dove. Though your heart shall be pierced, your soul will take flight. Sometimes plunged into suffering and darkness, you shall be permitted to ascend to the most high place of refuge, union with the Beloved.

This is your lot; what the Most High, Most Holy Trinity has chosen for you. Little dove, bow to the Creator; give all honor, glory, praise and thanksgiving unto our Thrice Holy God. Thank Him for His holy Mother who nurses us from her breast that God would be glorified in us. I am pleased to be chosen to assist you. It is good to be poor, little, pure and holy for God. Peace of Our Lord and Savior Jesus Christ be with you now and forever. Your brother, Francis (of Assisi)

Now, please write for your spiritual director and the prayer group."

30. **9-24-95** Assisi, Italy continued
St. Francis to a Priest, "I Intercede for You"

Saint Francis to my Spiritual Director.
"My brother,

I have been chosen to assist you in the area of restoring the Church, the Bride of Christ, and the one we have been committed to, the one we love. She is undergoing purification and shall be restored by a remnant of faithful little souls who have been given the grace from God to believe in His works in this age. You, my little brother, have been chosen for such grace. Your eyes have been opened. I have interceded for you, blowing on the little flame of love to excite it to a roaring fire within you. The radical, intense fire of love is God poured in you for the good of His Beloved Bride in her hour of need. I shall assist you in the area of complete abandonment to the Divine Will of the Most Holy Trinity. I intercede for you in the area of purity of heart and soul; detachment from your previous appetites; humility and gratitude; courage and perseverance.

My brother, fight the good fight. Prepare for battle. Pray for the courage to uphold all that you believe in. Pray for courage to speak when you are asked to speak on behalf of the truth, for the good of the Church. Drink of the everlasting fountain of life; die to yourself; love the Beloved; prepare. The cup of suffering shall not pass you by, but by the cup you will live forever in the company of all your holy brothers, priests, saints, and angels, before the throne of the Most High together with our Mother Most Holy. I am joyful to be of assistance to you. You serve with me at your side; not of your choosing; not of my choosing, but of God's choosing. To Him be all honor, glory, praise, and thanksgiving! He alone is wisdom. Peace of Our Lord and Savior Jesus Christ be with you, my little brother. Francis, servant"

St. Francis continued: "Now, please write for the prayer group."

31. **9-24-95** From St. Francis, in Assisi, for Prayer Group. 2AM.
St. Francis Assists Souls

"Little ones, I, the little poor man of Assisi have been chosen by the Most High God to assist you on your journey; to teach you the little way of holiness; to intercede on your behalf that God's perfect Divine Will be accomplished in and through you. I have accompanied you as you have journeyed to my home. The beauty and majesty of the Most High God is so abundantly displayed in Assisi. Set high above the plain, it rises like a monument to His Majesty and shines like a jewel chosen for the delight of the King. The radiance born of this area has reached the four corners of the earth and caused many a poor soul to rise above mortal existence to seek eternal life.

My little ones, you have been chosen to serve the Most High God by serving His beloved Bride, the Church. She is being transfigured in this age. A remnant of little souls have been raised and nurtured by Mary Most Holy to restore the Church into a brilliant light which will draw souls to her by way of love. You have been graced to be chosen to be part of the faithful remnant of little souls, forming the army, which will lead into the era of sanctification and peace. I have been chosen to assist souls in the formation of holiness through humility, purity of heart, obedience to the Divine Will of God, and courage to uphold the cross of Jesus Christ that saves.

I am your little brother in Jesus Christ. Our missions are similar. Ponder this in the light of contemplation. You will come to understand my words. I am joyful to assist you, individually and collectively. My spirit I share with you for you have been found worthy to uphold the cross of Jesus Christ in the service of Church and souls; interceding and co-redeeming. You are poor in spirit and pure of heart, full of incapacity and fearful like timid deer but the Most High, Thrice Holy One has chosen you. Thus, He will give you His strength and courage and show you the way with tenderness and mercy, teaching you to love which shall make you strong in Him.

Little ones, there will be trials, but you will overcome. You are a garden full of variety. Bloom to His delight. Sing His praises in your trials and joys. Be peacemakers and lovers. Souls will come to you then. I bless you in the Name of the Most Holy Trinity. Your little brother, Francis"

32. **9-26-95** San Giovanni, Padre Pio
The Love of God the Father

Inside the old church where Padre Pio said Mass, I sat in the back pew with my spiritual director. Intending to pray to Jesus, the Holy Spirit moved me to address God the Father instead. I said with deep loving affection, "Father," "Abba," "Daddy." With the utterance of each name, the presence of the Father was intensified until I felt wrapped up in His presence, filled with paternal love. I prayed, "Father, I love You. I know You are pure spirit, but I wish

I could draw close to You. How do I show my deep affection for You?" The Father intensified His Presence and seemingly enveloped me with His Love. I liken this to the way a parent would wrap a newborn baby in a blanket causing the baby to be warm, secure. Although the Father's presence in my soul was very "interior," it reached to all parts of my being and was felt physically also. I was given to know that I was deeply loved by the Father, my God. This knowledge was so tenderly received by my soul that it manifested itself in the spontaneous flow of tears. I remained all wrapped up in Him. He tenderly understood and accepted my desire to show Him love and affection and He mercifully returned it to me a hundredfold.

While the overwhelming attribute of the Father in my soul was His "Fatherhood" and my "childhood," His Majesty was intensely manifested also. This led to prayer of thanksgiving and offering of more love.

I prayed: "My Father, You have probed me, You know me and You are with me deeply now. You see that I am full of the desire to love You. It seems to me, my desire is overflowing, almost consuming me, but my capacity is so small. My Father, I long to love You more."

The Father intensified His presence in my soul. My heart was all aflame. He continued to caress and love His little creature. I felt all the more unworthy to be in His majestic loving presence. He gave me more of His Fatherly grace, pouring perfect, powerful love into my poor little soul. He is the Giver, always the Eternal Giver! I want to give to Him, but what can I give that He hasn't given to me? It is all His to give! The Father, Creator of all, Sovereign Master of the Universe is Love! He loves! He is so pleased when I permit Him to love me, to be my Father, to take care of me! When I am His little child, He is pleased and blesses me! It is pure and simple. Why do I examine it, analyze it, complicate it? Often I deny my Father His Fatherhood.

My spiritual director and I moved to the new church to pray before the Tabernacle, next to the statue of Padre Pio. I entered contemplation. In the deepest part of me, I felt a prompting; a welling up inside of me; a subtle but consistent "urging" to make myself an offering to God, there and then. I asked Padre Pio to assist me.

I prayed. "My Almighty, Triune God, I love You boundlessly! In that love, I give to You, all that I am; all that I possess. Do as You please with me. In my joys and sufferings, I am Yours. Do as You please with me. I love joy, but I want to love suffering. Suffering unites me to the passion of my Lord. Suffering in union with my Savior, saves souls. It is You, my Triune God, inside me now that leads me to say without reservation: Make of me, Your victim; victim of Your love; victim for sinners. It is You, my Triune God, inside me now, that leads me to say: "I am thirsty for the cup of suffering not for the sake of suffering but for the sake of love, for the sake of co-redeeming, for the sake of imitating my Lord. Amen."

33. **9-27-95** Rome, Italy. Pope's Public Audience.
A Pilgrim's Heart: Commitment to Love and Serve

3:30 PM Prayer in the St. Joseph Chapel of St. Peter's Basilica, Rome (Vatican).

My little, little ones,
I who am your Mother, have been a pilgrim with you. There have been no coincidences on your journey. Abundant graces have been bestowed upon each one. Some have carried a cross. Each has received precisely what was required to lead you to growth in holiness. This is the mercy of God upon you. I have been with you even when you could not sense my maternal presence. Often it is precisely when you cannot perceive my presence that I am closest to you. All the grace you have received has radiated through my Immaculate, Merciful and Sorrowful Heart.
Little ones, God seeks from you a profound commitment; a commitment to love; to serve; to grow in holiness and lead others to grow in holiness. You must not take this commitment lightly. It requires true sacrifice; it requires you lay down your life for souls. God will ask much of you, but He shall continue to uphold you and never forsake you. I will always assist you in your journey. Never doubt my intercession. Each soul is so precious to me. I love each one without distinction and seek only to draw you to God. You are a vital part of my army of little souls for these latter days.

My children, there is much suffering. Souls are in need. Alleviate suffering. Tend to the needs of souls. Be holy children. Live holy lives. Souls will be drawn to your holiness. Do the Will of God with much love and you will be holy. When you return home to your duties and vocations, remember always that you are but a pilgrim on a journey. Have a pilgrim's heart. Set your heart on God and heavenly things only. Recall all that you have witnessed. I was with you at the Eucharistic Miracle (Lanciano), adoring and thanking God for His mercy in miracles. I was with you as you visited each saint and walked on holy ground. Together with the saint, I blessed you and praised God for such examples of holiness. I rejoiced to observe your charity toward one another. I attended each Mass with you and knelt in prayer with you. You have walked on holy, holy ground. Take it with you. Make the ground you walk, holy! I bless you. I embrace you. I so love you and carry you in my Immaculate Heart. Peace be yours. Your Mother

34. **9-27-95** St. Joseph Chapel of St. Peter's Basilica, Rome
**Our Lady Speaks for a Priest on the Church,
Priests, and the Pope**

My beloved priest and son,
From this holy ground, I beseech you to pray unceasingly for the Church, for priests, and for the Pope. A quake has hit the Church. She is shaken, falling, and divided. The faithful are running from her. They run in many different directions. My heart is sorrowful to observe the condition of the Church. My heart aches to observe the hearts of priests. So many are barren hearts. Priests are suffering because they do not pray. Pray for them, my little son. Your prayers console my heart. I am always united to your prayers. You are beloved of my Immaculate Heart because you love. The Most Holy Trinity is glorified in you because you love. Continue to receive all that God grants you. Your soul is His resting place; a house of prayer. Let Him abide in you to the full. His presence brings all good things. Be holy for me, little son.
Let the Holy Spirit of God teach you continuously. He is making you holy. There is so little holiness on earth. God created man

to be holy as He is holy. In these times, which are so critical to creation, holiness is vitally important. It is the holy ones who will combat the darkness and save so many from death. Exist in my maternal heart where I can love you always and protect you continually. I am in your heart, son. I love you. Your Mother

35. **10-5-95** 7:45 AM (7-11 Store, getting coffee)
Spiritual Warfare of This Age

My children,
    You are battling the prince of darkness and his cohorts. War has been waged against you. You are surrounded by angels of light who guide you and protect you. And you are surrounded by angels of darkness who tempt you, disturb you and aim to oppress you, always attempting to divert your attention from the Divine Will of God. The dark angels are as real as the angels of light.
    You are being exposed now to the true spiritual warfare of this age. The closer you come to God, the closer you come to fulfilling your mission of drawing souls to love; the greater the attacks upon you. You must know the enemy in order to overcome him. The angels of darkness are liars and they are called angels of fear, angels of doubt, angels of jealousy, angels of rejection, angels of intimidation, angels of infirmity, angels of chaos, angels of addiction, angels of pride, rebellion, anger, hatred, murder, retaliation, blockage and so on and on. These are the ones you battle. But you do not battle alone. You fight darkness with light - the light of the Holy Spirit. You fight deceptions from liars with the truth, the truth of the Word of God. This is spiritual warfare; spiritual battle. The Holy Spirit of God is your protection for He gives His gifts to you so that you can discern the spirits. Using His light, you overcome the darkest of angels. Always engage St. Michael to assist you!
    God is Love. What comes from God is loving and peaceable. God never oppresses a soul. Oppression is from the devil. God always lifts the soul up and up! You are engaging in spiritual warfare, not merely for the good of your soul, but for many. The devil has a stronghold on many souls. The grace of God will assist you to free many souls from the strongholds of the devil. If the soil of

your own heart has been uprooted through attacks of the devil, know that it has been permitted for teaching and preparing because the evil spirits sense that God is about to birth new graces in you. God has chosen to make your heart a garden of goodness, full of love. He is making you into peacemakers and lovers of souls.

You are given to one another as gift to uphold one another. Together you will stand. Alone you will fall. Through your consecration to my Immaculate Heart, you are part of my army of little souls who are battling the forces of evil in the world. Pray together. The Holy Spirit is with you. Do not conceal your own weaknesses. Any secret kept in your heart will grow like a weed and choke off grace leaving you vulnerable to the enemy. Bring everything to the light. The devil flees the light for he is a creature of darkness. Thank you for engaging in war against the enemy. You have been prepared for this. Prayer warriors are my cohorts. I am always with you to overcome the darkness of the world. Soon, little ones, there will be only light. The darkness shall be no more. Pray for this coming. Be at peace. Love one another. Pray, pray, pray. Use your rosaries! I love you. Your Mother

36. **10-8-95** 8:30 AM Mass
Stand in the Gap Until All are Converted

At Holy Communion, I saw myself in a very realistic way on the cross, crucified. I was yelling from the depths of my soul the name of "Jesus," repeatedly. This scene came and went quickly, but it was very deep. I had no fear, only amazement in the power of the name of Jesus. After holy hour before the Tabernacle, Jesus said: **Please write.**

My Sacred Heart is a living flame of Divine Love. Infinite in capacity; it is love itself. Overflowing is My love for My creation; spilling over like a continuous fountain; searching for hearts that are open to receive; hearts willing to be victims of My love; willing to receive the wounds which penetrate a docile heart. For every heart who spurns My Divine Love, (and there are many), **I search for a heart willing to be My target. To this heart, I deposit My radiant Love; wounding such a heart;**

to love with My Love; depositing the essence of pure love; transforming the creature into love; inclining the creature to more love. These hearts are with Me on the road to Calvary; accepting My Love for every creature who refuses My Love. The docile heart loves for those who cannot yet love. The loving heart stands in the gap until each heart is converted to love. These hearts are fused to My Sacred Heart. Through these hearts, I am loving the whole of creation and in these hearts, the Father is glorified. These hearts fused to Mine, taste of My joy of loving and My sorrow in the refusal to love. Blessed are the hearts adhered to My Sacred Heart and great is your service for souls. I love you My creation. (long pause) **Little am I loved in return! Jesus**

37. 10-10-95 8:30AM Mass. Gospel: Martha and Mary
Do Not Worry: Be a Child

My Children,

I find your hearts are anxious about many things. Banish anxiety from your hearts. Anxiety about spiritual things is no less harmful to your heart than anxiety about worldly things. If you are anxious about spiritual things, you are lacking in love of God, knowledge of God, trust in God, abandonment to God. You have not yet turned yourself over to God. You have not yet understood spiritual childhood. You have not yet understood that it is God's perfect plan for you to abandon yourself into His loving and merciful arms. The Most Holy Trinity is over you, with you and in you. Do not worry. Be a child! The time you spend worrying, planning, analyzing would be much better spent saying, "I love You, my God. I love You." Never tire of saying, "I love You, my God." God never tires of hearing these words and blesses you in them. For these are the words which uplift your heart. When you say them from your heart, God never fails to respond with this His own "I love you, dear soul."

My children, do not be afraid of what God will ask of you. God never asks that which is beyond your giving. Always, His grace is sufficient. This is what is required of you; incline your human will to His Divine Will and desire to love with all your heart. You are but a human vessel. If you are full of anxiety, then you are not empty enough to be full of His love. You may think you are disposed to His Divine Will but in truth, you are still protecting yourself as if you are the one responsible for your preservation. My children, you are then not converted at all. Your heart must be so vulnerable, so docile, so open to be loved, to serve, and to give God's love away that you preserve nothing of yourself. Did my Son, our Lord and Savior, reserve even a drop of His precious blood for Himself, or did He shed it all for you?

To be converted is to die to your former ways of thinking and acting. To be converted means to become a little child, vulnerable and trusting completely in God. God must be the center of your heart, the love of your life. Fear and anxiety are not of God. You can become spiritually anxious when you analyze or compare your journey to your neighbor's journey. Each soul is created to give glory to God according to the constitution of each soul. Some are created more delicate, some stronger. But each is perfectly designed by God to accomplish His perfect plan in them. Accept yourself as God created you. Do not covet your neighbor's spiritual journey or gifts. Do not judge one another's journey. Rather appreciate one another's path to God, loving and upholding one another. As God has loved you unconditionally, without reservation or distinction, so too, you must love one another. Each soul is made beautiful only through love. Dismiss all from your heart except love. Walk in peace without anxiety, permitting God to be God. Only then are you truly converted. I love you. Your Mother

38. **10-10-95** 8 PM
Pray for Priests

My little daughters,
I am sending you as my voice, my messengers to my priests. Know that each and every priest is very beloved of my maternal heart. I await the conversion of my priests. I so love my priests. My heart is full of mercy for them. I implore you to love them as I do. I send you as messengers of my maternal and merciful love. Take them into your own heart. Pray for them unceasingly. Theirs is a

difficult journey. Their hearts are distracted by various duties of their vocation. If they do not pray, their hearts turn into barren deserts. Intercede for them. Assist them as I send you to them. Appreciate their sacrifice. Their paths are strewn with hardship and temptation of every kind. The devil makes them his special target. However, God's grace abounds for them to overcome every difficulty; to enable them to be good shepherds with joy and love of God within.

Conversion of their heart means so much to the Church, now and in the future. Therefore, embrace my shepherds with love, patience, and prayer. I will use you to radiate my own maternal love for them. I will permit them to see me in you. Therefore, be full of grace for them through your own holiness, purity of heart and humility. Only through prayer can you become the pure vessel of my maternal love. Therefore, live a life of prayer. Thank you for committing yourself to my service and theirs. I will always be with you, especially to minister to my priests. I love you. Your Mother

39. **10-11-95** 8:30 AM Mass. Gospel: Our Lord's Prayer
   to the Father
Mary and the "Our Father"

My children,

When you pray the prayer Jesus taught you to the Father, with love from the heart, you are truly disposing your heart to God. Let these words penetrate your heart. Do not say them without thinking. It is an offense to the Sacred and Immaculate Hearts to do so. Many claim to be praying from the heart. But few truly have hearts that are praying. Jesus teaches us to praise and honor the very name of God the Father. He is holy, holy, holy. We beseech Him then, "Thy Kingdom come." His Kingdom is love, peace, and justice. We implore Him, "Thy Will be done." Always a "fiat" to His Divine Will! We request the bread that sustains us, in body and in spirit. We beg forgiveness in proportion to the forgiveness we give others. Forgiveness is of extreme importance; forgiveness of yourself, your brothers and sisters, mothers and fathers, sons and daughters. We implore Him - "lead us not into temptation but deliver us from evil." Here we acknowledge our weakness and the reality of the devil so as to call upon His Divine Mercy always.

Dear children, do not recite these words with emptiness. But let this prayer be said with love and affection for the Father. These words revealed to you by my Son bring blessings upon your soul which are inestimable when prayed with sincerity and love. Often I observe you, my children, praying these words without realizing what you are saying. Prayer is then empty. The fruit of such prayer is emptiness.

I am calling you again and again to prayer with love from the heart. Prayer filled with desire is to be with God in union, in conversation, in relationship, in love! When you are with someone you love, your heart is alive and attentive. There is no boredom, rather there is a mutual sharing of the heart. This is prayer from the heart. It is full, not empty; alive, new and ever more beautiful. Therefore, say your prayers with patience, joy, trust and love. God is with you. But only in prayer can you come to realize this truth. Therefore, pray, pray, pray. I love you.

Your Mother

40. **10-12-95** 11 PM
A Prayer to Jesus For Strength

Jesus is very close and yet far away. The darkness is painful. I carry out all my duties joyfully. But deep inside my heart there is suffering; a pain only Jesus can take away. Nothing suffices except Jesus.

Prayer: "Oh My Jesus, I long for you, I ache for you. Love for you consumes my heart and soul. Jesus, You are my life, my everything. No matter how close You are, it's not close enough! The closer you come, the more I suffer. Jesus, how can this love I have for You cause suffering? Am I the toy of Your heart? Are you pleased to leave me sick with love? To gaze at your image only reminds me of what I do not have. I seek Your Holy Face everywhere. When I find it, I grow sicker. You have left me in exile. Yet you have given me everything; union with You. This union brings suffering, because it is not complete. We cannot consummate this love until You free me from this mortal life. If I am going to be the toy of Your heart, my Lord, give me strength. Please give me strength. As long as there is a veil between us, Lord, then wrap me in it so that I no longer see myself but only You. Keep me hidden and preserved for You. I live in the hope that there is a portion of Your love that is hidden and preserved for me. Jesus, I love You to madness it seems. Thank You for wounding me so. Be glorified in my weakness. I am Yours. Amen."

41. **10-13-95** Anniversary of Fatima Apparitions
The Father Speaks on the Woman Clothed with the Sun and The Cup of Justice.

During the Sorrowful Mysteries of the Rosary with my spiritual director, as Father prayed the Mystery of the Scourging, I saw interiorly, Jesus bound and whipped. Then God the Father spoke: **My children, there is nothing more offensive to Me than to observe one human being strike another human being. Observing My Son as He was scourged; His innocent human body assaulted with hatred, caused Me indescribable suffering. I Who am your Father, sent My Love to you and He was rejected. Yet, Love bore everything for you and purchased eternal life for you. Today, I observe you striking one another still. In every corner of the world, one man is lashing out to another man. The most innocent of victims are denied life itself. Breath is smothered in the womb. How long, My creation, must I observe hatred and death?**
On this, the anniversary of the apparitions of Fatima, I say to you: "Look up to the heavens for I am again sending the Woman Clothed with the Sun." Listen to her messages of love. In Fatima, she asked the prayer of the Rosary be said to avert terrible disasters. She taught you that prayer is powerful and can avert much suffering. She told the children at Fatima to "Look up to the heavens; to strive for heavenly things; love and holiness." She foretold of an era of peace that would arrive through her intercession and through her having crushed Satan's army. These are critical days for you. Days of decision; days of warfare between the Woman Clothed with the Sun and the serpent. In this time of mercy, the heavens are opening up

to you. You can avert much suffering through your prayer and your willingness to convert for good. Cease to strike one another. Cease scourging My Son who continues to suffer on your account due to lack of love. You must decide to accept what I am offering you; My Mercy, My Love. The cup of justice is full. Only love and repentance can appease My justice.

I, Who am your Father, bless you. My Love is for you. If you but raise your eyes and your heart to the heavens, you will see Me ready to grant all My Love and goodness to you. You must decide. I love you. Your Father

Carrying the Cross Mystery: I saw Our Lady literally holding the Pope in her arms. They were embracing one another in a most intimate and loving way. The Pope appeared to be weeping. Our Lady held his face in her hands and consoled him. Love was exchanged and strength imparted.

42. **10-16-95** My home, Rosary with Spiritual Director
Take this Sacred Heart of Mine.

Father prayed the Glorious Mysteries. At the Descent of Holy Spirit decade, with my eyes closed, I saw extremely brilliant light. All darkness vanished. The light represented the Holy Spirit. Then, I saw a river rushing. The river swept us into it. The river represented grace.

There was a pause then Jesus said: **Take this Sacred Heart of Mine which burns with love. And love Me for all the souls who spurn My love. Accept My Heart of Love for all those who will not accept this Heart of Mine. I gave words and teachings to (St.) Margaret Mary (regarding the Sacred Heart). I give the grace to you; the grace to know My Love; to accept My Love. Embrace My Heart and be one with Me. I so love you. Thank you for accepting this Heart of Mine. Pray for all souls. I love each soul as I love you, infinitely.**

Then, I saw descending from heaven, the Sacred Heart of Jesus, blood red, with streams of light issuing forth. At the same time, I saw our hearts depart and ascend up toward heaven. There was an exchange of hearts. Jesus said: **You have My Heart. I have yours.**

43. **10-17-95** 7:30 PM, My home
Die to Self: Let Go of Your Worldly Life

My children,
"Unless a grain of wheat falls to the ground and dies, it remains a grain of wheat. But if it dies, it produces much fruit. Whoever loves his life, loses it and whoever hates his life in this world will preserve it for eternal life." Jn 12:24
Unless you die to yourself, you will not rise to God. Pray to obtain the grace to endure the pain of death to self. Only then can God use you to bear much fruit for the kingdom of God. Put aside selfishness and pride. Pray for the grace to cast aside your own desires in favor of God's desire. He alone has perfect knowledge of your heart and He alone knows what is good for it. Death to self causes heartache. This heartache must be endured in patience and in love. Love overcomes the difficulty of dying to yourself.
Prayer is the way to know love and receive love. God reveals Himself in prayer. The sacraments procure grace for you to persevere in dying to yourself. All that is necessary is given unto you always. The grain of wheat that dies becomes food for others. You, too, must die to become God's instrument of love for others. This dying process continues daily. The seeds of self-interest and pride rise up to tempt you continually. Every creature has pride, which must be overcome. All that you are, all that you have, is pure gift. Therefore, be humble. Let go of your worldly life. Set aside your pride again and again and again. Be little and know God will provide for you. Be honest with yourself about your pride. Only then can you overcome it through grace. Bear fruit for God - all for His honor and glory. I will assist you always. Your Mother

44. **10-17-95** 11 PM, My home
An Attack Against the Messages

This morning my soul felt as strong as ever; as if it could endure anything for God. As the day progressed, however, this unusual strength left. I decided I would get the messages into notebooks. An attitude of negativity toward this work began in a subtle way but increased steadily. As I read the messages, I had an aversion to them. This escalated to almost a hatred of them. I persevered by sheer will, without prayer or realizing that I was under attack. It was as if a mist came over me, but it progressed into a dense fog, clouding my perception. The evil spirits were very subtle when others were around me. But when my family went to bed and I was alone, working on the notebooks, they seemed to rise up against me in one fell swoop. The attack was so intense that I wanted to go outside and scream because of the negativity inside of me. The only thing that I knew was that I was becoming sicker by the minute.

1. I lost my clarity. (Spirit of confusion.)
2. Strong aversion to anything and anyone spiritual. (Spirit of aversion to spiritual life.)
3. Hatred of this work. (Spirit of hatred.)
4. Absolute futility. (Spirit of futility and discouragement.)
5. Suspicion of spiritual director's discernment. (Spirit of suspicion.)
6. Extreme negativity of myself, almost self-hatred. (Spirit of self-hatred.)
7. Temptation to destroy the messages was extreme. (Spirit of anger.) (Spirit of rebellion and disobedience.)

I lifted my hand to push all of the messages off the table onto the floor. But I stopped, realizing the violence of the action I was about to take. I called my spiritual director. As I did so, I thought, "I hate to disturb him. Why can't I do this alone?" As soon as I heard his voice, I broke down. I was so wrenched I thought I would throw up. I was physically sick due to the attack. He prayed me through this for some time knowing exactly how to pray. The first release from this attack came when he prayed to St. Michael, the Archangel. The final release came when He called upon the Holy Spirit to come to me. Peace and love returned. I could never have done this alone. I could not pray by myself. I had to reach out for help!

45. **10-18-94** 8:30 AM Mass, Feast of St. Luke
Jesus: Your Conversion Must be Ongoing.

Soul, the more you are transfigured into My Image, the more sensitive you become to everything. I give to you My own Love that you may love souls. I give to you My own vision to see the needs of souls. I give you My own Heart that you have compassion and mercy for souls. You see spiritual realities, both the light and the darkness. Your sensitivity gives Me glory when it calls forth in you greater faith, hope, and charity. In this age, there is a great insensitivity; indifference, and hardness of heart. The converted soul can no longer exist in insensitivity. The converted soul is supple, docile. Such a soul is alive with love; living in faith; hoping in God and extends charity to souls.

On this day of remembrance of Luke, the evangelist and doctor, I say to you - converted souls have a great responsibility to share their conversion. Conversion of heart is a great gift, a miracle in a soul. These are the ones who live and spread the gospel of love. To these much has been given and much is asked. The conversion of one soul is for the good of all. I have said that you who have received the good news of the gospel of salvation are the light of the world and the salt of the earth; the leaven for the world. A single light set on a mountain can illumine an entire area of darkness. A little salt adds flavor to everything. A little leaven causes the entire bread to rise.

Through the intercession of the heart of Mary, there are many conversions in this era. The converted soul is called to spread the gospel of love by loving, serving, and praying for souls; living and trusting in abandonment to Divine Providence. Evangelize your environment by loving. Witness to the truth of the Gospel by living a life of great faith, hope, and charity. If you do this, you will be different. You will bring the kingdom of God which is within you into the midst of the kingdom of evil and dispel the darkness. Never doubt. The light will overcome the darkness. You, My beloved one, are a vital part of My light for the world. In weakness, I am glorified because then, I alone, am your strength. When you stumble, I will pick you up. Persevere with sensitivity. Your conversion must be ongoing. I love you. Jesus

46. **10-18-95** Rosary with Spiritual Director
Ordinary Souls

Because of yesterday's severe, evil attack, I began the Rosary
in a fragile state of being: very weak; extreme emptiness. As soon
as Father began the Rosary, I experienced a sharp violent stabbing
pain in my heart. Then I heard Jesus say: **"Divine Arrow of My
Living Charity."**
Later, Our Lady spoke:

My children,
Ordinary souls attain heaven by God's grace, which is mercy,
and God's Love. Ordinary lives filled with ordinary circumstances
are the occasion in which God's love enters and transforms souls
into love. Faithfulness to God's grace and obedience to the Holy
Spirit with acceptance of God's Love procures for the ordinary
soul, God's eternal kingdom. God provides the grace to transfig-
ure the ordinary into Love..
My children, God loves you in your ordinary souls; in your
ordinary lives. You need not strive to be extraordinary. Simply be
faithful little souls. Be faithful to God's grace; faithful to the inspi-
rations of the Holy Spirit; faithful to the Gospel of love and life.
Then you will attain your eternal reward. I will always assist you
in your journey to God. I anticipate with great joy the reunion of
all my children with God in His eternal kingdom; the kingdom of
love everlasting. I love you. Your Mother

47. **10-20-95** Prayer Group
Greater Love, Deeper Faith, More Hope

At the decade of the Descent of the Holy Spirit, there was a tremendous infilling of Divine Love.
Then Our Lady spoke:

My children,
Let your hearts be enkindled to greater love, deeper faith, and
more hope. In that faith and hope, trust as little children that I am

truly with you. I am always assisting you to walk in God's Divine Will. Please ponder the teachings I have given you for so long. These contain many rich teachings. Strive to live the messages I have given the world. The Father may soon require you to walk in darker faith. His grace will always illumine the path in the darkness of faith. You are being prepared for this; for all that will unfold. I will never leave you, but you may not always perceive my presence.

Persevere in prayer. Only through prayer can you draw ever closer to my Son, Jesus. Please offer your joys and sufferings in reparation for the sin of the world. My Son suffers still because so many souls refuse His love. You are fighting a great battle in which love will overcome every stronghold and darkness. Truly you are my prayer warriors. Great is your intercession. Many souls are saved because of your prayers and sacrifice. Be faithful to my Son by living the Gospel message of love. Come against all darkness with the light that burns in your heart - for that is where the light of God lives; where His love dwells. Radiate His light and love to all souls. Be secure in the knowledge of His infinite love for you. Be at peace. I love you. Your Mother

48. **10-22-95** My home
In Secret and Silence There is Union

I am keenly aware of the evil spirits that are surrounding and attacking my soul. The battle is intense and exhausting. I am assailed by spirits of doubt and negativity. I turn to Jesus and Mary constantly. Grace is sufficient enough that the attacks do not crush me. I am growing so weary. I called my spiritual director but could not reach him.

I began to pray the Rosary and entered a deep state of prayer, a state of stillness, silence and love. This lasted about an hour. When I awoke, I was very refreshed. I prayed to Mary and Jesus for help against doubt of some of the prophecies about the Church. I surrendered myself again, begging them to give me confidence in their works of this age.

Jesus spoke: ***Soul, in prayer this night I opened the door to a hidden chamber of My Sacred Heart and I usher you within. This secret chamber of My Heart contains profound stillness** and sacred silence. I darken your senses that you may enter this secret chamber of My Heart. The light in this chamber of My Heart (which is like a deep, deep well) is the light of My Divine Love. Here your little heart is lost in union with My Heart of infinite love. I ushered you to this deep and hidden chamber that I may, in secret, thoroughly press your little heart into the ocean of My Love to permeate you with Myself. In secret and in silence so profound, you believe you are sleeping, your soul is truly alive in Me while your heart and your will are made one with My Heart and My Will. I annihilate your unbelief and cast out your fear. I fortify you with My own love which is My strength. Divine Love is full of power. My Majesty reigns in you and you offer no resistance. This hidden, silent, dark and deep chamber of My Heart is where you and I are formed into deeper union. I give you My orders in so secret a fashion that you cannot yet perceive what I have already given you. This is the mystery of My love. And it is for you. Therefore, go in My peace with the confidence that you are My beloved and I am with you always. I love you, *Soul. Jesus

Now please continue to write as My Mother speaks to you.

49. **10-22-95**
Do Not Doubt the Prophecies About the Church

Our Lady spoke:
Dear Child,

I am aware of your difficulties. You are not walking this journey alone. You are given much grace from heaven. Please do not doubt the prophecies given to you about the Church and her trials. Your vision is limited. Consider the prophecies are given by Jesus and me, who know precisely what the Church must pass through on her way to glory. The foundations which must be laid are well underway now. These are the foundations which will preserve the deposit of truth in the Roman Catholic Church while she is attacked from within and without. This must come to pass on the journey to her glorification and restoration to love. Her purification will lead to her resplendent beautification. It is God's mercy that permits the prepara-

tion of the faithful so that the remnant are not denied the food of life during future trials. Like the prophets of old, the Holy Spirit is upon you and many others, so that souls are spared because they have been forewarned and instructed on preparing themselves for such purification. There are signs all over. Already the sheep and the goats are being separated. The Church herself, deep within her structure, knows well of the trials in her midst and those soon to come. Indeed, the Holy Spirit is preparing the way, forewarning all of creation, converting hearts to know the truth.

Dear ones, do not be overwhelmed or worried. The Holy Spirit and I, your devoted Mother, accompany you that you do not falter due to deceptions from the enemy. As my cohorts, you are unified and fortified in my Immaculate Heart. Lean on your Mother and I will impart my own limitless confidence in God, granting you the virtues of my Immaculate Heart. Rejoice that you are prepared for battle. Rejoice that you will usher in the glory of God through the glorified Church. We are birthing the era of peace where my Son will reign and Satan will be chained that he may not attack your souls again. Be at peace in my heart. I am with you always. I love you. Your Mother

She gave the Scripture Jeremiah 13:15-17 when I was doubting the prophecies about the Church.

Jeremiah 13:15 Give ear, listen humbly, for the Lord speaks.

Jeremiah 13:16 Give Glory to the Lord, your God, before it grows dark;

Before your feet stumble on darkening mountains;

Before the light you look for turns to darkness,

Changes into black clouds.

Jeremiah 13:17 If you do not listen to this in your pride, I will weep in secret many tears;

My eyes will run with tears for the Lord's flock, led away to exile.

50. **10-25-95** 8:30 AM Mass and before the Tabernacle.
My Church will Undergo My Passion

Soul, My Church, My Body on earth will undergo My passion on the way to her glory. She will be betrayed from within and without as I was betrayed by My very own. She is being

scourged now. The scourging is carried out by those who have accepted the rebellious attitude of the enemy. The enemy's cunning is such that the traitor's rationalize their rebellion and pride to be for the good of the Church, for her improvement. They want to embellish her, but instead, they are ravishing her and rendering her members impoverished. She will be crowned with the crown of mockery as I was crowned with thorns. Just as the head was not recognized as King, so too the body will not be recognized as the radiant Bride of the one true King until she passes through the darkness of Good Friday leading to the glory of the resurrection.

The enemy is in a frenzy knowing the time is near. He has set out to divide My House so that she cannot stand, but Divine Providence has provided for her. The Holy Spirit together with My Mother, who is Mother of all, has prepared the way. Throughout the world, foundations have been laid to provide for the faithful members throughout the days of trial when they will be persecuted for the faith.

Yes, My faithful remnant will stand. You will proclaim the truth of the Gospel and uphold the cross of salvation in the midst of persecution because I, Myself, will uphold you. I will make of you a refuge of Truth. You will not falter because Love has provided for you and love will empower you. The love within My members will overcome the final attack of the enemy. When he is bound in defeat, My Church, My Body will rise in glory. Do not be scandalized when I expose the traitors and cast them out. Pray that you may be fortified for battle. Already you can rejoice because the victory is Mine and yours. Love is with you. Love Me and love one another. Love will make you strong. My peace and My Love. Jesus

51. **10-27-95** Prayer Group
Immerse Yourself in the Most Sacred Heart

My children,
    Tonight I invite you to immerse yourself in the Most Sacred Heart of my Son. His Heart is an ocean of love. Enter and permit

yourself to be permeated by His Divine Love. Become saturated with love from His Heart, then you will find yourself fortified for your journey. Then you will be enabled to do whatever He asks you to do. Love will make you strong in Him who is your strength. By the blood of the Lamb you have been washed clean. His mercy has made you pure. Now the Holy Spirit fills you with His light and guides you along the path of the Divine Will of the Father.

My children, you will find yourselves being persecuted for the faith in the very near future. The Church will be tried. The faithful will be persecuted. I want you to be full of hope. You can rejoice in the resurrection and the victory that is already yours. Whatever you pass through on the way to the resurrection, will only cause you to grow in faith, hope, and charity. Do not be discouraged on your way.

Union with God is your goal. Persevere toward this one goal, enduring all that He permits to enter your path. Know that God's grace will always be with you to carry you through the greatest of trials. Cling to my Son. Love God. Seek Him always. If He leads you to the desert, rejoice. He teaches you in the desert that you may love Him because He is God - worthy of all your love. He teaches you detachment in the desert dryness. Only in detachment can He reign in you. All that He teaches you is preparation. You are being healed that you may heal others. You are being tried that you may help others during their trials. You are being loved that you may pour love upon others. One small step at a time, my children. One day at a time. Walk in love.

Tonight I weave you in and out of one another to form a beautiful wreath of fragrant flowers to present to God. I rejoice in your littleness. You are pure of heart. Pray always that souls will come to know and love God. Pray for the Church. She has great need of your prayers and sacrifice. I bless you in the Name of the Father, Son, and Holy Spirit. I love you. Your Mother

52. **10-31-95** 9 PM, My home
Do Not Be Afraid!

My children,
 I have made a covenant with you, an everlasting covenant. I will uphold My own in every trial, persecution, and hardship.

Truly, truly I say to you, do not be afraid. I will shelter you. I will pour out My grace and you will not falter. As the chaos of evil escalates, so too, My grace increases. In the darkness and devastation that will come to purge the earth of evil, I will protect and guide My own with a continuous outpouring of grace from My Heart of love. My own shall not be afraid. You will stand like a fortress because I am your foundation and your pillar of truth. You will not walk in darkness though darkness surrounds you. I will set My light within you. You will know I am in you. Indeed, you will give My light to one another.

O My creation, My creation, My creation! I love you in My perfect and infinite way; a way you do not comprehend. Though you refuse Me, I do not refuse you. I never turn from you as you turn from Me. I shall continue to pour My Love upon you. There is nothing I would not do for you! What appears to be punishment will be My mercy for you. I shall permit purification that you will be drawn to Me for good. O My creation, I shall give you the grace to accept My justice as wisdom and mercy for souls. Though all will suffer and some will perish, I shall sustain you in My love.

When the cup of divine justice is poured upon you, My own will praise My holy Name trusting in My wisdom, goodness, and love. The lukewarm will see My power and majesty and become fervent, and I will save you. You who refuse Me then will have chosen your own demise. Already you are making choices day by day. That is why My Holy Spirit is upon the earth with an outpouring like Pentecost. That is why I give to you again, My Mother upon earth. She is with you to assist you in your choices, preparing you that you are found with oil in your lamps. I am the oil. Your soul is the lamp. If you have surrendered, then I have chosen you and you have chosen Me. Then I am in you and you are in Me. Then your forehead bears the mark of My own. There is nothing to be afraid of. Yet there will be weeping and wailing. I, the Lord your God shall weep for you who will refuse Me even unto death.

O My creation, I shall continue to provide every grace for you, but you have a free will. Accept My grace that I may rejoice in you; that we may live together, in love, for an eternity of joy and peace; that you may enter into My kingdom on earth, the earth restored to love. O My creation, I am faithful to you. If you will accept My grace, you will be faithful to Me even in darkness, persecution, and hardship. In all things, in every circumstance, I will uphold you. Even if you fall, I will pick you up. There is nothing I would not do for you! I love you. I love you. I love you. **Your Jesus**

When Jesus said: **You who refuse Me will have chosen your own demise,** He made a point of showing me that He gives every soul the opportunity to choose Him. He does not condemn. The soul condemns itself in the light of the truth of God's Love and Mercy.

53. **11-1-95** Feast of All Saints 8:30 AM Mass
You Are Called to Sainthood

My children,
Today is your feast day. There is communion between the saints in heaven and the saints on earth. The saints in heaven behold My glory while the saints on earth hope in My glory. O My creation, you should depend on the intercession of the saints who have gone before you. Truly they intercede for you. Truly they are in communion with Me, with one another and with you - My saints in formation. Rely on their assistance. Learn from their example. They fought the good fight. With My grace they attained their goal. They are one with Me and I with them. My glory is theirs. They are lights for you. Permit them to illumine your path. Today, they rejoice in you. You are living in an era of great importance. In this era, I am forming an army of saints. Sainthood is accomplished on earth. So this is your feast day, My children. I am with you to remind you - you are called to sainthood.

O My creation, I am today, transfiguring you into My holiness. I am making of you a holy people. All the earth shall be made holy; holy for Me. For, I, the Lord, your God, am holy, holy, holy. Again I say to you, I the Lord, your God, am making you holy. I alone can form holiness. You have only to preserve yourself from sin, desire My Divine Will and accept My divine grace. Then My Almighty hand will form you into My own holiness. As My own children, My Body on earth - I, your Head, your God, bless you this day in communion with all the saints in heaven, all the choirs of angels. The complete citizenship of heaven under the queenship of Mary, anoint you this day with the oil of Divine Love. The mark of holiness, sainthood is upon your forehead. Walk as citizens of heaven. I, your Triune God, am with you. I love you. Jesus

54. **11-8-95** Rosary with Spiritual Director, my Home
Persevere in Faith

Sorrowful Mysteries: At the beginning of the Rosary, I saw hundreds of black darts aimed and fired at us from all sides. Yet when fired, they could not penetrate a protective shield that surrounds us. Our Lady spoke at the fourth decade, Carrying the Cross.

My little ones,
Persevere in faith. Carry the cross and go forward in the Will of God. Do not be paralyzed by temptations, attacks, or the pain of the cross. Bear everything with patience and love. Do not count the cost. Persevere. Love is with you. One step at a time, go forward to fulfill the task at hand. You are yet being formed by the hand of God. Truly, He is fashioning you into His own image. Do not doubt. You have one another to uphold, protect, guide and love. You are surrounded by heavenly protection at all times. The fury of the evil one has been unleashed. You will endure many attacks. Yet, as you exist in my Immaculate Heart, he cannot harm you. More will be required of you, as more is given unto you.
The fountain of God's mercy is being poured within you. The river of Divine Love is flowing through you. The Holy Spirit is guiding your path, feeding you wisdom and knowledge while keeping you aflame with love. Love will fuel everything you do. All will be for love and in love. Love is the source. Love is the means. Love is the goal. You need not understand. Obey! Trust! I am with you! You will not falter! Thank you for your prayers, your heart

and especially thank you for your fiat of love. Be at peace. I love you. Your Mother

55. **11-14-95** 8:30 AM Mass
The Enemy Deceives but My Love Heals

In prayer before the tabernacle, Jesus began to speak in a "pleading" disposition.

*Soul, My Own,
The riches of My Heart are far greater than all the riches of the world combined. One drop of the blood I shed for the salvation of the world is more precious than all the gold in the world. This blood is with you still in the Eucharistic Sacrifice of the Mass. Does the world value it as much as it values gold?

I, the Redeemer of the world offer to you, My creation, this very Heart of Mine. My call is from one heart to another heart. If you would open the door to your heart, I would enter. I will impart My own Heart of love to yours. This Heart of Mine will heal your brokenness by the gentle power of My love and goodness which takes away the hurts and the pains you hold in your heart. If I can enter your heart, from here all will be healed; that is, your soul, your mind, your will, and your body. The heart holds the key to the rest of your being. Your heart can harbor either darkness or light; sickness or wellness. The heart carries the burden of your life within. If I can heal you here, then all will be well with you. If My voice can penetrate your heart, it will respond as it will recognize the voice of its Creator. You must permit yourself to "listen" to your Creator.

My own human Heart encompasses every human heart through the power of My infinite divinity; enfolding all of humanity into My own divinity by means of this Heart of Mine. How long must I observe your human hearts to be full of every kind of illness, sin, and unforgiveness? Must you cling to your suffering and sickness? Why then, do you repeatedly refuse the healing ointment, the cure of My Divine Love and Mercy?

My own Sacred Heart is for you! My Heart is in My hand to place it within your own heart. Not that we are two hearts side by side, but that your heart dissolve into My Heart so we are one heart. My Heart is an infinite abyss of love containing every goodness you require. Why then, do you guard your heart from the One who loves you? Perhaps your heart is so full of the world that there is no room for its Creator Who is Love. Such a heart is very sick indeed. To be sick and unaware of your illness is a very dangerous state of being. Yet this is the kind of sickness I observe in you — My beloved people. This Heart of Mine aches for you to turn to Me. Listen. Hear. I am calling you -one heart to another heart. Must you harden your heart to My call?

O how the enemy deceives you into holding on to your fears, sickness and sin. His deception is a stronghold on your heart. From here your entire being suffers. There are two great deceptions in this age. First, the enemy convinces you that he does not exist. He does this so that you do not come to recognize him or his deceptions, therefore, you do not battle them. He is safe co-mingling with you. You are deceived and unaware. The second, He has convinced you that I (God) do not exist or if I do exist, it is to condemn you and oppress you with My laws.

From the beginning, he is a liar! I exist. He exists. He is not the opposite of Me. He is the opposite of Michael, the Archangel. He knows He is condemned to death. His goal is to take as many souls with him as possible. He leads you to death. I uphold you for life - eternal life. My laws set you free. His lawlessness binds you. I am Love. My Word proclaims this and it is true! I am Love. I love you. You are My own. I give to you this very Heart of Mine. It is pierced by your sins and scorned by you still, yet it is for you and with you forever and ever. My love is everlasting. Open your heart. I love you. Jesus

I asked, "Jesus, is the heart the place of conversion?" He said, **The will is the place of conversion but the heart is the place of initiation. The spark in the heart will ignite the will to conversion.**

56. **11-14-95**
Surrender More

In adoration, out of deep silence, Jesus said: *Soul, surrender more. I said: "Dear Jesus, What more can I surrender? You are everything to me." Jesus said: **Surrender more. Be more childlike. Be a little, little child.**

I pondered this. My surrender must be ever new and at every moment. I am too analytical and lacking in childlike trust. To be a child is utter abandonment to God. Even when I perceive I am doing this, perhaps I am not. The death of myself is not a moment in time, but a continuous, slow death process. Too often I rely on preconceived notions. This puts me ahead of God. The grace of the present moment is to suffice for me. I am nothing. God is everything. This reality is what surrender is about. And it is opposed to my human nature. Jesus is merciful to constantly remind me of the truth.

57. **11-15-95** My home, Rosary with Spiritual Director, 3 PM
Meditate on The Passion

First we prayed the Chaplet of Divine Mercy at 3 PM. Our Lady spoke at the Third Sorrowful Mystery.

My son and my daughter,

Blessed are you who are all aflame with love. Love Himself burns within you. As your Mother, the guardian of your hearts, I rejoice to observe my Son alive in you. His presence permeates your being and this gives glory to the Father. From above I observe few souls burning with true love of God. It is a great benefit to your soul to meditate on the passion and crucifixion of my Son.

The great mystery of the cross is a school of prayer. It is love unlike any human love. It is for you because the Father so loved you that He sent His Son as ransom for you. Your soul benefits greatly when it looks at the passion and the cross.

Receive all that God is giving you with much gratitude. Ponder it in your heart and rejoice that He has called you out of the world and made you His own, uniting you to Himself. You are wounded by love. This is a most precious and rare blessing. It is preparation for the future. Many will come to you. Many will draw from your love. Drink of it now. It is painful because God is increasing your capacity always and your entire being is acted upon as He continuously causes you to grow in love and union.

As your Mother, I remain with you and take joy and consolation in your hearts. This is a time of great mercy for you. Thank you for responding to God's call. If you could see the angels that surround you and all the heavenly graces within you; if you could see all the saints who pray for you, you would cry for joy! Persevere. Above all — love. Continue to surrender in totality. The smaller you become the more you can receive. I bless you with the oil of my maternal love. Truly my arms embrace you. When you pray the Rosary with such love, you are embracing me. Thank you. Your Mother

58. **11-16-95** 8:30 AM Mass
Vultures: Death of Self

At Holy Communion Jesus said: ***Soul, observe yourself on the cross with Me.** He refers to a vision I am getting of myself on the cross with Him. First is the wood, then Jesus, then me, hanging on the cross. I observe vulture-like birds coming at me and tearing at my flesh. Again and again my flesh is torn from my body. I am in agony. I do not suffer silently. I cry out from the depths of my being. I scream with pain. I cry out the name of Jesus. Jesus, have mercy on me! Finally, I am just a skeleton on the cross. My flesh is all gone. Then my bones begin to rot as well. Jesus says: **Now, you can fly like an eagle! The flesh cannot weigh you down. By the cross-I have set you free. Now with Me, you can ascend toward heaven. Like an eagle you can look directly into the sun and fly toward it.**

My beloved, every trial, burden, temptation, persecution, humiliation, insult to your flesh, all that I permit to come at you will serve to set you free from yourself. You no longer live for you but for Me! You cannot soar to the heights of union until you die to yourself in every way. I have chosen you for the heights. My tent on the highest mountain you will enter. The

Will of the Father will be your only appetite. You will read My Heart for the life of the Church, for the souls you will gather for Me. My love sustains you. From no human being will you draw as you draw from Me. But many will draw from you. All the while, in your suffering I am holding you, pressing you into Myself hanging on the cross for love of you. Suffer in silence as I suffered for you. Do not defend yourself. Endure for love of Me. Trust. Out of your suffering, I will make great good. I will impart My own beauty to you. How radiant you shall be for Me. My Divine Love has the power to adhere you to the cross. You are never alone on the cross. I am always with you. I love you, My beloved, My own. Jesus

My interior suffering is immense. I am dying! My flesh wants to live! It does not die silently. Exteriorly everything appears to be fine. Many would envy my comfortable life. But no one knows the interior suffering that God has chosen for my soul. He demands everything, never settling for a portion only. Still, the union that comes from the interior suffering is too sublime for words. It is pure love and pure joy. I would give my life for it. Indeed, at times, it seems I am.

In the state of extreme suffering interiorly, as I drove from the church, Satan said, "See, He (God) causes you suffering, suffering, suffering for what? He will give you cross after cross after cross. He is killing you! You want to live! Live! You are in the world to live. You will die later. Such suffering in this life is useless." I rebuked him saying, "No, no, no. You are a liar. Be gone from me." Then I prayed to St. Michael. Satan was gone.

In a way Satan caused me to focus on the truth of the great good Jesus gave me in this vision. My flesh weighs my soul down. I find in me, a love of comfort, a desire to be esteemed, to be loved by creatures. I am too sensitive to the words and opinions of others. In me, there are too many judgments and opinions for other souls. I am detached to a certain extent, even for the most part, but God requires everything. He desires no rivals. Sometimes I delude myself to think I am surrendered only to find myself resisting the dying process that is occurring by the hand of God because it hurts. It is not easy. There's a part of me that says I want to live!

God offers me true life in Him, where I can soar like an eagle, after I die to myself. In His great mercy He takes me to the wood of the cross and places me with Him. I suffer, yet I live, because wherever He is, I want to be. If He is with me, then I can endure.

He is there, hanging between heaven and earth to become the bridge that souls can use to get to heaven, our true home. He is there in the greatest act of love. For me, He died. So too, shall I die for Him. This is not an exaggeration. I will that anything that comes between God and my soul, be put to death. I live now for the consummation of this love. I know this is what the Father has willed for me. He created me for this. It is His Will. I belong to His Son. In this He is glorified. By the power of your Holy Spirit, Father, let Your Will be done. Cause me to be one with Your Son! All honor, glory and praise be Yours, My Triune God!

59. **11-17-95** Prayer Group
Little Lambs are Prayer Warriors

During Chaplet of Divine Mercy, Our Lady said:

My dear children,
I bless you as you have responded to my call to prayer for the salvation of the whole world. Thank you for permitting me to use you as prayer warriors in my army of little souls who will overcome the spirit of darkness and evil, bringing forth the era of peace, restoring love on the earth. You are answering my call now. I have formed you to be my partners in the peace plan for the world.
I warn you of the attacks that will come at you. You are protected by my Immaculate Heart. Satan cannot penetrate you. Still, you must learn to know the enemy so that you can battle him. This will be done with ease if you rely on the grace from the Holy Spirit and not on your own strength. The Holy Spirit is your strength. Never battle alone. I will raise you up that you may have far reaching vision for the Church. You are my little lambs and I am joyful to be with you as your Mother. Draw from me. You are an offering that is pleasing in His sight. Remain in Him. Be at peace. I so love you my children. Your Mother

60. **11-18-95** At Church after Mass
The Eucharist: Sacrament Most Targeted by Satan

Following Communion, Jesus said:

*Soul, My own,
The graces given in the Eucharist are inestimable for your soul. Truly you are eating the Bread of Life which is My Body for you. Your very being thrives on this food. My Body is the divine sustenance for your life. Bread consecrated into My Body on the altar by the power of the Holy Spirit is meant to draw souls to Me like a magnet. Souls who partake draw from the very life of Me. It is the essence of My Divine Love for souls. By means of grace, I give to you a hunger, a thirst for My Body, My Blood. This is the sacrament of union, of salvation. By means of this sacrament, your soul is made pure and holy; your heart is enkindled to love with My own Love inside you; your will is inclined to the Father's Will; your body is fortified as My temple. Even in heaven, souls cannot comprehend the unfathomable good of Holy Communion made in the proper state of grace. So great a gift has the Father given the world in and through the Word Made Flesh, who remains in the world in the Holy Sacrifice of the Mass, in the consecration of bread and wine into My Body and Blood; that this is precisely the sacrament most targeted by Satan.

In this age, Satan attacks this sacrament by means of desecrating it in many devious ways. There is blatant desecration of the Host by friends of the enemy. His followers are many. They delight in profaning the Host.

There is widespread subtle desecration by means of souls who receive in the state of mortal sin. Many of you who call yourselves My friends are living a lie regarding the state of your soul.

There is desecration by means of denying the True Presence of My Body and Blood in this sacrament. Many of My own believe it to be a symbol of Me only.

There is further denial of this truth by means of souls so full of pride, they fail to see their need to eat and drink My

Body, My Blood. Even some of My priests are compromising their belief in the True Presence.

These deceptions pierce My Heart, because I who am the Word Made Flesh know the eternal value of this sacrament for your soul. It is vital to the life of a soul and to the life of the Church. Truly, it is being compromised as the importance of it is diminished. Indeed, today you do not value the true reality of My love for you, My creation.

Pray, little one, each time you receive Me in this sacrament, pray with all your heart that it will always be available for your soul and for all souls. If My very own give into Satan's deceptions, there will come a time when you will secretly search for the true sacrament of Holy Communion.

O My creation, repent! Be reconciled to Me, your Triune God. Do not be deceived. Love the truth. Do not accept a lie. In that I have already given you all that is necessary, the truth itself, know that there will be consequences to your decision either for the truth or for the lie.

Especially, pray for the shepherds that they will remain in the truth and never compromise the truth even in persecution of it. The truth will stand. Those who stand with it will live even if they die. But those who deny the truth or compromise it for the sake of a lie will be swept away together with the father of all lies. Just as Judas betrayed Me and he was My own, so too, My own today are betraying this sacrament. The pain of this is all the greater as it comes from My Own. My Heart is wounded and bleeding because of you. Still, I love. I love. I love. Your Jesus

61. **11-29-95** My Home, 11 PM
Divine Mercy for America

*Soul, the message of Divine Mercy is vital for all souls. Let it be proclaimed in your country now. The message of mercy can free more souls from the clutches of the evil one than any other message of this age. The age of Divine Mercy will lead into the time of divine justice. Both are acts of Divine Love.

Many souls can be diverted from the path to perdition by means of My Divine Mercy.

The future of America depends upon its response to grace available now. If America continues on its present course, there will be much to suffer. Unfathomable graces are available to souls who turn to seek My Mercy now. Mercy and reconciliation go hand in hand. As revealed to Blessed Faustina, the message of mercy is more than devotion, it is an offering to the Father that appeases divine justice for the world. The Father sent Me into the world that all people would be reconciled to Him through Me. I am the ransom for all.

In the Chaplet, a soul unites himself to Me and again, I am the ransom, the offering Who mediates the soul with the Father. Satan opposes this message because it renders him powerless, because by the cross on Calvary, I overcame the death he desires for souls. Through the Chaplet (of Divine Mercy), My sacrifice for the world to the Father is offered again and continues to call forth mercy. Souls are saved and freed from the devil who has caught many souls in his net. The pride, lust, hatred, and idolatry in America escalates. Like wild fire, evil spreads its poison infecting more souls daily. The deception is great as Satan gloats over souls that perish daily.

The message of Divine Mercy will arrest the deception that binds souls who believe that I am an unforgiving judge who condemns. The truth remains. There is no sin so scarlet that it cannot be covered by My unfathomable mercy. You have only to seek mercy and reconciliation through repentance. Land of plenty, humble yourselves. I, your God, will restore you to love. My Mercy is for you. Turn to Me now.

Child, I will bless all your endeavors because it is My Will that the message of Divine Mercy spread as far as possible. Pray that the cup of divine justice be reduced as many drink from My Divine Mercy to be converted to love. You who proclaim My mercy must be a sign of mercy for all. Pray that the darkness of your country be penetrated by the rays of Divine Mercy now! Blessed Faustina intercedes for you. I love you. Jesus

62. 11-30-95 Rosary with Spiritual Director, My home, 2 PM
You Need Not Understand, Only Surrender!

At the decade of the Ascension, Father prayed about the balance between longing to go to God and staying here in accordance with the Will of God. Jesus said: **My son and My daughter, the secrets of your hearts are known to Me. Nothing is hidden. My light illumines your entirety. All of heaven can see My Light in you. Your longing for consummation of our union is balanced by the grace you receive to accomplish the Divine Will. I long to satisfy you as I bend from heaven to feed you a foretaste of the divine banquet. Already you partake in union. You have My Heart. All that I have, I share with you. Yet you are growing that you may have more of Me.**

The Father has chosen you each by name, to be a light for the world. Radiating My love, your light will be seen by many. It will illumine the Church in the hour of darkness. Your very longing is love. In it, I am glorified. Always long for Me. Always receive My Love, knowing, I too, long for you.

Suddenly, I felt a sharp stabbing from my left shoulder blade into my heart. Jesus said, ***Soul, make Me an offering. Give Me the pain.** I said, "Jesus, all I can think of is the pain of it." ***Soul, partake in My suffering for love of Me. Will you offer this?** "Jesus, please give me the grace to do so."

***Soul, you need not understand. Only surrender. United to Me, I use this offering to save souls, to avert souls from the path to perdition. I have prepared you for this. I have called you, My altar, My *Soul of the cross, foretelling of our union in and through the cross of suffering. I asked you to be "charity" for souls. *Now the time has come that indeed I make of you, My altar, so that by the cross you are My charity for souls. I shall make of you a radiant and pure bride by means of the cross of love. I love you My *Soul. You are Mine. Thank you for your fiat. Surrender into My arms. I will uphold you. I am your strength. In Me is your rest. Be still and offer no resistance. I give to you, My Peace. Thank you *Soul, for your offering.**

63. **11-30-95**
Bring Everything to the Light

At the Coronation, Our Lady said:

My children,

Thank you for crowning me with your love, surrender, and obedience. Thank you for bringing everything to the light. Trust, I who am your Mother, never leave you unprotected. My veil of protection surrounds you. You are deeply endowed with the Holy Spirit. His light makes you transparent and pure. When even a shadow of darkness gets near you, it is made evident to me, to all the saints assisting you and to your holy angels. If God permits you to be tried and tempted, it is for your good and for teaching. You must learn to do battle with the enemy. You will do so with ease, never losing your peace, as long as you are open and honest, bringing everything to the light. You are children of the light. Be at peace. I love you. Your Mother

64. **12-5-95** 12:45 AM
Drink of My Eternal Love

I prayed silently for two hours before Our Lady. Then, I went to bed at 12:40 AM. Within five minutes, Jesus spoke: ***Soul, like a dam bursting forth, I will pour out My living water through you that souls will drink of My charity, and My mercy, drawing from you as you draw from Me. Now is the time for you to drink of My fountain of eternal love. Drink to the full.**

My bride, I want you to become inebriated with the wine of My blood that you may have My life in every fiber of your being. Why do I ask you to drink? Because it is My nature to give and yours to receive. What do you have that you have not received? You must draw everything from Me. The vessel is empty until the Creator fills it with life and every good thing from His own Divine Life. My beloved, draw from the wisdom of the Most Holy Trinity and be filled that you may be a mirror of the wisdom of love. Do this for the souls I will send to you.

Remember always, true holy wisdom is found in the love of the cross of salvation. I love you. Jesus

65. **12-5-95** 8:30 AM Mass
The Wisdom of the Cross

*Soul, the wisdom of the cross is this. Divine Providence has provided salvation for all by the power of eternal Divine Love. The abyss between God and man has been bridged by the Son of God, Son of man. The wood of the cross is the plank that forms the bridge. My Body is the gateway from earth to heaven. The blood and water gushing from My Body is your baptism into life and your salvation from death. Wisdom loves the cross by which all men know the love of God. Divine Providence has made you children of God, heirs to His kingdom. God is love!

Love and the cross are one. The love of the Father is the very magnet that holds the bridge in place drawing souls unto Him by means of the bridge from earth to heaven. At the entrance to this gateway is Mary standing with the Holy Spirit. Mary urges all souls to the Gateway. Like a mother hen gathering her chicks, Mary gathers the family of man. The Holy Spirit ignites the human heart to love while bearing witness to the truth through the wisdom of the cross.

*Soul, the simplest can look at the crucifix and behold - this is love! It is written in the heart of every man. Is it any wonder that I would take you, My beloved, and put you on the cross with Me, that we become one? I want you to be the reservoir of My love, overflowing. I will pierce you with My love that you will burst forth to shower many souls. Do not be afraid. I love you. The treasures of My Heart are yours. Jesus

"Jesus - I long only for Union!
I abandon myself to Divine Providence.
I surrender myself to the Divine Will.
I unite myself to the Cross of Salvation and the Blood of the Lamb.
I will to love above all else by the Power of the Holy Spirit.

I place myself within the Immaculate Heart of Mary to be adorned with her virtues.

I seek the assistance of the saints who have gone before me that I may never offend Your most tender and merciful Heart.

My Jesus, I love You endlessly."

66. **12-5-95** Rosary with Spiritual Director, My home
Silent Prayer: A Place of Teaching

Father and I prayed the Rosary. Jesus said: **Beloved, I have taken you into a deep chamber of My Sacred Heart. Here, you enter into profound rest and peace. I cause you to be still so that in the silence and secrecy of My Heart I may anoint you with the oil of My Love. I adorn you with fragrant perfumes each identifying a virtue of holiness, which I have chosen for you. Here, I fashion you into My own beauty and impart My own goodness. I teach you here. What I teach will manifest in due season. It is enough for you to know that I give Myself to you in this way.**

I know all that you are going through. My grace upholds you. Trust. I have given you peace of soul and profound abiding love that you may know these come to those who walk in the Divine Will of God. Therefore, receive all that I give! Trust! I will instruct you along the way. You are in My Almighty hand. I, Myself, guide you. I am the Master Builder. You are My building. Let Me lay the deep foundation necessary to endure the trials of the future. Then will you uphold My holy name. You will give Me glory according to My Father's Will. I love you, My bride. I bless you, My priest. Your Jesus

67. **12-6-95** Feast of St. Nicholas, Bishop. Rosary
with Spiritual Director, my home
The Cradle and the Cross: Ponder Them Together

As soon as we decided to pray the Sorrowful Mysteries, evil spirits bombarded my mind with one distracting thought after another. Suddenly, I sensed the presence of Our Lady as we were praying to St. Michael. She said: *My children, Satan despises your meditating on the passion of Jesus most of all. He knows the great benefit of such meditation to a soul. He will attempt to block such efficacious prayer. Please continue to contemplate the passion of my Son. I pray with you in gratitude for the sufferings of my Son, which sets all souls free.*

We continued the Sorrowful Mysteries. At the third decade, the Crowning of Thorns, I observed Our Lady anointing the wounds on Jesus' head. These were deep puncture wounds, which pierced His scalp from the crown of thorns. I could observe her ever so lovingly removing the crown of thorns. Then she tenderly cleaned and anointed the puncture wounds all around His head. As she did so, I saw that she was so united to her Son that she experienced the crown of thorns mystically. We continued the Rosary and then prayed the Chaplet.

After both, Mary said: *My children, through His passion, death, and resurrection, my Son has set you free. You have freedom to choose life or death. He has purchased eternal life for you. But you must accept the gift by choosing for God. You must cooperate with divine grace. If you keep His commandments, you will be free. He has chosen eternal life for you, but also you must choose life.*

My children, in this season of Advent think often of my Son, Jesus. His birth and His death are closely united as both are love incomprehensible. One would lead to another. The wood of the cradle, then the wood of the cross would be His resting place. Life sprang from both the cradle and the cross. Your heart and your soul benefit greatly to think of these together. Only in prayer will you grow in deep understanding of these two great acts of love revealing the love of God for mankind.

How do you prepare to meet my Son at Christmas or at Easter? You must pray and become very small. Humble yourself. Open your heart and speak to Jesus from your heart. Learn to be comfortable in stillness and in silence. Then will you hear the voice of love - the Holy Spirit. If you seek and knock in sincerity; if you hunger and thirst for love; then pray to God who is Love. Be His child. Whenever I observe My children attempting to pray, I am close to them to assist them if I am so permitted. Your hearts must be open.

My children, you have been given to know that I am soothing the wounds of my Son because He is today, still crowned with mockery. (Mary is referring to the prior image received.) *This season of Advent is to be a holy season of preparation, appreciation, and deep love.*

In America, there is little holiness, little appreciation and little love. There is preparation, but it is for a very commercial celebration. There is too much busyness and anxiety about many different things. Pray with me in this holy season. Pray in union with my Mother's heart, then your prayers and your love become reparation for all who offend the heavenly Host by lack of reverence and attention given to the Most Holy Trinity. Your sacrifice to keep this season holy appeases the Father's justice on a wayward generation who will not appreciate His greatest gift of love, the Word Incarnate, Jesus Christ. Be still, my children. In the silence, there will Love come to you that you may be one. This is my prayer for you. Thank you for permitting me to be your Mother.

68. **12-7-95** Chaplet of Divine Mercy, My home with Father. **Image of Church and Those Who will not Serve**

As soon as we began the Chaplet, I saw Jesus on the cross. He was covered with blood. The blood dripped down into a chalice. The chalice was pure gold and brilliant rays of light burst forth from it. The chalice was filled with Jesus' blood. It was then tilted slightly to be poured out upon the Church. I saw an image of a church with a steeple. The church was cracked in the middle. The blood from the chalice poured into it. On one side of the church was Our Lady, the Holy Father, and a few other souls that I did not know. On the opposite side of the church was another group of souls. There was smoke all around them. The smoke was black. I sensed the presence of dark spirits. Then above them appeared a caption reading: "I will not serve."

Our Lady spoke: *The time has come. The sheep and the goats are being separated. I would gather all unto my bosom if I could. You who will not serve are lost because you have decided against God. Your free will shall not be violated. I weep for you who will not serve because all are my children. All are children of God. If you have decided for God, accept no compromise. Your faith will uphold you. Though you may be persecuted, accept no compromise. Pray for all souls and for the salvation of the world. It is God's mercy to pour out the chalice of divine justice to divide what is His from what is not His* (by free choice). *After a time of confusion, division, and suffering, there will be a radiant Church from which all will draw; a holy house; a beautiful bride. The smoke will vanish. Pray for this day to come. Little ones, I am with you. Your Mother*

69. **12-11-95** My home, 9 PM
My Heart, Wounded and Healed

Jesus, my God,

My heart is like a swollen river overflowing its banks. The current is strong, moved by the impulses of Your Divine Love imparted by the powerful wind of the Holy Spirit. Every thought of You increases my pain and fullness. I love you and I desire more of You. My heart remains wide open to receive Your infilling. Thoughts of You bring more physical pain. Powerfully, You fill my heart as You whisper gently, **God alone!** Then more grace comes with more power and I hear **Take and drink to the full. My rich Love and unfathomable Mercy are yours.** I am overcome by You, Lord.

When I feel my heart pierced by sharp darts of love, I know You are sending me arrows of knowledge and wisdom to teach me truth. This truth bursts forth in all my being, grounding me in You who are the Way, the Truth, the Life. Though these darts feel as sharp as razor blades cutting up my heart, they heal and make whole with Divine Love. My heart is aching as You, my God, act within. It recognizes its Creator and it trembles at Your beauty and majesty. As you envelop me, I attempt to envelop You in response. As You have captured me, I attempt to capture You. But You cannot be captured except by Your own merciful condescension that permits me to embrace You because You will to be one with me.

Oh, Incomprehensible Condescension! Your love and humility are wisdom and power! Worthy to be crushed by You, You bend from heaven to cover me with Your divine touches and kisses. Touches that wound and kisses that heal and touches that wound again. When my heart reaches capacity, it overflows until You give to me Your own Sacred Heart. My little vessel is transformed by the Eternal Fountain. Oh, the sheer grace of your pure and holy love! My Jesus, My God, I love You endlessly.

70. **12-12-95** Tabernacle Feast of Our Lady of Guadalupe, **America: Satanic Sacrifice and Pagan Worship**

My child, this is a great feast. A day of remembrance to honor the Father's divine and loving Providence who ordained that I come to the new world, the Americas. He sent me as a vessel of His Divine Love; a messenger to proclaim to all, - I am the Mother of all! He sent me to intercede on behalf of all especially to overcome the Satanic sacrifices of human hearts. As the handmaid of the Lord, I bring the God-man, Jesus, to all creation. As Mother of all, I carry all back to my Son, so that together we can present to the Father, what belongs to Him - all the souls He created!

Today in the Americas, there is satanic sacrifice in the bloodshed of the innocent, the aborted babies. There is pagan worship of the gods of money and power. In the modern Americas, I find God's people, deluded in their sophisticated intelligence and despairing in their extreme spiritual poverty. This is the work of the enemy. Yet, in modern times many, even in the Church, deny the enemy altogether. It is easy to look back to the days of Juan Diego and recognize the errors and the enemy. It is difficult to see the errors in your midst and the enemy who still devours souls as rapidly as he can. The great miracle of Guadalupe given to the Americas is little remembered and even doubted by many in modern times. It is easier to doubt everything because to believe is to have faith. Faith is risky because it is not concrete according to modern times. Today, then, faith is very weak.

Blessed are you who believe. You are the lights of hope and you will burn brightly to illumine the darkness of this age. Soon, the Father, the Son, and the Holy Spirit will send another sign to the world. This sign will reveal that He exists. Many will repent

and be converted. Do not doubt. Do not be afraid. I, who am your
Mother bless you continually with my presence. With me you are
safe. I do not keep you for my self. I am a vessel only. I bring you to
Jesus, just as I brought Him to the world. You must permit me to be
your mother. It is a decision to be open to me that I may assist you.
I pray unceasingly for you, my children. Please be converted now.
The blood that stains your soil, America, will be accounted for.
Please cease to offend God in so grievous a manner. What greater
error than to promote death instead of life? Please repent. Your
suffering will be great if you continue on your present course. I
love you. Your Mother

71. **12-13-95** My home, Rosary with Spiritual Director
St. Bernadette's Obedience and Faith

At the Descent of the Holy Spirit decade, suddenly I saw the
Grotto of Lourdes. Then I saw Our Lady. She was dressed in tradi-
tional Lourdes gown with blue cincture. All of this was so clear. It
was as if I were transported to Lourdes. Her hands were folded
together in prayer with the Rosary between them as she stood in
the niche in the grotto. Then I saw little Bernadette kneeling and
looking at Our Lady. I observed Bernadette go over to a dirt area
and begin to dig in the dirt. She washed her face with the dirt. She
was being obedient to Our Lady's request to go over to the spring
and wash her face with water. However, at first, there was only
dirt; no spring and no water. Yet, Bernadette did exactly as Mary
told her. Then a spring did burst forth!

I observed this for the entire decade. Then Our Lady said: *My*
son and my daughter, could you give to me this much obedience?
This much faith?

I hesitated, then I said: "Mother, it would be difficult for me."
She said: *Truly, the day will come when this much faith will be*
required to be obedient to God's Will for you. Then she was gone.

We continued to pray the Rosary. At the Coronation decade,
when Father mentioned the word obedience in his meditation, Our
Lady showed me the Lourdes scene again. Then she said: *Truly,*
one day it will be required of you to have this much faith and obe-

dience in order to remain obedient to the Roman Catholic Church; to hold fast to the traditions of the Church as taught by Peter (the Pope). *I implore you to hold fast to Peter and the Church of Rome. Be obedient. After a time of persecution, a new spring will burst forth. The remnant will stand.*

I said: "Dear Lady, how will we know what to do?"

She said: *A great illumination will come into your heart and soul from the Holy Spirit. The chosen remnant will receive this illumination from the Holy Spirit.* (I was relieved at her words.) She went on to explain to me. (As if she didn't want me to be over-confident.) *Even with the illumination, the pressures and persecutions from the world will try your faith and obedience. Therefore, God is granting you much grace now that you will withstand the trial. Remember little Bernadette. I love you. Your Mother*

72. **12-15-95** My home
How He Suffered for my Sins

When I awoke, there was severe pain from my back through my front in the area of my heart. It felt as if a sword had pierced me and stayed within. Every breath I took caused sharp pain. I had to be very careful how I moved, trying to keep my upper body still and breathing very shallow so as not to feel the sharp pain. I had difficulty functioning during the day. Everything was labored. I had to concentrate on the simplest task in order to do it. I could think of only one thing, Jesus on the cross. How every breath must have caused Him excruciating pain!

I went to bed that night almost paralyzed by the pain of each breath I took. For two hours I did not fall asleep, but entered a state of union with Jesus on the cross. My limbs had chills going through them. They became very cold. Then my back felt a burning sensation in the shape of a cross; as if I was being "branded" by a hot iron in the form of the cross across my shoulders and down the middle of my back, stopping at my waist. I somehow was one with Jesus on the cross. I cannot find the words to express the union or the suffering of Jesus as He hung on the cross. Every soul who was, is, and would be created, was present to Him as He hung at

Calvary. All of creation weighed on Him! The love and the suffering is too much for words.

The next couple of days the awareness of Jesus hanging on the cross never left me. Every breath I took, free of pain, reminded me of what He suffered for my sins and I was filled with gratitude.

73. 12-16-95
Angelic Conversation

During the night, it seemed I was in a conversation with some type of angelic beings. I myself cannot believe I'm writing this. I know that it was not the Father, Son, or Holy Spirit, or Mary, or any saint that I recognized. Somehow I entered into conversations with a group of loving, helpful, joyful spiritual beings. I remember being in a dreamlike state. All this took place over the course of the whole night — it seemed to me. I heard nothing with my proper ear nor were any of my senses involved that I know of. All this took place in a deeply interior way. We communicated by thought. Without words, knowledge was exchanged. These beings were full of intelligence. They were with me to help me in some way.

Out of a sleep it seemed, I heard the words "Control - give up control." It seemed natural for me to respond. I was not afraid at all. I sensed only profound peace and abundant, brilliant light.

I said: "I thought I had already given up control?"

I heard: "You have given up control of yourself. You have placed yourself in the heart of Jesus. But you have not given up control of those you love most - your family."

I said: "I want to give up control of my family. Please help me to do this. I don't want to control anything. But aren't they my charges?"

I heard: "Yes, in a sense. You are responsible for the children, but by love - not control. You must love unconditionally. You must not expect them to be mirrors of your way of thinking or behaving. Are you ready now to trust God with them? Can you give your husband and your children to God? Will you give up control of them?"

I said: "I always dreamed my family would be a certain way - an ideal family."

I heard: "Unconditional love makes an ideal family. You love your family very much, don't you?"

I said: "Yes, very much. But you know I love God first."

I heard: "Yes. Then will you give up control of your family to God?"

I said: "I honestly didn't know I was being so controlling. Can you help me to give up control? Altogether?"

I heard: "That is why we are with you. God has a plan for your family. He will be in charge, not you."

I said: "Is this about detachment? I really sense I am detached from them."

I heard: "This is about control and has more to do with pride."

I said: "Then I want nothing to do with control or pride. I give up control. I give my husband and my family to God. They are His to do as He pleases. Please help me to live out these words. Can you do that?"

I heard: "Yes, we can do that. We are here to help you do the Will of God."

I said: "Thank you very much. You have revealed something I hid deep inside me. I could not see it. And it was not the Will of God. Thank you."

I heard: "You are welcome. You are blessed by God."

I said: "Yes. I am blessed by God."

Here, I seemed to enter a state of prayer of union with God. I was no longer aware of my heavenly helpers, only My Triune God. Once awake, in the morning, I recalled what happened in the night. But I really tried to deny it, to push it aside. I made a decision to forget it. Actually, I think much more was said, but I cannot remember everything. During the next couple of days, the thoughts, the conversation continued to "play" in my heart. It became more real. I told my spiritual director. Father asked me to write it down. So I have, with the grace from God. The day after this experience, before the Tabernacle, I asked Jesus: "What happened to me last night?" He said: **I sent My ministering angels to you.**

74. **12-20-95**
Impending Persecutions

At Holy Communion, I saw a fish on the altar. Then suddenly a bullet shot through the fish. Blood everywhere. Then a second bullet shot the fish again. It splattered all over. I asked my spiritual director to help discern the image. Father helped me to discern the image explaining the Greek word for fish, "ICHTHUS," to mean the following: (Spiritual director's words) Each letter of the Greek word for fish was used by the early Christians to express their faith. ICHTHUS means "Jesus Christ, Son of God Savior." The sign of a fish was a symbol used by the early Christian for their homes or meeting places to indicate to other Christians that here is a Christian home or church.

The fish shot could be: Impending persecutions
  a. All Christians (those who follow Jesus)
  b. The Church - living, concrete, and visible
  c. The Apostles (Bishops, etc.) - Fishers of Men
  d. Jesus Himself

75. **12-20-95** Rosary with Spiritual Director, my home
Mary Warns About Attacks Against The Eucharist

Joyful Mysteries.
1. Annunciation. Mary said: *I was given the grace from God to say "yes," "fiat," "Let it be done..." But Jesus has the divine nature of a constant yes - always the Will of the Father! My son and my daughter, accept the grace to give your fiat to the Divine Will. Say yes to all the inspirations of the Holy Spirit. He is your guide. He leads you the way of the Divine Will of the Father.*
2. At the Visitation, I was in the prayer of quiet.
3. The Nativity. Father prayed on what Mary must have felt to look upon the face of Jesus at His birth. Mary responded to Father's prayer. Her disposition was joyful. For a while I simply experienced Mary's joy. Then she said: *The most profound*

peace filled us (Joseph and I) at His birth that holy night. Light from heaven streamed upon us. The light Himself was born. In the stillness and the silence He came. Myriads of angels honored the newborn King. Joseph and I were filled with grace. We adored in wonder and awe! Love overcame my being. Though He was physically outside of me now, our hearts remained together as one United Heart of Love.

4. The Presentation. Mary's disposition changed completely now. I saw again, the image of the fish on the altar. First one bullet hit the fish and then another. Blood all over the altar. Mary said: *Here, on the very altar of sacrifice, the heart of the Church will be attacked. Already there are far reaching plans to attack the Holy Sacrifice of the altar. Receive my warning. It shall unfold quickly now. Pray for the Church, all her members, especially priests and religious. I warn you so that you will be prepared. It cannot be reversed, but it* (suffering) *can be lessened by prayer and fasting.*

5. The Finding of Jesus in the Temple. Father prayed for our families etc. caught in the web of evil. Mary said: *My children, I want you to trust completely in my maternal care of your loved ones. Your families receive much grace by your prayer and sacrifice. Do not worry, please. At the precise moment, grace will touch their hearts and they will see the truth. Your prayers have provided very much for them. God's Mercy is great for them because you have accepted His Mercy. You have accepted the graces to convert your own heart, which now is inclined to the Divine Will of God. Thus, you draw much grace upon your families. Please trust.*

76. **12-20-95**
Fire and Smoke

Chaplet of Divine Mercy — I saw red and white rays and observed the following. The earth's soil was covered with blood. This blood ignited to fire. The fire burned intensely over all the earth. Black smoke arose and formed a layer around the earth. White rays from heaven pierced the black smoke, acting like a vacuum.

The dark smoke was taken out, gone. White rays of beautiful light enveloped the earth. The blood had penetrated the soil making it fertile. Now it was like springtime - new and beautiful.

While there was black smoke, Our Lady said: *During a time of upheaval, there will be much suffering. Many things, which the world counts on, will collapse. People will be despairing, frightened. You must have faith and trust. You shall speak to many about faith, trust and patience, prayer and sacrifice. The light will soon come. Darkness shall be no more. Let your faith be strengthened now through all the graces you are currently receiving. Much has been given to you. Much will be required. I love you. I bless you and thank you for your prayers. Your Mother*

77. **12-25-95** Christmas Day 10:40 PM Rosary
Christmas Message From Mary

My child,

On this great Feast of the Birth of Jesus, I bless you in His Holy Name. The Word Incarnate dwelt among us. He is the message. God is Love and God is with you. Rejoice in God, Our Savior, born the infant King to redeem the world by His life, death, and resurrection! Oh, Eternal Father, You have loved us in this greatest act of love — the gift of Your Only Begotten Son! Light is born! The darkness is scattered. He enters in the silence of the night. He arrives poor and naked mirroring the human condition in every way but sin. The silence of His birth pierces the world and changes the course of humanity forever.

Oh, my children, today of all days, I would hope to find your arms empty and outstretched so I could put the infant Jesus in them with full confidence that He would be received in love and adored by you. But so many are embracing the ways of the world, I have difficulty finding the arms that are empty and outstretched in hope that the babe of Bethlehem might fill them.

Indeed, if I find you prepared, empty of the world and arms outstretched in hope of love Himself, I will place my infant Son in your arms. One glance into His eyes will reveal love - Himself is with you. In His eyes you will see the reflection of His creative love. He loves you into His image and likeness. Only in His love will you be what you are created to be - His child, His reflection. He alone is your salvation, your peace, hope, and joy. Why do I ask you to empty your arms so you can embrace and hold onto Jesus? Because with Him you are in the safety of love and with Him you have true life. Without Him, you are the vulnerable victim of the enemy whose goal is to separate you from God. His only goal is to divide man from God. Therefore, on the birth of Jesus, I warn you again. War is being waged over souls. In these days of transition, the enemy perpetuates his lies to entice souls from God; the God he refused to serve because He condescended to become a human being. The enemy particularly hates this feast. (Christmas) *Many fall into his traps in this holy season. Still, God's Mercy is abundant in this season as souls turn, if only for a moment, to think of His birth. Many return to the sacraments for this feast calling forth many graces. The good of even one Holy Communion brings incomprehensible benefits to all.*

My children, renew yourselves on this feast day. Embrace the infant King and press Him into your heart. Speak to Him of your love and gratitude and your great need of Him. Renew your commitment to do as He asks — to do the Will of the Father. Offer the gift of yourself again. Turn your life over to Him with new and deeper trust in Divine Providence. As your hearts fuse into one, let the fire burn intensely with zeal for souls and zeal for His house. Believe that your prayers and sacrifices free souls from the enemy's clutches. You are my soldiers in the battle against evil. Be fortified for battle through the graces of the sacraments and prayer. You will overcome the pride of the world with humility. You destroy the hatred of the world with love. You co-redeem when you become one with Jesus in the crib and on the cross. Then will your labor bear fruit that is everlasting. The radiance and wonder of that holy night in Bethlehem is yours today in the same person of Jesus who is with you especially when you keep His commandments of love. Embrace Him. He embraces you eternally. My little ones, please ponder my words and obey that you are prepared for the days ahead. I am with you. I love you. Your Mother

78. **12-27-95** Rosary with Spiritual Director, my home, 3 PM
Discern Every Spirit

Fourth Joyful Mystery, Presentation, Our Lady said, *1Cor.3.*
Fifth Joyful Mystery, Finding Jesus in the Temple.
Father was praying a meditation asking Our Lady to always help
us find Jesus even in the midst of chaos, confusion, and turmoil.
Our Lady joyfully said: *Listen my daughter, he prays according to
the Holy Spirit, not of himself.*
She continued. *My children, the Holy Spirit is with you. He is
your guide. Trust in Him. You have prayed according to the truth
and the light of the Holy Spirit, my son. I will always assist you to
find Jesus. The chaos, confusion,, and turmoil will increase all
around you. I have warned you often. There is a crisis of faith.
There is a great spiritual battle waging now. You will hear more
"voices" directed at you that will attempt to divert you from the
path chosen for you. Other voices may come from good people, but
you must not be diverted from your own mission. My Son instructs
you. He is your Teacher, speaking quite directly to you.*
*Discern every spirit. Evil spirits approach in seemingly good
ways. The only voice you are to follow is the one voice that brings
peace, profound peace. As the chaos around you increases and as
you draw closer to fulfilling your mission, greater will the attempt
be to divert you from your mission. Watch for the spirits of division, disorder, confusion, and doubt. You do not battle alone. I am
with you, protecting you. Still, you must battle, stay alert and discern every voice. The enemy never rests. Stay focused on Jesus. Do
not look to the left or to the right. Do whatever God asks and only
what He asks. Blessed are you who are directed by God Himself.
You have only to follow Him. All will be well with you - the wellness
that comes from doing the Will of God.*
*Rest, my children. When you are fatigued you are easily tar-
geted by the enemy. Be refreshed in the love and peace of Jesus.
Your journey will continue in the grace of God. Live in the present
moment. Be at peace. You know God has a great and merciful plan
for all mankind. All will be restored in the reflection of the beauty
of the Most Holy Trinity. My son and my daughter, you are very
blessed. Give thanks and rejoice. I am with you. You are never alone.*

And in spiritual warfare, you battle with the power of all the heavens at your disposal. I love you. Your Mother

79. **12-28-95** Rosary in Father's Office
Union at the Cross

We prayed before the image of Jesus on the cross. Jesus said: **Soul, from the cross I gazed upon My Mother. Full of love for her, My suffering increased in the knowledge of her union with My suffering. She was offered the grace to lessen her pain. But she chose to suffer in union with Me. Such was her love of Me. Such was her love for all that she co-redeems. *I know about the relationship between a son and a mother! I know!**
At the Mystery of the Carrying of the Cross, I opened my eyes to look at the picture again. Behind Jesus on the cross, it was as if the heavens opened up to reveal all their glory. Jesus said: ***Soul, embrace and carry the cross, but always look beyond to the glory that comes only through the cross — the Resurrection!** End of Rosary.

80. **1-1-96** Feast of the Mother of God
A Sword has Pierced Your Heart Today

My home at 11:30 PM. Our Lady spoke.

Child of my Immaculate Heart, hide yourself in the deep recesses of the Sacred Heart of Jesus. In Him you will have everything for your journey. Remember that it is a journey. Today's trials are but a part of it. Today, the feast of my Motherhood of God, I am with you and your family as mother, comforter and protector. A sword has pierced your heart today. Now your heart is made in the image of my heart. Let me be your example. The sword brings deeper union and infinite love. It is a school of wisdom opening your heart to even greater divine graces. You have now, the oppor-

---

* Jesus is referring to some concerns I had about my son and our relationship.

tunity to love the one who pierced you. And love is what you are called to do. Love above all, in spite of everything and great will be your reward. I rejoice to know of the unlimited graces available to you and your family. Turn the pain into love and you will soar like an eagle to the tent of your beloved on the highest mountaintop. Turn the rejection into forgiveness and you will be radiantly transfigured into the Beloved.

Child, your prayers have been heard. What is the greatest gift in your life?

I replied: "Mother, it is the relationship of love that I have with the Most Holy Trinity."

Child, how often have you prayed that this would be given to all souls, to each family member?

I replied: "I have prayed that daily since my conversion years ago."

Then trust that this soul will be granted this gift through the suffering of the trial at hand. Your prayers and sacrifice are necessary to melt the heart of this soul for the grace of healing. This soul has walked in the valley of darkness. Only now is the woundedness coming into the light. Your love can do so much. The enemy has oppressed this soul for a very long time. Deeply deceived, this soul is numb inside. Now is the hour of decision. God will grant much grace. Pray that it will be accepted.

Remember, the love required of you now is the gift you have been given by Jesus. The origin of the love required of you must be in Divine Love, the Heart of Jesus. Do not rely on your human heart. Draw everything from my Son's Heart. All my suffering turned into eternal joy. So, too, will yours. Persevere in your faith. Hope and trust every step of the way. Remember, the Will of the Father is your life now. His Will brings peace. In your suffering, you will have peace deep in your soul because Jesus surrounds you. He wraps His cloak around you and embraces what is His. No one will destroy what belongs to God.

My dearly beloved daughter, you belong to God. I will assist you to do God's Will. Your love can set your family free. My Son defends you. Rest in Him. His love is enough for you. It is everything. Truly I am blessing your family with my protection and love. Child, open up and drink of the fountain of divine graces available

*to you from the side of Jesus, pierced and poured out for love of
you. Please be at peace. I love you. Your Mother*

81. **1-5-96** 12:30AM
No More Self, Only Jesus

Awakened out of a deep sleep, I glanced at the image of Jesus
(The Shroud) and knew I had to write. These words were like a
fountain rising up within my soul.

Oh my Jesus,
I am lifted up on the cross with you now.
No more self, only Jesus.
By the power of the love You place in my soul
I will to remain with You on the wood, the cross that saves.
No more self, only Jesus.

You send the closest one to pierce my side.
I cry out in pain. I am dying.
No more self, only Jesus.
Oh, Eternal Father, be glorified in Your little creature.
No more prayers morning, noon, and night.
Every excruciating breath from the cross is prayer.
I am writhing in pain now.
No more self, only Jesus.

Father, thank You for providing the way, the means
By which Your little creature can die quickly.
No more self, only Jesus.
In the midst of the pain of dying
My soul rises because Love triumphs.
Lifted up on the cross my eyes are opened. I see so much
　　more now.
This self of mine wants to be lowered from the cross.
But my spirit says, "There is so much to learn from here!"
Rest on the wood and learn. Wisdom is here!
Glorify God in dying.
No more self, only Jesus.

Lifted upon the cross I see how fleeting is this life
As my soul sets itself on the life to which I am going.
Sometimes in the midst of pain and anguish I have a
     foretaste of my true home.
My soul bursts out in true joy then, though I am bathed
     in tears and blood.
Jesus, on the cross Your breath and mine are one breath
Penetrating all time. Love saves.
No more self, only Jesus.

Jesus, on the cross Your blood and mine co-mingle
And the cup we drink is the Will of the Father.
The Will of the Father brings peace. Peace in the midst
     of dying.
Oh, happy death that brings forth life.
Blessed be the Father who chose for me the quickest
     means of dying.
Blessed be the one who pierces my side and my heart.
He does my soul great good.
No more self, only Jesus.

He suffers more than I. I see what He cannot.
We both have the same God.
The God who permits both of us to be crucified with Jesus.
The sword touches each one.
And by dying, we will live.
No more self, only Jesus.

82. **1-5-96** Afternoon, my home.
Focus on What is Important: The Pain Passes

My children,
     Be ever mindful that I observe the entire family of man tar-
geted by the enemy. One family after another is targeted by divi-
sion and deception. Evil escalates everywhere. But so too, grace
abounds in these trying times. You cannot comprehend the grace
that is being made available to each and every soul. Your prayers

and sacrifices are needed that souls will accept the graces of mercy available to them.

So often God must bring His children to their knees so they can focus on what is important. What is important is eternal. Today, too few even consider what is eternal. The whirlwind of evil deceives many, many souls. You who are consecrated to My Immaculate Heart have a storehouse of grace available to you. Draw from me. Many will be transformed in these times by the weight of the crosses being sent. God will permit you to suffer because suffering brings you to Him. In Him, is life and love. The resurrection comes only after the death of self. The pain passes. The good is eternal. Be people of deep faith.

The spiritual life is the eternal reality. For this, you are created. Embrace the cross that brings you into greater union with transformations. Pray that many will convert. All of creation is being prepared for the transformation of the entire world. God will manifest Himself in many ways. Trust He is with you to offer abundant life, now and forever. The cup will pass. But what you drink remains forever. Love is everlasting. Love will triumph. Evil will be no more. Hope! All of heaven is available to you. Persevere! The battle will one day end and sooner than you think. I bless you, my children. Thank you for your prayers and faithfulness. I love you. Your Mother

83. **1-8-96**
Trust! Let God be God!

Words from my spiritual director: "Let God be God."

"In your situation, you are truly being called into a surrender of yourself in faith and trust to all occurring within you and around you. Beyond the ordinary help offered by yourself in love to those around you, all that God asks of you is to "let God be God." Only He can take the sickness of our soul and heal it into the obediential fire of love. Open your wounded and wearied heart and present its pain, its numbness, its grief, its many burdens to that Heart where all is consumed and you may enter into His rest. Do not fight the pain of the 'now.' Accept and surrender it to Him who wants you to allow Him to place it in His own. Offer it to the Father and accept all the souls the Father draws to Him from this pain embraced; given to Him in total love. Precious too, are the arms of the Mother that surround you. 'I love you, child,' are her words to you and they echo those of her Son."

From Jesus:

I love you. This winter of sorrow will give way to the spring of life giving warmth. Trust Me, Soul. Not one movement of your soul escapes My loving attention. I grieve with you, but the Father's Will must be fulfilled in you. I love you. I am here. I abide in you. Suffer in Me, in peace. All enters into your mission willed by the Father. My Mother will always help you. Her concern and love surpasses yours and is always present to you.

The soul wrapped up in Me, cannot but be oblivious to all else. The world that is falling apart around you will be restored in a new and more beautiful form. Please allow Me to work My Will in you and around you. Trust and be at peace in your sorrow. All will be well with you and your loved ones. You are Mine.

Please remember, soul, that when you come to Me in a surrendering love, you are not running away from the world to escape it, but only to be revivified, restored. And to go back to fight the good fight that My Paul has written of in his letter. Drink, soul, of the precious blood from My side. Do so daily. It is I Who fight in you. Your Jesus

84. **1-9-96** Before the Tabernacle
I Am Your Joy

My beloved, your joy is complete because I am your joy. Your joy does not depend on human love or human rejection, not does it depend on anything in the world. It depends entirely upon Me, your God, your Savior. In Me, your joy abounds. In you, My joy abounds. Joy is the fruit of My Holy Spirit. (Jesus is referring to a grace I am receiving in which I have abundant joy in the midst of terrible suffering. After nine days of intense interior suffering, He is granting me the grace of deep, abiding joy while on the cross with Him.) **My Holy Spirit is in you, living, filling, upholding you in Me. In Him we are united as a sacrificial offering to the Father. Union is Love. Love is union.**

My beloved bride, as you drink the cup of My Blood, your joy increases because you foretaste your eternal home, union with God. You are My bride. Mine forever. The cross you carry makes you radiantly beautiful in My sight. Covered in My Blood, you are made pure and holy for Me. My joy increases as you are transfigured into Me. My bride, I have provided so much for you. The source of love pours Himself into you. Drink of My love and live in Me. I will sustain and uphold you for Myself.

Beloved, your heart is pierced with pain. Already it had been pierced by Love. Thus, you were prepared. The foundation was built to withstand the sword of suffering. Your suffering has incomprehensible merit in My sight. Not only your family, but many will be healed by your loving endurance and sacrifice. Yes, I have provided generously for you. All that I have is yours. Draw all that you need in this life from the treasury of My kingdom in heaven. All the angels, all the saints together with graces from the Immaculate Heart, together with the gifts of the Holy Spirit, and the blessing of the Father are yours as you hang on the cross with Me. My chosen one, let My Heart be your resting place. Give to Me everything. Above all, give Me your will, surrendered in trust. You know that I am faithful forever. Already I have prepared a crown for you. It awaits you — made of the choicest flowers of My heavenly garden. Every flower is pure white, signifying "the bride of Christ." I give you My Word, rich and everlasting life is yours. Persevere in Me. Lean on the Church in the priest that represents Me. I love you. Your Jesus

85. **1-10-96** Rosary with Spiritual Director
Suffering, Victim Souls

During the Rosary, I received an image of St. Michael the Archangel shielding us from the dragon's fire. The warrior, Michael, is plenty of protection from the attacks of the enemy of all souls.

When Father prayed over me, he received an image of suffering, victim souls, turning into pure, gold bars. These had been purified in the fire and now formed pure gold bars, which were deposited into the treasury of Our Lady's Immaculate Heart. Prayers and sacrifices form jewels which form part of the treasury of graces. But suffering formed the gold bars of grace that Jesus and Mary give to souls in need of special graces.

86. 1-12-96
Do not Avoid Me in the Pain

A friend prayed with me over the phone because I was under attack. As soon as I hung up the phone Jesus spoke.

Soul, be still, My bride. I am with you. Where is your trust in Me? My Mercy draws Me to you in your hour of testing and trial. What bridegroom does not test his bride's love? Are you avoiding Me? I find you so preoccupied with your earthly situation that you are forgetting the Divine Lover of your soul. Have I not said that I love all souls as I love you?

Soul, what I have given to you as gift, I will take for a while for the good of both. Yours will be tried and strengthened with new and abundant graces. This certain soul will be recreated. Pray and fast. Remain as My bride, turning to Me at every moment. Your life is a prayer. Do not avoid Me in the pain. Talk to Me, My bride. Give everything to Me. I am here and we are One. Be still. Be at peace in Me. Learn the silence of My Mother. She is full of wisdom and understanding in silence. Imitate your Mother.

Remember your prayer, no more self, only Jesus? Continue to say that powerful prayer, which means God's Will only. Then you will not be the toy of the enemy who never ceases to try to take you from Me. You perceive that you are battling alone. If this were true, you would have run from Me already. My bride, many angels and saints are protecting you. I, Myself am defending you. You are Mine! Your family will remain united in My Heart. You must be the vessel of My Love for all of them. No more self, only Jesus. Father, Your Will, not mine.

You have been avoiding Me. This wounds Me. There are no secrets from Me. You are hurt and weak. You cannot hide this from Me. In the intimacy of our love, can you not share everything with Me? Please do so. I shall restore your family into My holiness and love. Please trust Me. All that you need is yours already. I am here. I am yours. Please write and record everything. This will help you and others as well. Consecrate your husband and children to Me every day. I will take care of them as I care for you. My Love and Mercy abounds for all. Be at peace. Rest in Me.

My bride, in your suffering I will take you deeper into the mysteries of your God. Depend on Me. We hurt together. We weep together. Everything is done as One. You are My beloved bride - forever. I love you. Jesus

87. **1-12-96** Prayer Group
Focus on Hope, Not Suffering

My dear children,
You have just prayed in a most efficacious manner. In meditating upon My passion, your soul received incomprehensible graces. My children, you meditate on My passion so that you will more fully appreciate the resurrection. It is not for you to focus on suffering. Rather, that you have hope in suffering, hope in the resurrection, and hope in eternal life. The fruits of remembering My passion are beyond your understanding. By means of union with My suffering, your prayers and sacrifices free many souls from the snare of the evil one. Trust, dear children, that the power within you is far greater than the power of darkness.

Thank you for offering yourselves as prayer warriors through the Immaculate Heart of Mary. Only in the next life will you know the good of your prayers and suffering on earth. Truly, I have gone before you. I have prepared a place for you in My Father's Kingdom. I love you unconditionally, just the way you are! I bless you this night with the oil of My love and the blood of salvation. Truly, you are marked with the sign of salvation. You are Mine. No one will take you from Me.

Please continue to pray for the conversion of the world. **Many who converted long ago are not growing lukewarm and impatient, putting aside the prophecies of this day and putting on the ways of the world again. This wounds My Heart. Many graces have been granted and many are unappreciative of these graces. Souls who convert and then turn lukewarm wound My Heart deeply. Please persevere in your calling. Accept your graces and crosses with gratitude and love. I am with you always. I shall continue to instruct you as you seek My Father's Will. Rejoice My beloved ones, you have been chosen for a great mission of Love. Many graces are ordained for you. I love you. Your Jesus**

88. 1-13-96
As My Lamb, None can Take You from Me!

Father prayed over me because I was having terrible temptations to retaliate against someone who is hurting me. I had to fight the spirit of retaliation and anger. As soon as Father placed his hands upon my head to pray, I sensed I was standing in a shower and being cleansed with the pure waters of the Holy Spirit. I received a long infilling of love, and peace came. Suddenly, there was sharp pain in the area of my heart and I had difficulty breathing. Jesus whispered, **Let Me breathe for you. Peace.**

Then I saw myself on an altar as a small lamb, pure white, peaceful and gentle. A stream of blood began to flow from the lamb, dripping down from the altar to the floor. The blood had beauty and life. Then I saw a multitude of demons approaching the altar aimed at the lamb. On the other side, I saw a lot of people aimed at the lamb. Just before they could reach me, I saw Jesus, as the Good Shepherd, scoop me up into His arms and hold me tightly. He said: **It doesn't matter that all the demons be unleashed upon you or if all the people of the world persecute you. None can take you from Me. I uphold you in My Almighty arms. With Me, you are safe.**

What confidence overcame my soul in the safety of Jesus' arms. But within minutes my thoughts turned again to a certain soul who is hurting me. Jesus said: **Let go. My eye is fixed upon this soul.**

I alone can do it. And I will. Trust. Be at peace. Your suffering makes you pure in My eyes. It is a great offering to Me. I bless you, your family and many souls through your offering. You are never alone. I sensed the company of many saints assisting me in this trial.

89. **1-21-96** My home.
Imitate the Lamb

I am under a severe trial. Jesus began to speak.

Blessed are you My beloved one, chosen by the Father before all ages to be a sign of My Love and Mercy in this age. Chosen are you, bride of My Heart, filled with high graces of Divine Love. If you could see how radiantly beautiful you are hanging upon the cross you would weep for joy. (I was weeping, sorrowful for my family.) **Your soul is resplendent with light breaking forth from your suffering. You taste but a drop of My passion. Your love is spurned. Your affection rejected. Your heart betrayed. Your person violated. You are one with your groom now. I suffered this and more on your account. Turn to Me and say, "Yes. Let it be done according to Your Word."**
    Bride of Mine, imitate the Lamb of God led to the slaughter in profound silence. Oh, the wisdom and power of such holy silence! This is your surrender. You die by the sword of waywardness. But by the power of the Holy Spirit you live; lifted high above the world and its ways. Taste of the heights of pure and glorious love. You are naked, scourged, and bloodied but your Eternal Groom covers you. My Love drapes your nakedness; covers your vulnerability. My Mercy wraps you in white garments befitting a bride of Christ. Your ring is gold, tried in the fire and made pure and precious. Your head is adorned with wreaths of pure white flowers; lilies and roses made from every sigh of pain, every tear that falls, as you endure the agony of being nailed to My cross.
    Little lamb, be still! Give to Me utter confidence. I work a wonder before your eyes. I have permitted you to know the

depth of darkness and deception that surrounds you. And on the day that I bring forth great light from the pit of deception, you will rejoice and give glory to Me. I uphold you. No one, nothing of the world will penetrate the center of your soul, for there I Am. Cling to the truth of My promises. Have great hope. All will be well with you. Be docile, silent, obedient, humble and pure for Me. I am feeding you wisdom and knowledge. You are drinking of My Blood and life bursts forth from you as you hang on the cross with Me. Drink and be filled. Many souls are receiving graces gushing forth from your sacrifice. Blessed are you, chosen and anointed by your Triune God. Do not fear. I am with you. Live in My peace. I am your Jesus.

90. **1-22-96** Rosary with Father, my home, 1 PM
Jesus on Families Suffering and Grace Through Mary

At the First Joyful Mystery, the Annunciation, I saw Our Lady of the Miraculous Medal with hands extended out and radiant light flowing from her palms onto earth. The light represented graces flowing from God through her. There were more streams of grace than ever before. She was like a pure white fire of love who was so full that she had to empty herself out; pouring grace upon grace onto the earth.

Then I observed the earth in a closer view. Many of the people on earth had a whirlwind of darkness around them, trying to pull them into it. The graces issuing forth from the hands of Our Blessed Mother were far more powerful than the darkness. I could see streams of grace going directly into hearts. God's Light would fill the people.

At the Third Joyful Mystery, the Nativity, Jesus said: **Children, the maternal milk of the Blessed Virgin Mary, Our Mother, is the food of holiness. Let her nourish your hearts. She will bring you to Me.** Then I saw a certain soul as a baby in a playpen. Inside the playpen was every kind of gift that this soul could want. Each gift was illuminated with light. But the baby could only see the gift that was outside the playpen. It was beautifully wrapped and alluring. This became the focus of the soul, that which was out of its reach, not meant for it.

Jesus said: **Dear child, all that this soul needs is already provided. Yet it is blind to this. The enemy shines a light on the gift outside My providence. The soul finds this false light irresistible; leaves what I have provided and falls into the trap set for it. But it is an illusion and leads to a path away from Me, away from what is good.**

There are many souls falling into this trap and families are suffering because of it. I must illumine the way back to Me; back to goodness. Families are being purified. You will witness turmoil and uprooting in many families. It is a time of purification which will ultimately strengthen families. Many will be united again. There is new life for families who believe, repent, and convert. I will show them the Way.

Pray and fast for families. Much healing is needed. And forgiveness is the key. Only in prayer can this be accomplished. Through prayer you will find My peace and the grace to love, forgive, and love again. I am with families in a unique way. Though you suffer, I will be your joy if you but trust.

91. **1-23-96** (A) Tuesday, before the Tabernacle
Resist the Enemy

I am in turmoil. There is a strong interior battle inside of me. My prayer time is unrecollected. Jesus began to speak in a firm tone.

Soul,

Seek only My Will. Every grace shall be yours. Walk in My Will. Resist the enemy tempting you to take care of yourself, to defend yourself. I will take care of you. I, The Lord Your God, will uphold you. Remember, no more self, only Jesus? Father, Thy Will not mine! Pray. Hope. Your soul is in My Almighty Hand. The Will of the Father is your existence.

The love of the Holy Spirit penetrates you and sustains you in every way. The cross unites you to Me. The cross is the ladder connecting the depths of love and the heights of union. United to Me on the cross, you plunge into the deeper mysteries of the love of the Most Holy Trinity. As you hang on the

cross with Me, Divine Love upholds you. Love, holy, unconditional, infinite and transforming is beyond your human understanding. Only in your true home (heaven) will you be shown the splendor, the majesty and the glory of Divine Love as it exists in the Three Persons of the Most Holy Trinity. You cannot see this now and live.

By the gift of the cross, you are crucified to the world and lifted up into the ways of the Most Holy Trinity. Transformed into the very love of your Triune God, you are recreated into My Image. The former ways of your living and thinking are to be put aside now. You are an entirely new creation. This is the cross that causes you to soar to new heights of union. You suffer and die by the cross. But you also live by the cross. Your life will be transformed by this cross. You will praise Me and thank Me when you see what I bring about through it.

The enemy tempts you to protect yourself, to seek comfort, consolation and retaliation. But I alone am your God, your Master. Resist the enemy. Go forward in courage and fortitude. You have chosen none of this. You did not seek to be perfected. I chose you. I chose to perfect you by the road all holy ones have walked before you; the road leading to perfection in Me. You cannot see the souls you are saving. There are many, including the one who persecutes you. Each soul must die to himself to be saved.

Souls that are deaf and blind become the toy of the enemy. The enemy has incited this soul toward its own demise for the division of the family and the destruction of your spiritual life. I will uphold you even as I upheld Job. I will restore you as I restored Job. Job was a witness for many in his day. Like the prophets of old, you are tried in the fire. Like the prophets of old, you have a calling in My Church. Your situation reveals to you the state of My own family, the Church. Apostasy and division have penetrated her as the enemy has set up camp even among the highest-ranking members of My Mystical Body. Purification paves the way for restoration.

My lamb, upon the altar you are resting. You are bleeding now. Your sacrifice not only heals your family, but also prepares you for your role as a restorer in My Church, My Body, divided and beaten like yours now.

My beloved, go forward seeking one thing only, My Divine Will. Dedicate yourself daily to My Divine Will. Find your joy in My Will. The cross of suffering is My gift to you. You were carefully prepared for this. I have provided everything for you. Rejoice in Me now and forever. Give Me glory by your sacrifice. I will give you My Glory forever. Be merciful as I Am. I love you. Your Jesus

92. **1-23-96** (B) Before the Tabernacle.
St. Paul on Persevering in Ministry

I was having doubts about continuing my ministry because of family problems. Suddenly I heard: "It is I, Paul, the Apostle. Live and proclaim the Gospel message of love with zeal for the ministry to which God has called you. Toil unceasingly for the sake of the Kingdom of God. Expect nothing but persecution from the world. The world crucified Jesus. Strive for perfection in Him to whom you are called. Fulfill your ministry with single-minded determination to be the reflection of your Creator. Toil as a true soldier of Christ. Draw close to Him through suffering. The battle continues. Fight the good fight. I assist you. Take courage. You are not alone. Your spiritual journey is the everlasting reality. The King of Heaven and Earth, the Almighty and Sovereign Son of God rested upon the wood of the cross. So too, His followers. Do not count the cost of discipleship. Discipleship is a total commitment to Christ. Go forward. There is much work to do. I bless you in the Name of the Father, the Son, and the Holy Spirit. His Apostle, Paul."

93. **1-23-96** (C) My Home
Encouragement from Many Saints

There is in me, a strong aversion to the spiritual life. Everything in my being is a resounding "no" to the spiritual life. I am weary from the interior battle and I am being tempted to seek consolation from other people. Prayer is almost impossible, yet I spend time trying anyway.

Father arrived to pray the Rosary with me. Immediately following, I heard my name and the words, "Fight the good fight!" These words had great power in them. Then I heard, "It is I, Paul." I thought, "But I do not know you, Paul." I heard, "I am close to you to help you fight the good fight."

Immediately I heard, "Soul, indeed this is how Jesus treats His closest friends. Suffering is the fire that produces wisdom, knowledge and love. Suffering borne in union with the Beloved produces rare beauty. It is I, Teresa (of Avila).

Then I received an interior image of St. Therese, the Little Flower, presenting me with a blood red rose. She radiated exquisite joy and love but did not speak to me.

Then St. Francis of Assisi entered the image. He held in his hands a beautiful white dove. He said to me, "Soul, be gentle and peaceful as this dove. I assist you. Peace." Then the interior image was gone.

Suddenly, I heard the words, "The fire and passion that burns inside you will sustain you always. It is His Love. I am Catherine of Genoa."

I thought, this is not real. This cannot be.

Immediately, a large group of saints said, "It is real!"

I thought, it seems real now, in this graced moment, but afterward, when I am alone, it won't seem real. Again the saints said, "You are never alone! Believe!"

Then Our Lady showed me the word "Fiat." I said to her, "Mother, I cannot do this anymore. Please get someone else to do this, or if you want me to continue, please do everything for me." Blessed Mother said, "*I will.*"

Then I sensed something trying to divide me from my spiritual director. Our Lady showed me a heavy nautical rope tied in a knot, very strong. She said, *Nothing will loosen this union of the spirit. I, myself, stand guard over it. It is necessary that God's work be accomplished. Be at peace.*

Then I prayed for my spiritual director because so many souls draw from him. Jesus said, **My priest drinks of Life in Me. He is a fountain of My Love and Mercy for many. I refresh him with living waters of the Holy Spirit for My Mystical Body.**

94. **1-25-96** 8:30AM Holy Mass
The Graced "Our Father"

During the beginning of Holy Mass, I was not recollected. When the cantor began to sing the "Our Father" prayer, something happened. Immediately my spirit burst forth praying "Abba," "Abba." It was a cry from the deepest part of my being. Suddenly, I experienced a "drawing up." It seemed that I was being drawn upward toward the Eternal Father. He was like the most powerful magnet. My spirit seemed to travel very rapidly up through a light tunnel. The tunnel seemed to have a life force that was peaceful, reassuring, powerful, yet gentle, and the light that seemed to make up this tunnel was full of love. There was nothing that would cause fear.

I somehow knew that the Father was the destination. Suddenly, I stopped midway. Though my entire being longed to continue upward to reach my destination, I knew that this was as far as I could go. In this grace, my human will seemed more united to His Divine Will than ever before. I would never ask to continue upward. Whatever He decided was perfect. I could never question His Will, it so thoroughly permeated me at this moment. Then, it seemed that I received the most tender embrace of the Father's Divine Love. My spirit seemed very strengthened. My longing for Him grew. This grace enkindled more love of Him, more knowledge of His Goodness, more confidence in His protection over me.

All of this happened during the singing of the "Our Father" prayer of the Mass. The Father is glorified every time I pray the prayer that Jesus taught His disciples. But it must come from my heart. The Father is interested in the heart of His creature. And he sees all that is within my heart, at every moment.

My Prayer: "O Eternal Father, Perfect Love, let your little creature be the praise of Your eternal glory. Be merciful Father. I am a beggar before a King. Grant that I may come into your kingdom by the power of the Blood of the Lamb that washes me. The Eternal Sacrifice ransomed my guilt. By His merits, find me acceptable, for I have none of my own. Receive me, Eternal Father, into Your Holy household. And let me live and die in You, my Creator who is Love. You will that I reach my destination. Grant that I never turn away from the Grace that will carry me home to You. My 'Abba,' my True Father, I love you. Amen."

95. **1-26-96** Prayer Group
God Wants to Restore Families by the Power of Love

My dear children,
Do not doubt the power of your intercession. Your prayers have great power because you pray in union with My Immaculate Heart. My heart prays unceasingly for all my children. Indeed, the world is in much darkness. The light that enters to dispel the darkness comes through your prayers and sacrifices. Most especially your suffering united to Jesus' passion, turns many souls from the path to perdition.
My children, you simply cannot pray enough. Make your entire life a constant prayer. Never leave God out of anything you do. Do everything in union with My Son. He lives in you. Do not deny Him the intimacy He desires. Do not keep Him waiting for you. Speak to Him and listen to His response. He always responds. Your prayers are always heard. Do not doubt this. If you suffer in union with Jesus, even greater is your intercession for souls. I remind you, my little ones, you did not choose to be intercessors. You were chosen by God. You were prepared by God. God is the One who gives you the grace to respond to His call. Thank you for your prayers. I take your burdens and intentions to the throne of Our Triune God. Pray always for the conversion of all souls. Many families are being purified at this time. This is the mercy of God. God wants to restore families into His Holy reflection. The fire of purification restores and beautifies.
If you are tried and tested, know God has even more blessings to give to you as you stand the trial and pass the test. Growth comes through maturity in faith. You must learn to fight the battle against evil as true soldiers of Christ with great faith and hope. Above all, you are called to love. Love that is sacrificial and unconditional. No one is exempt from the commandment of love. At the end of your journey you will stand before God to be examined according to your love. Love is the way and the means, the beginning and the

*end, the everlasting reality. Therefore, in all things, love above all!
Do not rely on your human love. Draw from the eternal fountain of
Love, the Heart of my Son, Jesus. He is with you always. And I am
with you also. Do not be afraid. The spirit you have received is not
a cowardly spirit but a powerful spirit. Love is powerful and transforming. I love you. I bless you. Your Mother*

96. **1-29-96**
The Trinity, Three Persons, One Being of Love

Reflecting by my fireplace, I had a sudden impulse of grace to
write. When I began, my hand cramped up, almost becoming paralyzed. I dropped the pen. I prayed, "My God?" Then I picked up
the pen and could write. The essence of this experience was like a
spring bursting forth from my soul, expressing itself in the following words. It seemed that I was drawn up into all Three Persons,
distinct, yet One Being of Love.

My God, My All
Your Presence, so pure and holy, permeates my being.
Oh, Unspeakable Beauty! Everlasting Truth!
You invade my nothingness
Drawing me up into pure Love.
Surrounding my soul with Three Persons in One.
One holy embrace that cauterizes and wounds at the same time.
In You I rest. Peace surrounds me.
Union and Love!
The banquet is never-ending abundance, always new.
My appetite is insatiable.
The more I ingest, the more I desire.
Oh, my God, I desire and adore You!
What glory is Yours. Yours alone!
Mercy draws me into Your glory and glorifies me
That I may glorify You.

Oh, Eternal Word! Oh Incarnate Wisdom! Jesus!
Oh, Breath, that creates!
Create to Love. My Father!
Oh, Love Himself. Oh, Holy Spirit!
Never let me go!
Keep me in Thee, now and forever.
Oh, Kingdom of God, Reign in my soul.
Wrap me in Your purity. Shroud me in Your Holiness.
Draw me up into the mystery of Your Divine Love.
You created me for Yourself.

My Divine Teacher, teach me
That I may know my God.
Incomprehensible Trinity!
Teach me to love like You.
Majestic Trinity, Lavish Love,
Conquer me, Conquer!
Eternally I will praise your name.
Oh, Holy One, my Triune God,
All glory and honor be Yours forever.
I love you boundlessly.
I live now, not I, but You.
My soul is all aflame.
The fire burns brightly.
May Your Light in me
illumine the darkness of this age.
A sign of Your Mercy am I.

97. **1-30-96** Rosary with Father at my home.
Victims of Divine Love for the World

During the Fifth Sorrowful Mystery, Jesus Dies on the Cross, I saw the heavens, open up very wide. Out of the heavens descended the Heart of Jesus, Redeemer of the world. His Sacred Heart had indescribable power. I cannot find the words. Within, there is an infinite abyss of Divine Love, forming a treasury of riches of goodness and beauty. The precious, perfect Blood of His Sacred Heart is true life for all.

Then, the Heart of the Redeemer opened wide and poured itself out, forming a gushing fountain of life-giving blood which fell to the earth. Though it was intended for all, it entered only some; those open to receive His Life for them.

I saw the words "Victims of My Love for the world." These souls receive His salvific Blood for themselves and also for others who are not yet open to receive. Victims of His Love drink from His never-ending fountain of life in proportion to their surrender and capacity. In His plan of salvation, it seems to me, that souls who will receive Him become "feeder vessels" for the world. There is a deep spirit of cooperation among these souls. They form His Mystical Body which serves all peoples of the world. The grace that emits from the Mystical Body goes out to believers and non-believers. And through it, by means of grace, many are drawn to the Heart of Jesus.

When Father finished the Rosary, as he prayed the Litany of Saints, I could see each saint as he named them. I could see the Communion of Saints, in cooperation with God, interceding on behalf of all souls. I saw the spirit of each respective saint. They were directing themselves to God because their intercession for the world is one, continuous act of union with God. Their intercession reached us through the Heart of Jesus, by the power of the Holy Spirit, in the providence of the Father.

Suddenly, I saw the Blessed Mother, poised halfway between the heavens and earth. I saw that all the graces from heaven flow to earth through her Immaculate Heart. Like the moon that is but a reflection of the sun's light, She is the facilitator of His grace for all creation. She is almost unnoticed by souls on earth. But Wisdom recognizes her to be the mother of all, the one who suffers (Co-redeems with Jesus), nurturers (Mediatrix of Grace), and pleads (Advocate for the people).

98. 2-13-96
A Heart Pierced by Love

Journal Entry: For several weeks , when Father and I pray the Rosary, I enter a state of prayer that renders me unable to pray aloud. I hear Father lead the Rosary as if in the distant background. I attempt to pray my portion of the Rosary, but I am rendered silent. It is as if I am drained of all energy to speak. If I attempt to move, it takes a concentrated effort. I am not sure what is happening to me. I enter into God's profound Silence. Other times, I am aware of One, Two, or Three Persons of the Holy Trinity. Sometimes, I am aware of nothing. I am so thoroughly stilled interiorly that it seems to spill over physically. All of this is very dark. I do not feel or do anything. I cannot cause it to begin or end. It seems to end when Father finishes all the prayers of the Rosary, prayer of St. Michael, and the Litany of the Saints.

Today, in the midst of the above prayer state, quite suddenly, it seemed that a large arrow was plunged through my chest, through my heart, and all the way through to my back in one quick motion. It is very painful physically. The arrow was pushed through and then pulled out. It happened so quickly, without any warning and it hurt. After this happened, I entered the same state of prayer. I felt weaker physically. God's presence intensified. My heart feels physically engorged and painful. It radiates heat also. I do not understand this. There is a continuous awareness of God's presence in my heart. There is also deeper recollection and a desire for silence. Is this a consolation? If so, it is a painful one, although the effect is sweet. It strengthens my faith, hope, and love.

99. 2-14-96
Jesus: On True Love and Mercy

Last week, I went on private retreat to a community in Nebraska. Two members of the prayer group and three priests traveled there. It was a time of prayer and discernment blessed by God and Mother Mary.

Today at Mass following Holy Communion, I suddenly saw interiorly, the Sacred Heart of Jesus. His Heart is utterly alive, an infinite treasury of Love. It beats unceasingly with Love and radiates to all of creation. I cannot describe the power! Light radiates while fire burns unceasingly. I can see that it is surrounded by a crown of thorns. Sins have crowned His Heart in this manner.

Jesus said: **Soul, I am crowned today with rejection from unbelievers; indifference from lukewarm souls and ingratitude from My Own** (believers).

Your heart is also pierced by rejection, indifference and ingratitude. Yet, even as the world crowns with mockery, the Eternal Father, crowns with glory. Why? Because we love the ones who persecute us. In being merciful, you receive Mercy.

I said: "Jesus, my pain is such that it seems I could die from it. Yet my rejection cannot compare to Yours. I carry the stain of sin. But You are perfect, pure, holy, worthy of all praise, honor, glory and gratitude. You are Love, worthy from the beginning to the end, for all eternity. Yet, You suffer rejection, indifference and ingratitude from the very ones You have created. Jesus, permit me to suffer if it alleviates even one drop of Your suffering. You have dealt mercifully with me. Is it possible that I could be merciful to You?"

Jesus said: **Soul, you are merciful to Me when you are merciful to My people, especially those who hurt you. You are merciful to Me when you show mercy to those the world rejects. When you choose love, then you alleviate My suffering Heart. For Me to observe the lack of love among you is My greatest suffering. My creation has looked to itself to find love. Love that does not include Divine Love is simply self-love, idolatry.**

For it is written, "You must love the Lord, your God, with all your heart, your soul, your mind and strength. Then, love others as yourself." I am Love. Love originates in Me. You must know My Love to love, as I require. Love that does not originate in Me is not love at all. It becomes attachment, usury, self-serving and without sacrifice. Your generation labels these "love." But it is a mockery to the Truth of Divine Love.

My bride, My lamb, I accept your sacrifice. Through it I bless you and many others. Together we are an offering to the Father. As you drink of the chalice of suffering, the Father shares

His Glory with you. Rejoice, favored one, the Mercy of God is yours. You will know the agony of Gethsemane. It leads to the Resurrection; true life in Me, with the Father and the Holy Spirit, forever. I bless you, My bride and victim lamb. Peace I give to you. Your Jesus

100. 2-15-96
The Father: The Angels Await My Command to Pour Out Justice.

During the Rosary with Father at my home, I saw two magnificent angels of light with indescribable power displayed in them and all around them. Next to them were other angels holding trumpets, ready to sound them. The two magnificent angels were holding large basins. They held them in such a position so as to be ready to pour their contents out. Then, somehow, I saw the throne of God the Father. The angels awaited the word of the Father, watching Him on His Throne and giving Him glory as they exist in a state of listening readiness.

I said, "Father, what are You showing me?"

I heard: **Child, these are the angels awaiting My command – the command to pour out My justice upon the earth.**

I said, "Father, what about Your mercy?" He said: **Child, observe.**

Then I saw the earth covered by a blanket of darkness. As if to unveil the world below, it was pulled back like a curtain and I could see the following. I somehow saw wars, murders, abortions, and violence. I saw hatred among people, division in families, among nations and the churches. I saw destruction of people, whole nations, through power and greed. I saw sins of every kind, impurity and lust. I saw a heavy-handed government that oppressed people. I somehow saw confusion and massive disorder. Good was presented as bad and bad was presented as good. There appeared to be a worldwide loss of equilibrium.

I said, "Father, My God, I know Your Goodness and Mercy. But as You reveal this to me, I am sinking into despair. It is overwhelming! Godlessness is over the earth. What is the good of prayer and sacrifice? What can one person do in the face of such overwhelming sin? Father, You are Just and Your creation cries out for justice but also, You are Mercy and Your creation cries out for Mercy. Please, my God."

The Father said: **Child, I do not reveal this to you so that you would fall into despair, but that you would hope for purification and sanctification. One man makes a great difference. Consider Abraham, Moses, and the Twelve. The faith and obedience of one man touches a multitude because I multiply the good of one just man and integrate it into My own Goodness. I am a Merciful Father. The trumpets have not yet sounded. My Almighty Hand extends the days of mercy. I am raising apostles of mercy. Proclaim it. Draw from the fountain of mercy through the Two Hearts, Jesus and Mary, before the trumpet sounds and the cup of My Justice is poured upon earth. My Divine Justice is merciful.**

The day is coming that all of creation will be purged. The darkness must end. The era of sanctification must begin. This is a time of transition wherein Mercy abounds for the asking. The key is "to ask." Few realize the necessity of asking. One just, humble, holy soul draws mercy upon creation by living the law of love, through faith, sacrifice, and prayer. Do not be afraid of the future. Daily, have hope and persevere.

I, who am your Father, watch over all creation. I am offended by My people. I grieve for you. I have given this time of Divine Mercy. Make good use of it. Pray and sacrifice for souls. Those who have received abundant graces are accountable for every one of them. It is a great responsibility. But do not be overwhelmed. In peace, accept the truth of Divine Justice to be poured out to purge the earth of its defilement. Live each day in faith. Trust in your Eternal Father. I am a loving and merciful Father, but My children have become unloving and unmerciful. I will bring My children back to Me. In My perfect time, it will be done. The angels await My command. They have their mission and you have yours. You have the ability to unite yourself to Jesus on the cross, to sacrifice and bring souls to Me. Even the choirs of angels cannot do this. All of you who accept your mission to bring souls to Me, do so

by the power of Divine Love, the Holy Spirit of God. Be at peace. But do not waste time.

I prayed, "My Father, help me to trust completely. Help me to believe that one soul can make a difference in the world today. I am confident of one thing only – You! You are my God, my Eternal Father. I know your Love for me. I love You in return, my Father. And I abandon myself to Your Divine Providence. That You would make good of me, is sure proof of Your Divine Mercy. You gave me the gift of faith. Father, keep me in the truth of this gift that I may never cease to believe in You, and Your Goodness. Allow that I would exist in the truth all the days of my life. For Your own glory, take my prayers, works, joys, and sufferings, and make good of them to increase faith, hope and love on earth. Father of all, loving Creator, I cry out for those who refuse You. And if souls will come to You through the purification which Divine Justice calls for, then let the trumpets sound. Gather Your people unto You, O God. Only in You will the earth be sanctified. Let it be done according to Your Word. Amen."

The Father said: **My child, you are My beloved daughter and I will multiply your offering for many. Trust in My Love, Mercy, and Justice. I Am.**

101. **2-19-96**
An Open Heart is a Reservoir of Grace

During the Rosary with Father I was "out" until the end when suddenly I heard Our Lady's voice. My heart leaped for joy because her voice is so sweet and reassuring. It is very distinctive, unlike any other.

She said: *Dear children,*
The rain falls from heaven and it lands on a variety of surfaces. (It is raining today.) *Some surfaces are hard and cannot absorb the rain. Some are soft and readily absorb the water. So too, the graces that come from heaven to earth. These graces can only be absorbed by a heart that is soft* (open). *If a heart is hard, no matter how much grace rains from heaven, it does not penetrate.*

In God's merciful plan of salvation, hearts that can absorb heavenly graces, do so and become a reservoir, a treasury of grace for other souls.

My children, you are such a reservoir. You are storehouses of grace for many who are not yet able to receive the graces God has ordained for them. But some day, they will. When you pray the Rosary as you do, your prayers are turned into pure love and many souls benefit from this pure love. As you meditate on each Mystery of the Rosary representing the Gospel, the mystery of the life of our Jesus, each mystery is imprinted upon your heart, soul, and mind. This imprint becomes a part of your being. The more you pray, the more it is integrated into your entirety. You are transfigured as you continually mediate on the Gospel mysteries, which form the decades of the Holy Rosary. This is why the Rosary is a most efficacious prayer. When prayed from the heart, you are sanctified while the prayers are turned into pure love, which is stored within you to feed other souls when they are ready, when their hearts are softened. I am always your prayer partner.

Dear children, God permits me to be with you in a most intimate way. I assist you always and protect you. You exist deep within my Immaculate Heart where nothing escapes my maternal vigilance. Be not afraid. I will help you so that you do not offend the most tender and merciful Heart of my Son, Jesus. Be reflections of my Immaculate Heart to the glory of our loving Father. I bless you. I love you. Your Mother

102. **2-21-96** Ash Wednesday
Jesus Said: This is Intercession.

During the Rosary with Father at my home, I saw the following. I saw Jesus hanging on the cross on Calvary, not yet expired. I saw the Eternal Father over the cross with arms outstretched embracing the cross with His Son hanging on it. I saw the dove of the Holy Spirit between the Father and the Son, with rays of brilliant light bursting down upon Jesus on the cross. Jesus, full of the Holy Spirit, radiated light upward to the Father and down to those around the cross. Love permeated everything.

Then I saw myself in the distance walking toward the cross where Jesus hung. I had been stripped of worldly garments and scourged severely. I was bloody and weak, but my eyes focused on Jesus. He beckoned me. Love drew me to Him.

The Eternal Father gave me to know that He willed me to be properly prepared and presented to Jesus. Suddenly, the Blessed Mother appeared and began to walk with me on my left side. She took my hand in hers leading me toward Jesus. Then my spiritual director appeared and walked on my right. He was dressed in his priestly vestments, representing the Church. I observed the following. Every prayer that Father prayed for me formed a white veil. This seemed to form out of the very utterance of his prayers. Prayers, thus wrapped around me, formed the proper garment. Thus, I was prepared for Jesus. This priest was to present me to Jesus on the cross. The Holy Spirit overshadowed everything. The Father's Divine Will embraced everything. And Mother Mary interceded for everything.

Then Jesus spoke to Father: **She is breath of My breath; fire of My fire; dove of My heart; blood of My blood; seed of the Father; flower of the Immaculate Heart and she is your spiritual child. As My priest, you will present her to Me. Now you accompany her to My cross, covering her in prayer that is of the Holy Spirit, adorning her in love that is from Me. She takes her place on the cross with Me. The more she is pierced by the sword, the more mercy is poured upon the earth. My mercy shall gush from her for many. She is a sign of My mercy. She is My bride. You, My priest, form her for Me. You shall be by her side presenting her to Me, to the Father, in the Holy Spirit. When her mission is fulfilled, you shall finally present her to the heavenly court to the glory of the Father. You are united in this manner: you represent My Church, she is wedded to My Church. Her formation, her sacrifice and mission is made in, with, and for the Church. As My representative, you are her teacher, guide, protector and minister. You are united in the Church and for the Church. I, Myself, guide you in guiding her. My priest, My bride, My Church are all one in Me by the power of the Holy Spirit for the glory of the Father.**

I proceeded to Jesus on the cross. Along the way, my tears and blood fell to the ground and formed rose petals that fragranced the

Way of the Cross. This is the path the children of God must walk and we fragrance it for one another. I took my place upon the cross with Jesus. Love fastened me there. But the prayers of Mother Mary and Father empowered me to remain there with Jesus. Jesus said, **This is intercession.**

Then a sword was thrust through my heart. And I knew who was the instrument to pierce me. Immediately, mercy flowed from my heart. It became like a fountain. It covered many around the cross. From the cross, Jesus directed me to look closely at Father's hands. They bore the marks of one who had hung on the cross. He had suffered much; his life, a sacrifice to God. I saw other priests similarly marked. Jesus said, **What would My Church be without them (priests)? Intercede for them as they do for you. My bride, remain in Me. Here, on the cross with Me, there is power to save souls. Do this for love of Me. Peace. I love you. Your Jesus**

103. **2-23-96** Prayer Group Rosary
Intercede That Love be Restored

Dear little children,

Blessed are you little ones, who offer yourselves as intercessors for all souls. You are precious in my sight! You are a pleasing offering because your hearts are very pure. Purity of heart is a rare gift. It is most pleasing to God and to me. You are offering your hearts to God in intercession of His Perfect Intention. Do you see that His intention is that all souls would be transformed into Love? Then the world would have peace and joy, which stem from Love. Few know the truth of God's Infinite, Unconditional Love for souls! This is what you are interceding for, that Love will be restored to all people. I, who am your Mother, continue to intercede on your behalf. Each one of you is being transformed into Love Himself. This is a process, which is individual and precise for each soul. The goal is the same for all – union with God who is Love. But the journey is varied for each.

Tonight I have carried your intentions to God. Thank you for offering yourselves as a sacrifice to cover the terrible offenses made against God in this age. Each one of you is a rare and beautiful flower in the garden of my Immaculate Heart. Please never doubt the good and the power of your prayer. Prayer saves souls!

I will assist you to grow in love so that you will endure and persevere through many trials. Be of strong faith! The Spirit of God is with you. You shall not falter. Remain as little, little children. You are full of poverty, but you shall be made rich in love! Peace be yours. I love you. Your Mother

104. **2-23-96** Church following Mass
Jesus: Do You Love Me?

Following one hour of silence before the tabernacle, I heard:

Soul, do you love Me?
Yes, Lord, I love you.
Soul, do you know that I love you?
Oh, yes, Lord, I know that You love me.
Look at the Crucifix. What do you see?
I see the Father's love for His creation.
I see the Son of God embracing the Will of The Father for
   pure love of all creation.
I see the Spirit of the Living God burst forth from Your
   Being to cover mankind for all ages.
I see the waters of Baptism showering the children of God.
I see the blood of salvation covering the sins of mankind.
I see eyes that embrace all suffering for the sake of Love.
I see mercy gush forth from Your heart to forgive all sinners.
I see the King, humble and obedient.
I see tenderness and profound peace flowing from complete
   submission to the Will of the Father.
I see the Wisdom of the Most Holy Trinity.
I see a mystery that can be pondered into eternity without
   comprehension, but with some understanding of the power
   of sacrificial Love.
I see the Majesty of God.
I see the revelation of Your love for me as I observe the Divine
   Love of the Most Holy Trinity revealed in and through
   Your self immolation.

And in my heart and soul, I am drawn to You on the cross, no
longer content to look up and ponder. I have done this. I
must now be One with You on the cross to ponder all that
You observe from high upon the wood.

I want to explore You and all Your wounds.

I want to examine suffering from Your perspective.

Why? Because love for You moves me to desire Union!

Union that moves me to love as You love, to do as You do.

That I may be another You for the glory of The Father.

The Father chose me for You that the Holy Spirit that
permeates You will permeate me.

Then the fullness of the Spirit will be increased on earth, for
the Church, for all souls.

**Soul, already I have placed you on the cross with Me. From
here, what do you see?**

(Here, it was as if I was truly one with Jesus on the cross, so as
to see from His perspective with vision that comes from the Holy
Spirit.)

I see indifference! I see indifference to You and to the cross.
Few are in love or adoration of You on the cross where You pur-
chased eternal life for us. But the few that I observe truly love You.
They burn like fire. They love and pray and sacrifice attempting to
start more fires. But for the most part, hearts are cold, very cold.
Most are completely indifferent. Your Love is spurned, O Lord.
Have mercy.

Soul, who can change this?

Jesus, You promised the Holy Spirit would be with us to show
us the way, to teach us the Truth and to cause us to Love in response to how we have first been loved by You and the Father.

**Go then Soul, and baptize people in the Holy Spirit. Ignite
fires that burn with Love. One person ignites another person.
One by one will love be restored. Thus, will the heart of My
Church become inflamed with love, pure and holy. By no other
means will souls be drawn back to the Church, but by the fire
of the Holy Spirit that brings forth all the gifts of the Spirit
required by all the members of the Mystical Body. The crisis of
Truth will be reversed by the Holy Spirit of Truth, converting**

one soul after another. I shall place you in the heart of her (the Church) where restoration must begin and spread everywhere throughout her members. Thus will a remnant be raised to restore My Body and a multitude will be affected in the age to come. I send you like a lamb among wolves but I, the Good Shepherd, accompany you. By My Voice will you fulfill the mission ordained for you as part of My chosen faithful remnant, all of whom are soldiers in the army of little souls gathered in the Immaculate Heart of Mary.

This army will navigate the Church through the stormy waters with Mary on the left and the Eucharist on the right, both standing on the ancient pillars of Truth; carrying to safety, the deposit of Faith and Holy Traditions, fully alive in the new outpouring of the Holy Spirit who creates Fire. Fire that does not consume but melts the coldest heart and gives life to the dead. Thus will indifference be overcome. The Kingdom of God will reign upon earth. The Church will be the Heart that pumps life-giving blood to all its members. Go now in My peace. I bless you, My bride and My victim. I love you. Jesus

105. **2-25-96** 10AM My Prayer Room
Jesus on Patience!

I was praying to Jesus for a healing in my family, when He said: **Soul, patience is a holy virtue. It is a willingness to suffer, endure, and surrender. Patience is a most necessary virtue in the spiritual life. The spiritual life is outside of time. It is the human condition that works within time constraints. The spiritual person rises above these constraints. The Holy Spirit gives vision that is superior, far reaching, timeless. In the spiritual life, impatience is a true hindrance. It is not of the Holy Spirit. The Spirit brings patience to the soul. Patience is little valued in a world that values busyness and fast results. Nothing that lasts comes quickly.**

The spiritual life is a journey that leads into eternity. I am outside of time. So, too, is the spiritual life. Growth in patience is necessary for all souls. Many are diverted from their spiri-

tual life through a lack of patience, which is an unwillingness to suffer.

I find My creation unwilling to suffer even the smallest things. Many rebel against the very monotony of daily life by impatiently filling time with meaningless busyness. Souls are impatient due to selfishness, pride and a lack of sacrificial love. Holiness requires patience. The world does not preach sacrifice, discipline, or patience. But I, the Lord, your God, require sacrifice, discipline, patience, endurance, longsuffering, perseverance. All these are fruits of the Holy Spirit in a soul. The enemy tempts souls to impatience. Many fall into this temptation. Often this causes a serious fall in the spiritual journey. A soul runs ahead of Me. There is no waiting to hear My Voice. No waiting to receive the prompting of the Holy Spirit. A soul goes forward, not in My Will but in theirs.

I have a magnificent plan for each individual soul. But the spiritual life includes many hills and valleys, seasons of darkness and of light. Each season has its own beauty, gifts and trials. Each leads to growth in the knowledge of Me and of self. Each season is wrapped in My Divine Love, Grace and Presence! You are never alone! Your soul created by the breath of the Father is dignified by the Holy Trinity and receives a magnificent angelic being to accompany you from the moment of your birth to your passage into eternal life.

Oh, My creation, if only you would accept the gift of My Holy Spirit, you would have Love! All the gifts of the Spirit would be yours. The journey would be filled with faith, hope, and charity. All would be joy! You would patiently endure all things for the sake of Love. You would be secure in the knowledge that Divine Providence cares for you. If you could see the magnificent reality of the spiritual, angelic world in beautiful motion all around you, all would be converted!

Then would you see the reality of the Spirits of Light and the spirits of darkness. You would see the ugliness of the devil and his cohorts; the ugliness of sin and its effects on your soul. Then would you see the truth and the beauty of the Angels of Light, the ministering angels that lead you to Me, feeding you My Grace with tender love for your soul.

Your guardian angel knows and sees the dignity of your soul. Imagine how loved you are by the angel that tends to you at every moment of your life. Most are utterly indifferent to such a magnificent being of light!

Oh, My creation, I have provided for you in ways incomprehensible to you! Awaken! Open your hearts, your ears, and your eyes! Yes, I require faith! I do not permit you to see the reality of the spiritual world except through the eyes of the Holy Spirit. He is the one who gives you to see and to hear and to know the Truth of the spiritual world. The Holy Spirit descended upon the world at Pentecost and He is with you unto the end of time. Receive Him and Live! Only in Him will you have love, peace, joy. Be patient as I am patient with you. Seek the Holy Spirit with all your heart, soul, mind and strength. He will come to all who invite Him. He will lead you along the journey to Me and to the Father. It is a journey of ineffable love and profound peace. It is Life abundant! Come. I love you. Jesus

106. **2-26-96** 12:30AM
Interceding: Heal Us!

I was sleeping soundly when suddenly a sharp piercing of my heart awakened me. Whatever pierces usually passes in and out quickly and leaves a wound. But in this case, the instrument that pierced, seemingly, remained lodged inside my heart. Intense heat began to overcome it. My chest was burning up. After a time, it seemed I was placed on the cross with Jesus.

Upon the cross, we were as one offering to the Father. The Father's presence increased. I found myself addressing the Father in a very labored manner, as if I was truly hanging on the cross and suffering excruciating pain. My cries to the Father became increasingly more powerful until it seemed to me that my cries from the cross could pierce the heavens and the earth. I cried out, "Father, heal us! Abba, Father, heal us! Father, glorify Your Son – now is the time – heal us!" I continued to cry out in this manner with great intensity for a long time. My breathing became labored because I was physically and spiritually exhausted. After a while, I could no longer cry out. There was a time of silence, then Eternal Father said: **Daughter, open your mouth. Drink of His Blood. I will pour it inside of you.** So powerful was His command that I think I physically opened my mouth and began the gesture of swallowing the Blood of the Lamb. During all of this, the arrow of fire remained in my heart until I thought I would burn up. Eventually, I fell asleep pondering the mystery of God's grace in my soul. There is so much I do not understand. I yield to grace. That is all.

107. **2-28-96**
Mary: Together We Gather Souls

When Father and I prayed the Chaplet of Divine Mercy, another stabbing arrow seemed to pass through my heart with great intensity and fire. It was extremely painful. It entered like a sharp arrow, delivered intense heat and rendered such violence to my heart that it felt like a grenade went off and my heart exploded. Seemingly, it became one open, bleeding, painful wound. But this wound is one of Love. It is a constant reminder to remain open to love; to overcome the temptation to close my heart. I am in the midst of a situation in which it would be natural to close my heart to love.

I went out during the prayer of the Rosary. In the beginning, I sensed two angels take my hands and lift my spirit with great ease to go with them somewhere. All was silence, stillness, peace, and love. I do not recall anything until Father began his meditation on the decade of the Coronation of Mary.

Then, I saw our spirits halfway between heaven and earth. We ascended toward heaven in the form of a cross (arms outstretched). Our spirits were transparent and light surrounded them. I became aware that we carried other souls with us, many of them, and that we were not going to the Lord but to Our Lady. We were to form part of her crown.

Our Lady said: *All who embrace the Divine Will of the Father become part of my coronation. By means of your consecration to My Immaculate Heart, you form part of my crown, glorifying the Father. I love you, dear children, and together we gather souls for the Most Holy Trinity. I will lead you closer to God. Allow God complete freedom in you and He will raise you up. Continue to pray as much as possible and offer everything to God. I love you. Your Mother*

108. **3-6-96** Rosary with Father, my home.
The Immaculate Heart, Intercession, Co-Redeemers

As Father led the Joyful Mysteries, I became aware that I was in a place of silence and stillness and Father's prayers were as if in the distant background, like a whisper.

Our Lady said: *You are in my Immaculate Heart. Rest! Rest in my heart.* I was enveloped in the security of her maternal heart and remained at rest in profound peace and silence until the end of the Rosary. Toward the end, I could hear Father's voice again. I listened to his prayers. Then Our Lady said: *Yes, child, listen. Does he not soothe the heart?* Our Lady was truly listening to Father's prayers and seemed so joyful because of them. She said: *His prayers have power because he prays from a heart full of love. His love soothes my heart. And you are in my heart. Receive love and peace from within. Rest and be refreshed for the journey. We are here for you.* (The Church, Father and her.) Then Father said: "I love you Mary, my mother." And Our Lady said: *I love you, my son.*

Then I saw a high brick wall. Parts of the wall were coming down. I saw myself on the cross then. A drop of my blood and sweat fell on the brick wall. One by one, the bricks began to break apart and the wall began to come down. Behind the wall I saw a human heart. Our Lady said: *This human heart represents those of you who try to protect yourselves through self-sufficiency and pride. You are deceived by the enemy if you think you can protect yourself from suffering by building a wall around your heart. You suffer all the more because the wall prevents the receiving and the giving of true love. Do not be afraid to receive and give love. If you build a wall around your heart, you are a prisoner of fear and pride. The intercession of victim lambs who unite to Jesus on the cross can cause the walls to come down around the many hearts dying from lack of love. Brick by brick, the walls will come down. This will open the way for Love.*

Then I saw the globe of the earth. Then a large cross arose from it and rested on top of the globe. I saw myself on the cross with Jesus. I cried out to the Father, "Father, forgive them. They know not what they do." I never looked down at the world, but fixed my eyes upward to the Father. I continued to cry out, "Father, forgive us!" My heart suddenly filled with intense love and compassion for all God's creatures. I willed to suffer in intercession for each little creature. It became an overwhelming desire. I was passionately crying out on behalf of the entire world. This continued for a while, then the heavens opened up and the voice of our Triune God spoke very slowly, deliberately; not as a human would speak, more like a breath. I somehow saw the breath of God breathe upon the world. He breathed: M e r c y. I watched the word form out of air from His breath. His breath of mercy descended upon the earth. The Father honored my prayer. The world was touched by His Mercy.

Jesus said: **Such is the power of a soul who lays down his life in imitation of Me. The Father seeks sacrificial victim lambs to worship Him in spirit and in truth. These lambs are chosen and purified in the fire. Their sacrifice is pleasing because they are transfigured into Love, into My Image. The redemption of the world continues through the sacrifices of victim lambs. I am the Redeemer. You are My co-redeemers.**

109. **3-8-96** Prayer Group Meeting
Put Aside Fear. Trust!

Fifth Sorrowful Mystery, Jesus' Death on the Cross.

My dear children,
My Mercy descended upon you long ago. The fountain of My Divine Mercy has saturated you. You have witnessed My Love through many graces which many have never witnessed. So it is, that you have received much in these critical times of unfathomable Mercy. So it is, that requires much of you. I have done great things for you, My beloved ones! I raised you by My Own Hand for your sanctification, for My Glory, for the good of the souls you serve now and in the future.

The time has come that I shall require of you, a deeper level of trust because I have already demonstrated in so many ways, the depth of My Divine Mercy and Love for you. I have done this individually and collectively. Through your deeper trust in My Mercy, you will draw more mercy upon your families, the Church, and the world. The more you trust in My Mercy, the more I will bless your trust with new and abundant graces.

My Mercy gushed forth from My side pierced on the cross and opened up for the salvation of the world. If you too, wish to draw mercy upon yourselves and your loved ones, then you must be pierced and opened up to become a fountain of mercy for others. Now is the time to trust. Do not put off trusting. Do not put off proclaiming My Mercy to others because these are the days of extraordinary Mercy. Many can avail themselves of graces in and through your intercession — if you trust at a new and deeper level. This is what I require of you now! You have been prepared by My Own Hand to do as I ask. I will enable you to trust boundlessly if you but seek to put aside all fear! Fear is the obstacle to trust. Perfect Love casts out all fear. Fear is the tactic of the enemy. The enemy will do all that he can to cause you to be afraid. He knows the power in a soul that trusts, especially, in My Mercy! The enemy hates Mercy!

Do not worry about where you are going. I am leading you. That is enough to know. Look at all that I have done for you already. Are we not closer in love today than we were yesterday? Yes, My little lambs, each of you has grown in love and union. I am delighted that the intention of your heart is pure. I see that you each long to love Me and to serve Me fulfilling the Divine Will of Our Father. Therefore, trust that the water and blood flowing from My Heart for you is all that you need to accomplish all that I ask of you.

Drink, drink of the endless fountain of My love and mercy! Be full! Truly I say to you, you will do great things in and through Me. Many will be saved by your love, prayer, sacrifice and trust. I promise, the more you trust, the more you will be used by Me! Trust is absolutely necessary! I want to use you to be apostles of My Divine Mercy so that through you, mercy will be poured out to many. But I can only do so if you turn to Me in complete trust.

Pray, dear little children, that the world will avail itself of My Unfathomable Mercy now. As it is today, many would perish if the cup of My Father's justice was poured out now. You see how important it is that you pray for those who cannot, that you love for those who refuse to love, that you believe for all unbelievers, that you trust for all who live in fear and darkness. When you trust through times of difficulty, you touch My Merciful Heart and I am moved to increase the flow of mercy upon the world. I bless you here and now and always. I am with you. I love you. Your Jesus of Mercy!

110. **3-10-96**
Suffer Silently

During Mass, I am numb with pain, spiritually and physically. It feels as if something very heavy has been put upon my back. My neck, back and shoulders are in knots from the weight of it. When I received Communion, everything seems to disappear and I am overwhelmed with the love of Jesus. Then, I received an image of a certain soul with a whip, scourging Jesus. I bury my face to hide the tears that begin to flow. To my core, I am shaken to observe this soul beating Jesus.

Jesus remains silent and continues to love and forgive. Jesus looks into my eyes. Tenderly He says: **Soothe My wounds, soul of My cross. Your love can soothe My wounds. Thus will you draw mercy for those who continually carry out the scourging of My Body.** I continue to observe this soul scourge Jesus. His blood flowed all over. I have a strong urge to speak this to the person.

Jesus says: **Silence, soul of My cross. It will not be heard now. You are to soothe My wounds with your love and mercy. This is what I ask of you, My beloved bride and victim. Your suffering is drawing unfathomable mercy for many souls. Thank you.**

At one time, you also held the whip in your hands, then My Mother and other victim souls interceded for you. And The

Holy Spirit enlightened your mind and heart so that you would no longer offend Me. Now you and Mother Mary intercede together, for many. Countless souls are offending Me in the same manner as this soul. You are suffering for all of them. You are carrying the weight of the cross of sin. Many chosen and prepared souls are sharing in the weight of the sins of this generation. Through you, My Mercy is being given to many.

I love you, My victim lamb. How radiant you are in your suffering! My own beauty is yours as you are made into My reflection. I suffer with you, soul of My cross. Every tear has meaning to Me. Every sigh of love touches My Heart, soothes My Body. Every temptation resisted by you increases the fire within you. You grow in love, purity and strength. The weight of the cross on your back carries souls to Me, souls that otherwise would not have reached Me but for your sacrifice. Loving Me as you do affects souls in ways incomprehensible to you. Trust. It is true. Never doubt the good of your suffering for the sake of Love. It may seem to you that your greatest suffering comes from loving and serving Me. Consider that My greatest suffering was for love of you!

Love endures everything. Your heart can endure much for the sake of the conversion of souls because I have given you My Own Sacred Heart of Love. Your heart is secure within Mine. You say to Me, "It seems my heart is shredded into pieces?" And I say to you, "It is My Heart that is shredded by lack of Love from My creatures." You are sharing My pain. Are we not One? Why then do you differentiate "your" pain or "My pain"? We are One! I bear the burden! I share but one drop with you! Do lovers share everything? I say to you, lovers become one and share everything! That is how it is between God and every soul! I am present to everything in every soul. I, who am Infinite Love, am subjected to unloving, impure, and evil ways inside the very hearts that I have created, sustained, and destined for loving union.

Oh My bride, if you could see the sin of the world, the evil I see at every moment, you would be willing to suffer again and again, to even be chopped into little pieces, to cover the wounds inflicted upon My Heart at every moment! And you would zealously seek other souls to love, to suffer and make amends for the atrocities against My most Sacred and tender Heart! Love unreservedly, My bride! Do not count the cost, count the good. Count only the souls you will carry to Me so that My tender Heart will be soothed by love, love, love!

I love you infinitely. Eternally, you are a part of Me. You have My Heart and I have yours. I suffer with you. With Me, you have Life. Your suffering will turn to joy eternally. Pray and fast for your family and for all souls who are My family. In eternity you will see that you suffered but for a moment. In My mercy, I make great good of it! Soul of My Cross, you are loved by He who is, who was and always will be! Your Triune God upholds you. My Love will sustain you. Rest in My merciful Heart. Give to Me, your trust. In silent and patient endurance you will rise to Me. Will you do this for Me?

"Jesus, I will trust in You because I love You so very much."

I am delighted in you. Continue to respond. I shall do everything else. Yes?

"Yes, my Jesus, yes." Then my heart was pierced, becoming swollen with Love.

Note: I suffered very much this weekend from the strong sense of not belonging to this world. I do not seem to fit anymore. Everywhere I turn I see things that grieve the most pure Heart of Jesus. I cannot escape the knowledge of the sin of the world grieving the Father, Son, and Holy Spirit. It weighs heavy on my heart, though sometimes I try very much to push it aside. I cannot. No matter how I am occupied, I sense the sin, the disorder and the pain that comes from it. I think my spirit prays at every moment asking God to heal all of us.

"Oh, Sacred Heart of Love, there is none like You! Innocent Lamb of God, let this little, poor creature of Yours tend to Your wounds. Let my love anoint Your scourged Body. Oh, my Jesus, You have already answered my request. Thank You, my Lord and Savior! Oh, that I could love You more. Amen."

111. **3-13-96** My home
Toward a New Pentecost

Right before Father and I began the prayer of the Rosary, I received a sharp piercing pain in my heart. As soon as I received the piercing, it was as if I was transported to Calvary. It was as if I experienced a portion of the piercing that Jesus received and I felt pain through my side and heart like a burning sword inside of me. It was as if I was opened up and poured out. It felt like blood was gushing out of my side. My blood was to give life to someone else. I began to have extreme chills and became cold all over. After this, I entered another prayer state immediately. I was "out" completely during most of the Rosary. But toward the end, I began to hear some of Father's prayers and received the following.

The first image I saw was of myself lying on an altar. Then God the Father said: **My daughter, you are the sacrifice on the altar. You are an acceptable offering to Me.** His disposition was extremely gentle, loving, and accepting. I offered myself again saying, "Father, let me be Your victim for many." He approved.

Then, I saw three crosses on Calvary. I was looking from a distance. There was mostly darkness everywhere on earth. Then lightening and thunder struck all around the three crosses. Jesus' cross became brilliantly illuminated in light that was very alive. Jesus was on the cross while the beauty of the Light radiated all around. The lightening and thunder grew more intense. Again, the earth was full of darkness. Then Jesus said sorrowfully: **I come to separate the sheep from the goats; the good from the evil.** Here He pointed to the good thief and then the bad thief on either side of Him. Then He continued: **Do not be scandalized as you witness more division. The time has come. Evil must be exposed and separated from good.**

Then, I saw a ladder that reached from earth to heaven. The ladder was formed by intercessors who laid down their lives to form the rungs of the ladder. Then, souls could journey from earth to heaven. The ladder, made of beautiful, little souls was full of Life and took many souls to help form it. The saints of old helped form the ladder also. All of heaven shined light upon the ladder illuminating the way to the entry into paradise. There were souls on earth waiting to climb the ladder. But it was disturbing to see that the number was few compared to the souls that were indifferent.

Then, I saw the earth enveloped in fire. The fire was not destructive. It did consume, but only that which needed to be purged. Jesus said: **This is the fire of Perfect Love. It will envelop and transfigure the earth. It will be transmitted from within; one soul to another. The fire is the Holy Spirit. He will descend upon the world and cause a New Pentecost.** Then, I saw the heavens open up and fire fell like rain upon the earth. It was beautiful. What was dead came to life. What was alive became more alive. Evil was consumed. Goodness overcame everything.

Then, I heard God the Father again. He said to my spiritual director: **Thank you My beloved son. Thank you for your love and sacrifice. My favor is upon you. I accept your prayers, your offering. You are united to My Son; one by the power of the Holy Spirit. You are for Me; for My honor and My glory. You are an offering for many souls. I am over you. I love you eternally. Receive My paternal blessing.**

Then, I saw the globe of the earth. From the heavens high above, I heard the powerful voice of God resounding throughout the heavens and earth. His utterance seemed to pierce the entire universe with His Majesty as He said: **My creation! My Covenant is everlasting! I hear your cries, your wailing! Your Father hears you! You suffer and wail as if you are orphans. You cry out as if to the air, to a God, a Father, you do not know. You do not know Me because you do not know the Word. When He was among you, you did not know Him. Now the Spirit is with you and you do not know Him!**

Oh, My creation! I have given you everything! Still you cry out like a fatherless generation. Oh pitiable state! My Mercy is for the asking. Turn! Repent! Receive My Spirit and forgiveness is yours. Lament over your sinfulness instead of lamenting over being forsaken. I shall never forsake you! Oh, My creation, turn to Me. Reconcile with Me that I may welcome you into the embrace of My Paternal Love and forgiveness. You are not orphans. Your Father loves you! Receive My Love, My Word. Do not wait. I am your Eternal Father, the Alpha and the Omega.

112. **3-13-96** AM, Tabernacle
My Mystical Body is Being Scourged

My children,
   My passion continues as My Mystical Body is continually scourged due to lack of love and unity. Her wounds are deep. They penetrate My Heart. Many innocent souls are the victims. My little ones, you, who know My Voice, shall be the salve; your love, the healing ointment; your sacrifice will close the wounds. I have chosen you for My Church. I shall be your Guide. Pray together, confident that prayer bears much fruit. Your work shall produce an abundant harvest of souls. Pray for the Church and her leaders. Pray for unity. Division has penetrated and the result is confusion among the faithful. The Holy Spirit will raise up a remnant to heal her. The Spirit will accomplish the work. Pray and live in union with My Holy Spirit. I am with you always. To the priests I say, "Open your hearts." Trust. I shall reward your humility. You shall not falter. Love is with you, blessing you every step of the way. Thank you, My beloved ones, for desiring the Most Holy Divine Will. I love you. Your Jesus

113. **3-19-96** AM, Tabernacle. Feast of St. Joseph
St. Joseph Carries the Weight of the Church

   I am the Head. The Church is My Mystical Body. Joseph's position in the Body could be likened to your feet. He is a humble, hidden worker, graciously carrying the weight of the Body (Church). Your feet carry you where you want to go. Joseph carries the weight of the Church, directing it along the path of the Divine Will of the Father. Joseph's role is unique among all saints. He was My just and faithful guardian, My earthly father. He was the just and faithful guardian of the Blessed Virgin Mary. He was united to Me in those years of hidden union and love. In Nazareth, Joseph tended to the Word Made Flesh. Now in heaven, the Word embraces Joseph in a unique way.

Joseph intercedes with Me at the right hand of the Father. Mary Immaculate is the mother of the Church and Joseph, is the unique father of the Church. Theirs is a unique relationship even in heaven where they intercede together for the Church, for the world. When you pray with Mary, you honor Joseph. When you pray with Joseph, you honor Mary. When you seek their intercession, you give Me honor and you glorify the Father. They are the Father's vessels of election. When you honor the saints by acknowledging their lives as exemplary, and you seek to imitate their holy virtues, you acknowledge the Will of the Father that all would be one holy family; one heart of love breathing in union with His Divine Will. There is wisdom in praying with and through the saints because they obtain for you many heavenly graces. It is their mission and their pleasure to assist you. They seek to draw all souls to God so that you enjoy what they enjoy - My Eternal Presence. It is My Will. And the saints are one with My Will in heaven. Be one with My Will on earth and you will know love and peace as a member of a loving and holy family. I love you. That is My Covenant and it is everlasting. Your Jesus

114. **3-19-96** PM, My home. Feast of St. Joseph
Intercede for My House

During the Rosary with Father, I was "out" until the last part of the Rosary. During the Mystery of the Presentation of Jesus in the Temple, I saw the scene as if I was present at it. The focus was on St. Joseph. (It is his feast day.) I saw how protective he was standing next to Mary holding Jesus in her arms. He radiated strength, his eyes full of unconditional love. He was beholding a mystery. He would ponder this mystery in his heart during the years with Jesus in Nazareth. I somehow observed the union of heart that existed between St. Joseph and St. Mary as they presented Jesus in the temple and it is indescribable. The Holy Spirit knit them together. Joseph radiated the light of obediential love.

Jesus said to me: **Soul, recall when I called you in the spirit of Ezekiel? Recall the dry dead bones spread all over the ground.**

Recall I said; "Prophesy over them." I said breathe over them and bring them to life. Recall the scrolls I gave to you saying, "Ingest these scrolls." And you did. They contained the Will of the Father. You are chosen: a prophet and intercessor for the people. Look little one. Then I saw the image of the Church. I saw people leave. Father and I were called to intercede for those who had wandered away.

Jesus said: **Remain in My House to restore and embellish her. She will be made beautiful. Love will draw them back inside. Remain within My House, My priest. Pray and offer the Sacrifice of the Mass and make available all the sacraments. My lamb, remain within My House to pray and sacrifice; prophesy and anoint. Your house is part of Mine.**

I received an image of the Church. I saw the Most Holy Trinity inside; Mary and St. Michael above the top of the Church; St. Joseph on the bottom; St. Peter on the right. (St. Peter was the Peter of today - Pope John Paul II.) St. Paul was on the left.

I prayed to Jesus, "Lord, what will penetrate the hardness of their hearts and cause them to see the Truth and turn back to you, to Your House? Jesus said: **Observe.** Then I saw the globe of the earth. Halfway between the earth and heaven, I saw Jesus on the cross with His side opened wide, blood and water gushed out and poured over the earth.

Then I saw, between Jesus and earth, more crosses with people on them. I saw myself and Father and other people that I recognized as people of prayer. Each was pierced; opened up so that blood poured onto the earth. Intercessors were living on the cross in union with Jesus. I observed the blood of the victim souls break down hard hearts, one drop at a time. As I observed all of this, the Dove of the Holy Spirit radiated His Light onto the hearts. Light entered the darkness of many hearts. I said, "Lord, You could do this all in an instant if you wanted!"

He said: **Yes! But it is the divine plan that salvation requires cooperation with grace, relationship with Me, relationship with one another. You must help one another as the family of man. My creation is a family. You break My covenant of Love when you do not see yourself in relationship to your brothers and sisters.** I said, "Jesus, if their will is against Your Will and Your Way, what then?"

Jesus said: **I, who am Lord and Savior of all, open and close doors around them according to My Divine Will. My grace surrounds them to penetrate as soon as there is a softening of their own will. Then I can incline them to My Will without violating the dignity and freedom of the human will. Prayerful intercession facilitates the graced moment of conversion. I patiently await the human will.**

Soul of My cross, the evil spirits attack your family to murder your spiritual life and mission in My Church. The prayers and Masses offered by your spiritual director are most efficacious in freeing your family of the demonic attack upon it. My bride, I will restore your house and you will assist Me in restoring My House. I love you. Continue to walk in faith, hope, and love. I guide your every step.

During the Chaplet of Divine Mercy, I saw us prostrate before the throne of the Eternal Father. We prayed "For the sake of His sorrowful passion, have mercy on us and on the whole world." Then the Eternal Father asked His priest to stand before Him. Jesus wrapped Father in a blood red cloak. They embraced. Then Jesus blessed Father on the forehead with the sign of the cross in Precious Blood. Father returned to prayer, prostrate again. The Eternal Father said: **This is your call, your mission: Love. And lead souls to Love. I bless you. I am your Eternal Father.**

115. **3-22-96** Prayer Group
Come to Know the Father's Love Through the Cross

My little ones,

Thank you for pondering the mysteries of My passion suffered for love of you. I so desire that you come to know more fully the depth of My Divine Love for each one of you. I would die for even one, but I died for all. The more you come to know of My love for you, the more you will love Me in return. This is the desire of My Heart – that you and I are united in a deep bond of love. Above all things, I desire that you come to know that you are truly loved by the Father who created you for Himself. All else flows from this. This is the fundamental Truth that

facilitates love! If you know this, you will love. If you do not know this, you will not love. And the more you know it, the more you will love. The more you love, the more you will endure for the sake of love.

Each one of you is carrying your cross during this season of Lent. None have escaped the cross. The cross is My gift to you. Truly your cross unites you to Me in ways incomprehensible. All that you endure bears fruit that you may or may not see in this life. But in the next, it shall be revealed to you. Great will be your joy and Mine. As I share the intentions of My Heart with you, you become a reflection of Me. We intercede together to the Father for the world. Thank you for your intercession.

The world has great need of your prayers and sacrifices. Faith is fading even in the Church. When you walk in faith and trust, you make up for the lack of faith in My Body. Oh, My beloved Bride, the Church! She is suffering and she will continue to endure many trials and attacks. Many are abandoning her. Many are trying to recreate her. But I will raise you to assist her. Great will be your ministry to My Mystical Body! I shall restore her! And I will use each one of you to beautify her. Now I am beautifying you by the way of the cross; here does the old self die and the new self emerge. How beautiful you are as My new creation – a creation of love, pure, and holy. I give to you, My Peace. Rejoice! I am with you. What more do you require? I love you. Your Jesus

116. **3-23-96** In Church, PM Mass and Holy Hour
A Sacrificial Lamb

At Holy Communion, I prayed: "Lord, You are with me. I beg You, look upon my neediness and have mercy. You are my Teacher. Instruct me. Help me to understand Your Perfect Divine Will in my family. Then I saw a lamb on an altar bleeding profusely. The body of the lamb was terribly bruised. Jesus said, **This is you, My beloved.**

Then I saw a shepherd with a staff approach the altar. He picked up the lamb and embraced it. His charity helped to heal some of the wounds on the lamb. Jesus continued: **My Church provides the charity, tending to your wounds and enables you to endure much suffering for the sake of My Kingdom. Your suffering is not in vain. I make great good of it. You suffer in My Name for love of Me. For love of you I pour grace upon many. You are drawing My Mercy upon souls! My Bride, can you not recognize the profound peace in your soul as My Presence within you? Such peace comes only from Me. I have hidden you in the depths of My Heart that you would be enveloped in My Peace while you drink of My Divine Love.**

Recognize the love of the Father who has provided for you. The Father is glorified by one thing only – Love. Do not be afraid to accept all that comes from the Father. Do not be surprised by His generosity. He provides that you may endure silently, without resistance, becoming a sacrificial lamb for the salvation of souls. I am in the shepherd and the shepherd is in Me. I am in the lamb and the lamb is in Me. Love is with you always but especially in the painful hours of your immolation.

I asked, "Lord, what about my family?" I saw four corners of a square. Then a circle was drawn around the square. Then a dot appeared in the center. Jesus said: **The four corners are the members of your family. The circle is the unending love of the Trinity. The center dot is the Blessed Mother. The rays of love emanate from the circle of the Trinity into the Heart of the Blessed Mother and then back to the Trinity. Everything inside the circle receives constant grace, protection, and love. Though the four corners seem far apart, the Immaculate Heart of Mary will draw you all together according to the perfect time designated by the Father. She is watching over your family and all exist in My Love. Do not worry. Trust.**

*Soul, thank you for being the victim of My Love. Your fiat resounds in My Heart. My bride, I am with you. Do not tremble with fear. One who lives within the intimacy of My Heart rests in My Peace. I am here. Your Jesus

117. **3-27-96** My home
My Spiritual Director's Prayer

I was suffering very much and Father prayed over me. Spirits of rebellion and negativity toward God were tempting me. He prayed, "Protect her from the demonic spirits that surround her. God, Our Father, come and embrace her with peace, strength, security, and love. Clothe her in garb fitting a bride of Your Son." Then Father looked at Jesus on the cross and said, "Please Lord take her into Your Heart." Then he heard Jesus: **She is Mine. She will always be Mine. I do take her into My Heart. From there she will love; she will give mercy. From there, she will have gentleness, kindness and peace. From there, she will see the suffering of the world and she will love to overcome it.**

118. **3-29-96**
Agony in the Garden of Gethsemane

Driving home from Prayer Group Meeting, in the car alone, I was suddenly overcome with a deep, deep sense of loneliness. My spirit was plunged into utter loneliness. This was an entirely new experience. It was deeply spiritual, not emotional.

I understood immediately that I was tasting of Our Lord's Agony in the Garden. As I drove home, it was as if I had been stripped of everything and everyone, so that I existed in nakedness in a world in which I was all alone. I arrived home. I was alone in the house. The family was gone. I slipped into bed and the loneliness was so heavy that I burst into tears of extreme agony.

But suddenly, Our Lord stopped me from crying. Instantly, my tears dried up. He did not want me to release the pain of the loneliness. He wanted me to experience it, just as He did in the Garden, for love of me. Here, for the next twenty minutes or so, I was plunged into darkness and loneliness, which could not be comforted. I became one with Jesus and began to taste and feel just as He did in the Garden.

Oh, Desolate Garden
Utter darkness of the Night
Oh, Garden of Loneliness
Oh, night of Agony
Drowning in sorrow
Piercing isolation
Oh, weight of the world
Sin so deadly
Humanity so fleeting
Death so promising
Oh, torturous sacrifice
Oh, silent suffering
Resounding stillness in the night
Chill penetrating my bones
Heart abandoned, body trembling,
Blood and sweat dripping
Have You forsaken me, Father? Take this cup from me.
Not mine, but Your Will be done.

Wind that whispers of torture
Sin of all ages
Bearing down upon me
Obedience overcoming disobedience
Love overcoming everything
Death unlike any other death
Surrender, my soul, Surrender!
Father, the hour has come
Glorify me that I may glorify you
Eternal life be purchased
I am the ransom
Receive my offering eternally
Now all shall have life
Let the darkness of this lonely night
Cover the lonely darkness of man
Agonizing Love to cancel man's sin
Oh, how I love, I love, I love
Alone I am. Alone, I am not.

I cried out to the Father, here. The Father's embrace surrounded me and I fell asleep in Him.

119. **4-2-96** My home
Our Lady's Heart

During the Chaplet of Divine Mercy with Father, the Blessed Mother revealed her Immaculate Heart to me in an interior vision. I saw her heart surrounded by the crown of thorns. A sword pierced it from the top and a fire burned in the depths of it. She gave me to see that my heart was aligned with hers and the sword that pierces touched us both. She revealed that the fire in the depths of her maternal heart is the fire of love of the Most Holy Trinity. By means of this love we are united, mother and daughter, In all of this, God is glorified.

She revealed that her heart was so aflame with Love that it has the power to protect souls who take refuge in her heart. Though legions of demons assail these souls, there is protection in her heart because God ordered it. Then I saw legions of dark spirits attempting to surround her heart and aim at the souls within it. What amazed me about these evil spirits was their constant motion. They never ceased movement. They consistently plotted against the Immaculate Heart of Mary and all those souls within her heart. I could sense their deep hatred of the Blessed Virgin Mary and those souls open to her maternal love and assistance. They are afraid of her. Mary was still and silent. Joyfully she protects all the souls who take refuge in her heart. Mary said: *If you permit me to be your mother, I will shelter your heart and soul in my maternal love and take you to my Son. I love you, dear children.*

Later in prayer, Our Lady requested that I pray as much as possible for a certain soul in great need of her maternal intercession. This soul had persecuted me very much and I really did not want to pray that much for this soul. But Our Lady implored me to do so. She said: *Daughter, ask me to help this soul. This soul has great need of your prayers and sacrifice. It makes me very joyful when you pray for this soul.* I did as she requested.

120. **4-9-96**
Infidelity and the Human Will

Father said Mass at my house and this message was received.

My child, great is the infidelity of the children of God, all of whom are my children also. Many have broken the covenant and turned their minds and hearts toward other gods. The human will can become like iron. It can will its own way without regard for God's Way. Iron is melted and molded in fire. God's Mercy will call for the iron human will to be encompassed by the fire of purification. This suffering will melt obstinate hearts. This is a wayward age! Purification will come to make obstinate hearts convert to docility. Unless you become like a little child, you cannot enter the Kingdom of God. A little child turns to his Eternal Father. The enemy helps to prop up the human will. But the human will leads to folly. When one falls, Divine Grace is ready to teach and guide, to pick up the heart and soul.

You are interceding on behalf of many wayward souls. Thank you, daughter, for your abandonment to the Divine Will. I know of your suffering. By doing God's Will in this situation you are being clothed in virtue creating beauty in your own soul. The Divine Bridegroom is attracted to such virtue. He is with you always to oversee His creative beautification. In the Father's eyes you are a jewel shining brightly; a light in the darkness. The Blood of the Lamb has transfigured you into another sacrificial lamb.

Silence, little lamb. Silent suffering resounds in the heavens. And the heavens rejoice in the sacrifice of love, opening up to pour down grace and mercy. More light, more love comes to souls.

Daughter, you weep because you think you are not loved. Remember when St. Peter denied Jesus? Did he mean what he said in that moment of confusion and fear? Fear motivated him to say what he did not mean. This is the case in your situation. What is said to you does not come from the true heart but from a tormented mind.

What you witness in your own family is but an example of what is happening in the family of man and in the Church. Mankind is walking in fear. It is evident that the world is heading for disaster. No one can control or prevent it except God. Beyond any cataclysmic disaster, the disaster man experiences in his heart is the lack of

*love and peace within. Man is becoming more frustrated and des-
perate for true love and meaning. For all the sophistication, intelligence, money and power, you cannot find happiness. You race
like mice in a maze and end up fatigued and empty. Then you feed
yourselves on more ways of the world so you can continue the race.
Where are you going? My poor children! Your infidelity to God
and His Covenant of Love leads you to emptiness.*

*Jesus' passion ended in humility, in obedience to the Will of
the Father, when he died only to resurrect! My children, your suffering is prolonged because you refuse to humble yourselves to
obey God and His precepts. Your own law is disordered. My children, disorder is touching every aspect of your lives. Are your hearts
not aching for lack of love and peace? Your cries are growing louder
daily. More victim souls are needed for reparation. The just and
little ones are interceding for a multitude of souls on the brink of
eternal death.*

*Oh, my children, God's justice is coming! Your ways are unjust.
The Father will set justice before you to teach you the Truth. You will
see what you have done! A light will pierce your hearts and illumine
what is hidden within. The truth of your ways will be evident.*

*Yield your human will to the Divine Will now! Grant this gift of
yourself to God. Exchange your disorder for God's order. This is
not easy. God knows. But if you desire it with all your heart, grace
will accomplish it.*

*The enemy is constantly tempting you to have your own way.
The human will desires the path of least resistance and the way of
human reasoning. It does not desire the perfect way, which is difficult and involves self-sacrifice. Forfeit the imperfection of the human will to receive the Perfection of the Divine Will.*

*Because faith is lacking, people do not embrace God's Way.
Because faith is weak, you do not believe that God is Love. If you
believed in Love, in Jesus, you would embrace His Law of Love
and trust in Divine Providence.*

My children, what must be done that you might have hope?

*Believers must pray and sacrifice for unbelievers. Victim souls
must intercede for sinners, those offending God the most. The
humble ones must break the bondage of the proud. Children of the
Light must illumine the darkness of the world with Love.*

Restoration will come through purification. Purification will bring much suffering and this will bring the resurrection. Many will be lost while many are saved. They will be lost who separate themselves from God by sin without repentance. These are the ones who befriend Satan and refuse God's Love and Mercy. Love alone will triumph! God will raise a faithful generation and a glorified Church.

The Father made an everlasting covenant with you, His people, forever. You have the Word Incarnate in the Sacrament of Holy Communion. You have the Holy Spirit who is Love, breathing life within you. Unite, God's family, by the power of His Love and live! Become small and surrendered as a child who is sorry for offending His Father.

You will have peace on earth when your infidelity changes to fidelity to God's Love. This is my prayer for you, dear children. Being faithful to God will bring you joy! I love you. Your Mother

121. **4-11-96**
Prayer and Divine Mercy

In the beginning of the Rosary with Father at my home, I entered the peace and silence of the Sacred Heart of Jesus. I rested there. All was Peace. His Heartbeat imparted strength to my weary heart. The steady rhythm of His pure Divine Love infused my soul. I received sharp piercing of my heart and entered a sleep-like state, no longer able to hear Father's meditations. While Father was finishing the Rosary, I received the following image.

I could see a multitude of people assembled for Mass. It was Divine Mercy Sunday in the image. When the priest raised the consecrated Host, looking up to the Eternal Father and offering Jesus to Him, immediately blood and water flowed from the Host onto the people gathered for Mass. Jesus' blood and water touched everyone present. So great was the outpouring of blood and water that it formed a river, which filled the facility and then flowed out of it. The priest was completely overcome by brilliant light. Jesus said: **My Divine Mercy will heal and transfigure My creation to Love.** While observing all of this, I received a deep understanding of the need to be merciful and loving not only to others, but to myself as well.

122. **4-12-96** Prayer Group Meeting
A Mission of Love, Message of Hope

Our Lady said: *My dear children, praised be our risen Jesus! Thank you for your prayers this night. You have prayed according to the Holy Spirit. This gives glory to the Father. When my Jesus ascended to the Father, He left the apostles with a direct mission to proclaim the Gospel message of love. The apostles could carry out His command only after the Holy Spirit descended upon them to empower them to fulfill their mission. You have a special mission. You must rely on the One Source for direction and He is The Holy Spirit of God. Desire one thing only - the perfect, Divine Will of the Most Holy Trinity. Do only what God asks you to do. Always seek the Holy Spirit in prayer from your heart to discern the Divine Will for you. Seeking spiritual direction and community discernment is a great protection to keep from being deceived by the enemy. Do not walk alone or in secret or you will walk in darkness. And the enemy will certainly misdirect your path away from the Truth! The enemy will present many attractive things to you; activities that appear to be good. But if it is not the perfect will of God, you are not called to do it.*

Often the Divine Will involves waiting, praying and patiently enduring suffering. What God seeks from you will be brought to your doorstep. You need not seek to "do" for God. God desires that you "be" for Him. He does the doing. This requires prayer, humility, wisdom and peace of soul. Only through prayer can you properly discern the spirits operating. Never discount the spirit of your human will. It is very powerful. And it must be forfeited for the sake of the Divine Will. Only in the Holy Spirit of Truth can you battle effectively. In Him, the victory is yours. If you have purity of heart, God will protect you every step of the way.

Your mission is important in the Church. It is for the Church, Christ's Mystical Body on earth. It is necessary that you be fortified by prayer and the sacraments. I am with you in a special way to guide, protect and raise you up in the virtues of My Immaculate Heart. You draw grace for many who are in desperate need of God's mercy. When you are docile and obedient to the movements of the Holy Spirit, be assured that your endeavors will be blessed beyond your expectations.

Thank you for your sacrifice. Your obedience and purity of heart gain much grace for you individually and collectively. You have an important collective mission within the heart of the Church. And each of you has a very particular, individual mission as well. Your individual mission is to love and to be One with God. Your collective mission is to make Love known. My children, cause souls to love the One who is Love! Love alone will change the face of the earth. Love alone will restore the Church.

Thank you for proclaiming the mercy of God. This message of Divine Mercy is vital for this particular time. Man will not have peace until it turns fully to the mercy of God. Pray that all will be reconciled to God through repentance and conversion. Intercede with me on behalf of the salvation of the world. Carry your crosses with love and you will bear much fruit for the Kingdom of God. The cross reveals God's Merciful Love. Carrying the cross chosen for you requires the graces of the Holy Spirit. Take courage and persevere.

Be my little, little children. Thank you for permitting me to be your mother. Many of God's children deny this privilege to me. Trust! You are in my heart of love. Do not be afraid. You shall live eternally in joy in the presence of Our Most Loving Triune God. I love you. Your Mother

123. **4-15-96** Before the Tabernacle
Prayer from a Wounded Heart

Jesus, my Lord and my God, Savior of my soul, you have taken me through an exercise of suffering which is so deep it has plunged me into the depths of Your Sacred Heart in order that I exist moment by moment. Your Almighty Hand is fashioning me into another You and how painful it is! My deepest desire is to be one with You. Is there any other way but through the cross?

My beloved Teacher, I desired to be taught to know You through Your Passion and now You have willed it for me. Divine Light so illumines my heart and mind and soul now that I see how necessary it is for me to suffer and die to myself and the things of the world. This hurts very much Lord! This self of mine is stronger than I ever imagined and it wants to live. Dying is an agony! While I am living this death constantly, I feel myself more alive in You, in a union so close that I cannot perceive where You leave off and I begin. You are my life, Lord. My All! You are my Eternal Breath! Through this exercise of suffering, You have taught me that I am truly a citizen of another world. Now I know on earth that I am a pilgrim.

My heart has seemingly been shredded into little pieces. Was this necessary that I could have Your Sacred Heart to be mine? Indeed! Jesus, I have cried out to You in the excruciating moments of my scourging which has been permitted for months, repeatedly. Somehow I knew that as I cried out to You in my agony that You would use that cry to free a thousand souls. This is the source of my perseverance; knowing that You would take each tear, each cry from my anguished heart and make great good of it.

Lord, it seems there is not a portion of myself that is not riddled in pain and You alone know it. What profound detachment has been accomplished in this exercise of suffering! Born of this also is the most profound love and appreciation of Your Church. Through Your Mystical Body, You are ministering to my wounds and healing me through the sacraments and her faithful ones. So deep is my gratitude in the midst of great anguish, I find myself crying out, "Thank you, My Lord and My God." This amazes me!

Jesus, more than anything, I desire to learn to embrace suffering. I desire to put my arms around suffering so that I can be the offering to bring many souls to you. But, instead, when I suffer, I cry out for Your arms to embrace me and console me. My weakness is astounding. Daily I walk as one barely alive in this world. I cry "Uphold me, Lord!" And I am met with Your silence. How beneficial that silence is to my soul! You cause me to walk in faith that is alive, exercised! Faith is no longer a concept but a lived reality that keeps me going.

You have caused me to hope in a seemingly hopeless situation. I never realized how important the virtue of hope is to life itself.

Faith and hope have become the two pillars, which uphold my life in this most difficult trial.

But at the heart of the matter is charity! Lord, I did not know how difficult charity would be until you required that I love one who persecutes me and torments my heart. At one time, these virtues seemed easy. They require the utmost effort and grace in this trial. Once the virtues of faith, hope, and love lay like flower petals floating on the surface of my soul. But now the storm arises and powerful waves, violent motion, cause the petals to go deep into my soul. In the storm of suffering, these virtues have motion and life in my soul.

There are days when I have had to exercise great faith, hope and charity to get out of bed and get my son to school. Lord, You know this to be true! In the midst of this painful trial, you require that I continue to walk in faith and serve You in Your Mystical Body. Your Love is demanding, My God! And it is only by Your grace that I remain in You, having to become very little and self-less. In my need, You are with me. And I grow.

Jesus began to speak. ***Soul of My cross, you gave to Me a most courageous act of mercy when you embraced the one who hurts you. You chose to love in that moment when you felt only the pain that has been caused by this soul. You could have decided to remain alone in a safe place. But you reached out to a tormented and confused soul. You did as I willed! You saw that you could offer Me one more act of mercy on this Feast of My Divine Mercy and you gave it to Me. Little did you know that this little act of mercy would be highly valued by My Tender Heart! When I received this act of mercy from you, I made this the offering to free hundreds of souls from the place of detention** (Purgatory).

I bless you my bride and my victim. All that you do, all that you are is for Me. In the midst of your own crucifixion, you are radiantly alive and beautiful in My sight. I am with you to cover you in new garments of holiness woven of your sacrifice and the virtues you exercise. You are wounded, but your bleeding is life for many souls. It has an eternal meaning. *Soul of My cross, you have become little so that I can take you into the deep recesses of My Heart of Love. I will continue to teach you.

Desire Me. I will it! Your fragrance penetrates My Heart and I am moved to shower you with more grace. I am increasing everything in you. You perceive that you are almost dead, but truly I say to you that you are fully alive in Me. Rest in Me. You are My bride and victim. I am your hiding place. We are one. I love you. Your Jesus

124. **4-16-96** Before Tabernacle following Mass
Obedience and Discernment of Spirits

I was praying for the truth of a particular situation when I received the following image. I saw a certain soul, a person of prayer, in a beautiful garden and the greatest portion of it was hers to enjoy. However, there was a portion of it, which she could not have according to God's Perfect Will. Then I saw dark spirits surround this soul. They tempted her so that all she could think of was what she could not have. Her own desire grew strong within her. She was overcome and even in prayer believed her desire was from God. But this was a deception.

I observed this soul enter the portion of the garden which was not intended for her. The forbidden portion of this garden did not yield its delights to her. She became frustrated and began to work feverishly to gather the fruits and flowers for herself. While she did, the dark spirits laughed secretly and encouraged her to have her way saying, "God wills it!" The deeper she entered what did not belong to her, the more turmoil welled up within. When she would lose her peace of soul, the dark spirits would say "You deserve it. You have done so much for God." False peace overcame her as she was deceived every step of the way. I saw within a great storm arise.

Jesus said: **What a soul does in secret will come to the light. Pray for this soul. Forgive. Disobedience is the downfall of many. This soul walked alone and became the easy prey of the enemy. Satan knows exactly how to push the human will. She did not submit to spiritual direction and desired to have it her way. I want you to learn. Obedience is required. It is of the highest importance to Me. Always subject yourself to spiritual** direction and obey! There is much useless suffering due to disobedience and lack of discernment causes great harm to souls. Learn from this situation. Pray for this soul and I shall grant My Mercy.

Little one, your obedience to My Voice wins the abundance of My grace. I desire obedience in all matters, big or small. Never walk alone. Discern the spirits through your spiritual director and with the community I have provided for you. The enemy is clever, but if you bring everything to the light and obey, you will not falter. Obedience is the hallmark of holiness. Be holy for Me, My beloved bride and victim. I love you. Your Jesus

125. 4-17-96
The Sacrificial Life of a Priest

Last night brought painful turmoil in my family, but I was upheld in grace and God turned the situation into a time of love and learning. Regarding the one who inflicts the pain, God grants me the grace to be patient, merciful, loving, and silent. I am astounded that this is possible in the midst of this painful trial.

Today at Holy Communion, my soul experienced a deep sense of well-being. A certitude overcame me that all things work for good for those who love God. My joy became full and peace was with me.

In prayer following Mass and before the Tabernacle, I thanked God for the graces in Father's soul. The more I pray with my spiritual director, the more I am in awe of God's grace in this priest. Suddenly, I received an image of the heart of this priest. Right before me I observed his heart open up as if for my viewing. The first thing I noticed within was a roaring fire. Buried deep within the flames was an indestructible treasure chest. The chest was full of divine graces formed into most precious jewels. These are jewels he is meant to share with the Mystical Body of Christ, the Church. The treasury was abundant! But then I noticed that this treasure chest was counterbalanced by another one, which contained the treasury of his suffering. Inside this chest, I saw tears and a heart twisted in anguish representing the times of his life when he suffered the agony of Christ's passion. I saw lonely moments. I saw silence that hurt. I saw a confused mind representing the times he struggled for clarity in his vocation. I saw scars from battles between self-will and God's Will and wounds from the battles between evil spirits and his own. I saw him deposit the gift of himself repeatedly into the treasury. I saw moments of doubt, futility, and longing. I saw hunger for love and thirst for knowledge of God. I saw many books, worn from the study and searching. I saw a human will committed at times and sometimes, not so committed. I saw his youth spent at the monastery in silent obedience and utmost sacrifice.

All the while, I saw Our Lady of the Holy Trinity stand and guard the treasury of this chosen life dedicated to God. I observed Our Lady, with her own hands, deposit the jewels of his suffering and sacrifice into the treasury of Divine Grace. Her heart and his soul contain within the fruit of his sacrifice. Over a lifetime, this treasury has grown abundantly. Our Lady must distribute the treasury to other souls. She does this constantly and joyfully. He drinks of the fountain of Divine Grace; the water and the blood that pours out from the Heart of Jesus so as to alleviate His own thirst. I understood in this grace, the Most Holy Trinity would not deny this priest because he has not denied the Father, Son, and Holy Spirit. May You be praised and glorified, My God! Thank you, Mother Mary.

126. **4-17-96** My Home
The Faithful Ones will be Persecuted

During most of the Rosary, I was completely out in prayer and did not hear Father's meditations. Toward the end I saw the Blessed Virgin Mary. She was a being of radiant light, dazzling, beautiful beyond words, almost all light. She exposed her Immaculate Heart and poured out graces, which manifested as powerful beams of light directed at us.

Then I received an image of myself being scourged as Jesus was during His passion. Our Lady was present and close to me. Then I observed Father and other people being scourged as well. Mary spoke. *My little children will suffer much because of their faith in Jesus. My little ones who remain faithful to the Roman Catholic Church, all her tradition and teachings, will suffer persecution by the ones who refuse to be faithful to her. I will pour out graces upon all who are persecuted for the faith and Love will uphold you. I am the Mediatrix of Grace!*

127. 4-20-96
The Devils in the Mind

Father was in turmoil today and asked that I pray with him. This is what I saw when I prayed over him.

I saw inside of his head, what appeared to be two impish devils. They had their hands on a nerve vessel in his mind. One said to the other, "Let's take away his peace and joy!" They each grabbed an end of a vessel and crisscrossed it, and tied it into knots. One said, "Now he has fear and confusion." They were pleased to observe this in his mind.

I bound the spirits of self-doubt, fear, and confusion. I asked Our Lady for help. She entered his mind and untied the knot. She held the vessels, kissed them and put them in their proper place. She remained to oversee his mind so that he would have peace and joy again.

128. 4-25-96
Silence! Who can Hear a Conversion of the Heart?

After Holy Hour, Our Lady said: *My dear daughter, be at peace in My Son, Jesus Christ. I see your heart, pierced and bleeding. You are suffering, my daughter, but not in vain. O, what a sweet offering is coming from you, little flower of God! My child, I watch over you as a mother would her only child. At night when you toss and turn in pain and suffering, I am with you. My heart envelops you as I impart to you the virtues of my own Immaculate Heart. Suffering is the fertile ground in which the virtues grow. Through your suffering, the garden of your heart bears fruit for many and you are beautified to the glory of God.*

My dear little child, do you not know that all things work for the good for those who love God? It is written and it is true! You love. Therefore, believe and trust that He will bring good out of your suffering. He will bring light from the darkness. You are battling a fierce war over this soul, but you do so with the power of God. There is nothing weak about a victim lamb bleeding on the altar. Dear child, there is power in the victim lamb; an invisible power that can overcome evil!

My daughter, you are God's little instrument. Do not confuse your silence with weakness or inaction. Silence is a great action bringing forth abundant power! Silence speaks volumes about a soul, revealing a close union with God who speaks in silence. God's greatness is manifested in silence!

Who can hear a conversion of the heart? The words that you would speak and action you would take would be full of imperfection while the Silence of God moves in the perfection of His Divine Will.

My little child, while I was to observe my Son's public ministry leading to His Passion and Crucifixion, a great silence filled my soul permitting me to be one with the Divine Will of The Father while agonizing with Jesus as His perfect, Divine and Human Being underwent a tortuous death and apparent defeat. But look at what Divine Providence brought forth in and through Him! We, created beings, must rely on the Eternal Father. His Wisdom is beyond our understanding and His ways far above ours. My little child, your gracious God provides for you always but especially in your hour of great need and time of formation. Dear little one, resist discouragement!

When you cry to the Father in prayer, say to Him, "My Abba, increase my faith, hope, and charity and in your loving goodness let me find my joy."

Draw from my Immaculate Heart and grow, my child, in wisdom, knowledge and understanding! Be holy for love of the Most Holy Trinity! And for sinners, be a vessel of God's Merciful Love. Be patient with God and yourself. Dear little flower, your suffering increases your radiance. You are being raised in the very protected garden of my Immaculate Heart. All that you learn during this trial will benefit the Church in the future. Rejoice, my little one, you are chosen by God! I love you, your Mother

129. **4-26-96** Prayer Group
The Prayer Cenacle is a Family

My dear children gather together in My Immaculate Heart. I, your Mother, desire to teach and love you, my very special prayer warriors. Though you are very little, you have within a great power. The power of God is within through the Person of the Holy Spirit. He is with you always. His Presence within your souls attracts the enemy. You are his targets because you are full of God's light. The enemy desires to extinguish the Light. His tactics include division, fear, doubt, discouragement, sadness and distraction.

A house divided cannot stand, my little ones. And the enemy seeks to divide in every instance. The Holy Spirit of Love unifies. Union of heart is necessary for every family. This prayer cenacle is a family. Together you are under my mantle of love. Reject division of every kind. This is possible when there is great sacrificial love present. Humanly, it is not possible. But in God's Divine Grace it is done. Lay down your way and your will in sacrifice for the Perfect Will of God. God's Will is Love, a selfless, sacrificial love. I am with you and shall remain to teach, protect, and guide you because you have been chosen by God. You are called to be in the center of the heart of the Church in ministry to God's people. All that you are undergoing is part of your formation. Your ministry will be vital in the Church. Remain very little! Humble yourselves and always strive for perfect obedience. You are learning very much through your suffering, temptations, and trials. Each one of you is being beautified by God. I embrace you all and press you into my Tender Heart. Remain as powerful intercessors for the salvation of many souls. Embrace one another as I embrace you. Look to the Holy Spirit within to keep you united as one heart, one family. Resist the enemy with all your strength. Let the Spirit of Wisdom be your guide. You never battle alone. The heavenly court is at your disposal. Be my children of joy. I take great delight in each one of you. I love you. Your Mother

130. **4-29-96** Feast of St. Catherine of Siena
Various Scenes of the Catholic Church

As Father led the Rosary, I entered a sleeplike state of prayer and in this state, I saw and heard the following. I saw Pope John Paul II sitting in a kingly presider's chair in his private chapel in Rome. He was in deep prayer. Suddenly, the scene changed. I saw only the chair. The Pope was no longer visible. But now, on the chair rested the Queen's Crown of Mother Mary. This Holy Father had already placed the fifth jewel in the crown representing the Fifth Marian Dogma of Faith. The crown was radiantly beautiful with five prominent jewels representing the five Marian Dogmas. From this, the Chair of St. Peter and the Crown of Mother Mary, radiated tremendous light directed at the entire world through the Catholic Church.

Later, I was somehow shown an overview of the Catholic Church in Europe. I saw many empty Catholic churches throughout Europe. A great apostasy had taken place and a true crisis of faith existed. Then, as if in contrast, I saw an overview of the Catholic Church in the United States. The Catholic churches remained relatively full. I had the thought that the Church in the United States was much stronger than Europe. Immediately I saw, in an image, at least fifty percent of the churches were empty in America and understood that the Roman Catholic Church would suffer a great apostasy in the future.

Then I saw the Good Shepherd and He said, "I Am the Gate." I observed as He pastored the sheep. Some passed through the gate while others did not. I observed the Good Shepherd divide the flock. Those who entered through the Gate were only a remnant, His Own. The other's did not know His Voice and went off to follow "other voices." Then I noticed that the remnant had something in common besides knowing His Voice. They had the fingerprints of Our Lady upon their hearts. She had prepared and formed them so that they recognized the Voice of her Son, Jesus, The Good Shepherd.

Then I saw a great storm come upon the Church. Like the vision of St. John Bosco, it was portrayed now as a large ship on the ocean. The remnant flock was on board the ship and would steer it though the stormy waters. On one side of the ship was a pillar with the

Eucharist and on the other side was a pillar with the Blessed Virgin Mary. The ship was tossed about in the tumultuous and dark storm. On board were many saints and legions of angels of light. Prayer fueled the ship. Then I saw a large pendulum swing. It moved from "Church Suffering" to "Church Glorified." Then Our Lady said: *My daughter, you shall witness all that has been revealed to you.*

131. **4-29-96** Feast of St. Catherine of Siena
St. Catherine of Siena Helps Me

"Dive soul, dive into the ocean of His Divine Love contained in the open Heart of Jesus! Let your memory be immersed and inebriated with Divine Goodness so that eternally you shall give praise to His Goodness made known to you.

Drink soul, drink of His Precious Blood so that His Life is in you, transfiguring you at every moment into His Holiness. Immerse your intellect in the mysteries of His Divine Love so that you may know Him whom you love. And therefore, love Him all the more, as your understanding of Him deepens leading you to an altogether complete surrender of yourself. Let your human will be swallowed up by the ocean of Divine Love. Drown in Him. Then He will give you His Perfect Will and it will be your life.

Hide soul, hide in the open Heart of Jesus. In that secret place of union, be lost and found. Live in Him. Live for Him. Hide in Him and He will use you for His Church for the good of all souls. Rejoice. You are His bride and so am I. Thanks be to our Triune God who is Love. I am Catherine of Siena, a ray of His love for you."

(Note: The first time I heard this in the morning following Mass and before the Tabernacle, I rejected it as impossible and put it out of my mind. The second time I heard it in the evening at my home, I believed it was Catherine of Siena but did not record it. Finally, I wrote it down when I heard it for the third time before the Tabernacle again. St. Catherine repeated it three times and it seemed to me that in some way, she appreciated my skepticism.)

132. **5-1-96**
Battle Against Evil

My little ones,

I am continually preparing you, guiding and leading you in the battle against evil. You are my army! The battle is fierce over souls and the salvation of the world. All that you undergo in the way of trials and suffering strengthens you for greater battles to come in the future. So much depends upon your surrender to the Divine Will of the Most Holy Trinity. Your decision for God now affects your own salvation and that of many. My army, chosen by God and prepared in these days of His Mercy, will carry the Church and the world into the era of sanctification. The Kingdom of the Divine Will will come. It is being birthed now. Birthing involves suffering and sacrifice. You, my littlest ones, are suffering already. Soldiers must undergo strenuous training exercises so that they are fit for battle. Battle you will! Do not let the enemy discourage you. You will be prepared for battle. I am gathering my little soldiers from all parts of the world. In prayer and in my Heart you are one, united army.

Love is your weapon! It is your greatest defense. Love alone will overcome the present darkness. You may find yourselves being tried in the ways of love. The love required is truly sacrificial; an altogether selfless love which manifests itself in zeal for souls. By means of your consecration to My Immaculate Heart, you are united in me. I am your refuge! Through my Heart, which shall triumph, a great victory shall be won. What do we win my little ones? We complete the victory won by my Son, Jesus, over all evil and darkness. The earth will be free. Love will reign. God is Love and the world will know and serve Him in humility. In glorifying the Eternal Father, He will glorify us with eternal life in Him. Your joy will be complete forever. I love you and grant you my own courage for the days ahead. Your Mother

133. **5-6-96** Prayer Group
Many will Convert and Seek Spiritual Help

Dear little ones, there are many ways to learn, and it is the Holy Spirit who teaches of the spiritual reality. The quickest way to learn of spiritual warfare is to put on the armor of God and engage in the battle against evil, led by the Holy Spirit. You are in the midst of a battle. Please persevere in the good fight. You are learning quickly. You are pleasing to the heavenly court watching over you as you are raised to be prayer warriors. You have already rescued many souls from spiritual death. Because you are effective warriors, the enemy encamps around you. The battle will intensify in the days to come. Many will come to seek your intercession and help. The Holy Spirit is releasing His power on earth to overcome the present darkness. The Spirit of Truth will reveal to each soul their state of being before God. Faced with the Truth, many will convert and seek spiritual guidance and prayer. Many will be freed from evil spirits, which have oppressed them for so long. You will provide spiritual assistance to many. God will use His faithful ones to pray with those in need.

I am grateful to you who have responded to my call in these days of visitation. Great will be your reward in heaven. You console my heart. Many little ones are turning away from my call, but you have responded. You do not waver. You endure and sacrifice. I am with you to help you to endure the trials and overcome temptations. We are victorious, my little ones. Rest in my heart and regain your strength. But never cease to pray for the zeal to work as God's warriors against evil.

You cannot see the fruit of your labor; the good of your prayers. But I ask that you trust in God and I can reveal that already your harvest is plentiful. Yet, there remains much work to be done. Together, let us glorify God by working in His vineyard, and together we will praise His Holy Name with thanksgiving for the privilege of serving Him. Let us do this joyfully, peacefully, humbly, and lovingly. I love you. Your Mother

134. 5-7-96
Purchased by the Blood of the Lamb: Identity

Following the consecration of the Mass, the Eternal Father said: **You have been purchased by the Blood of the Lamb.**

After Mass Jesus said: **My beloved ones, you have been purchased by the Blood of the Lamb. I, Your Lord and Savior, provided the sacrifice. You hear these words often. Your mind may know it. Until your heart knows it, these words which are Truth, do not take root in your soul. Because you do not know that you are Mine, you suffer. You suffer in the way an orphan suffers. Your true identity escapes you. You do not know who you are until you know that you are a child of God.**

In this age, many have taken paths away from their true identity. This ends in futility. You have squandered precious time on emptiness. The result is a great thirst for love. The fountain of My Divine Love is in you. You have not tapped into it because it is locked in your heart and your hearts are hardened. Today, you are led by your mind. It is in your mind that the spirit of the world operates. You are easily led by this spirit because you are not rooted in your own identity. You are not rooted in Me, your Lord and Savior.

The Holy Spirit is within your hearts. Because you do not go within your own heart to seek your true identity, you do not find Me and you do not live in the power of the Holy Spirit. Yet, I am with you and great is My thirst for your loving response to My Presence. I, your Savior, have a deep longing for you, My creation. Discover Me within you because I have loved you and chose you from the beginning! When you open your heart to see Me within, realize that I have covered you with My Precious Blood and marked you as My Own, so that in Me, you discover your true identity. Then, you come to know that you are loved and that Love Himself is in you. The Father ordained that we be in relationship; that Love be exchanged between Creator and creature; that Life be shared on earth and in heaven; that we live as family.

Why do I long for you, creation? Because Love draws all things to Him; because Love is relationship, communion, union!

My joy is complete eternally, in the Father and in the Holy Spirit, but your joy is not complete until you enter into the eternal circle of Divine Love, The Most Holy Trinity! Through baptism, you enter. But you must stir up the grace of Baptism through continual conversion and not remain immature in your faith, hope, and love.

Drink of the fountain of Divine Love! My Blood covers you. Take courage! I shall not forsake you though you forsake Me. My Love is abiding and perfect. It can not be compared to human love with all its imperfection.

It is necessary that I permit you to suffer because in suffering you stop running away from Me and run toward Me. Often, only in suffering, do you open your heart to Me at all, then I become known to you. Knowledge of Me becomes personal and intimate. We have a relationship and love is exchanged. This is when suffering becomes a great gift. Your suffering is the result of sin. You perpetuate suffering in your obstinate refusal to listen and obey the promptings of the Holy Spirit within.

The Most Holy Trinity awaits you. The longer you put off discovering your true identity in your Creator, the more you will suffer. Only those whose identity is rooted in Me, can withstand all of life's trials in peace and confidence.

I am the Water of Life and the Saving Blood, but I cannot cause you to drink. You must will it, humble yourselves and open your hearts. Then will the fountain of Divine Love quench your thirst and bring you to Life that will never perish. How long, beloved ones, must I await your response? You have been purchased by the Blood of the Lamb, but you must decide to enter into your inheritance. I love you. Your Jesus

135. **5-8-96** Church
Jesus on the Sacrament of Reconciliation

After Mass Jesus spoke. **Please write for My people.**

I am the Divine Bridegroom of each soul. When you approach the altar to receive My Body, prepare yourselves! A bride does not approach her groom without preparation. There is preparation in body and heart with attention to every detail. Taking such care of your body, why do you care so little for your soul? You esteem human love and union above Divine Love and union with Me, your Lord and Savior. Has the spirit of the world and the prince of darkness deceived you? Perhaps you are convinced that holiness is beyond you. Do not accept a lie. I, the Lord your God am Holy and have called you to holiness through union with Me. My Grace makes it possible for you to be the saint that you are meant to be. You are destined for heaven where all are saints. I did not create you for anything less.

Did I not forgive the thief on the cross at Calvary? If you turn to Me in repentance and seek My Mercy, it is yours!

When you approach My altar to partake of My Body, come to Me after cleansing yourself in the Sacrament of Reconciliation. Unburden your heart of the sin that weighs you down so that your soul can soar unencumbered to the heights of My Love in Holy Communion. Do not rationalize your faults and sins away! However small or hidden to you, I see clearly all sin. And all men sin. That is why I provide the means by which you cleanse yourself of sin and bathe yourself in forgiveness. The Sacrament of Reconciliation is My great gift for you! But in this age, it is forgotten or little appreciated. Your generation is unwilling to acknowledge sin! This is the greatest of offenses! Great is your pride and arrogance! Satan has perpetuated a lie to convince you that you do not sin and do not require repentance or mercy.

He was banished from the heavens in his pride and refusal to serve. He takes many to the abyss of eternal darkness because of the same sin. Do you keep My Commandments, My law of Love? My dearly beloved ones, you cannot imagine the graces, which are available in the Sacrament of Mercy! If you could see the good it does in your soul, you would approach the confessional regularly with great appreciation for the sanctifying grace given in this sacrament. Sin obscures grace which would flow freely through a clear vessel. Your mind is darkened if you have no appreciation of the Sacrament of Reconciliation. How is it that you flee from My Mercy and cling to your selfishness and pride? You are like prisoners shackled in a cell. I, the Lord, your God, offer to cut you free of the shackles, but you choose to remain a prisoner rather than admit your guilt and accept My forgiveness.

If you seek My Mercy in all sincerity, humility, and repentance, you are forgiven. Full restoration is available for sinners. Do not avoid Me in the Sacrament of Reconciliation! Take this gift of My Mercy and cleanse your soul in My forgiveness. Boundless is My Love for you, My creation, and boundless is My Mercy unto all ages. Approach the altar of sacrifice with expectant faith, but first acknowledge your guilt and seek My forgiveness. Trust in My Mercy. I am the Divine Bridegroom of each soul and I am calling you to conversion. Repent and believe in the Gospel! **Your Jesus**

136. **5-15-96** Home
The Garden of Heavenly Grace and Union

As Father began to pray the Rosary, I entered a sleeplike prayer state. My soul, in stillness and silence, sensed the Hand of God the Father reaching to me. I lifted my hand to Him and He seemingly lifted my spirit which ascended upward with Him.

Suddenly, I was walking with Him in a most beautiful garden, utterly content. He led me to walk through this exquisite garden of which I could not perceive a boundary. It seemed natural to commune with My Heavenly Father. I was filled with one thought at first, "How much I love You, My God!" For a while, in silence, I walked with Him. Then I wondered, "Where are we?" After more silence, He said: **My little one, you like gardens, don't you?** "Very much" I replied. **This is the garden of heavenly grace and union. Your spirit is drawn to be with me. I, your Eternal Father, enrich your soul.** I was amazed that all of this seemed so natural and appropriate. It was as if I had become a very small child, full of trust.

Then I noticed a tree at the entrance of the garden. It was a tree trunk with a crossbeam at the top, which formed a cross. The Father said: **No one can enter this garden of grace without spending time on the tree of suffering. It is by means of this tree of suffering that the mortal self dies to gain immortality. The Di-**

vine Will cannot reign in your soul unless your human will has endured a kind of crucifixion. Whoever enters this garden of grace and union has spent time on this tree. I asked, "Is suffering the only means of entry to this garden?" He said: Love reigns in this garden of heavenly grace and union. And love must be tried to be true. Suffering that is redemptive, purifying, and transforming is the means of entry because this is the catalyst of True Love. The Divine Will is perfect Love, perfect Peace, and perfect Wisdom. The Kingdom of the Divine Will is My heavenly Jerusalem. It shall come down from the heavens to reign on earth. Little one, look below to the earth. What do you see?

"I see vast desert lands, dry, and parched. Very little water on the earth. Everything appears to be dried up. I see very little life, little good. Everything is obscure." The Father said: Observe, child. He breathed a breath of wind upon the earth. So powerful was His breath that the entire earth was covered by it. The wind descended upon the earth. Life began anew. Water began to flow abundantly. Former wastelands were made fertile. This new life was not life, as we know it now. It was an entirely new life, an enriched, sublime life that is fully awake in God and deeply immersed in Him. Humanity was renewed. So, too, the entire earth and everything in it. There was radiant beauty on earth, born of His Breath that never existed before in the history of man. There was freshness that thoroughly permeated every one and everything. There was clarity and fullness like never before.

The Father said: Through My Love, through the Blessed Virgin Mary and the Church, through the sufferings and sacrifices of holy souls on earth, through the prayers of pure and humble hearts, there is great intercession at this time, calling down the reign of the Kingdom of the Divine Will, the new and heavenly Jerusalem. The Wind of the Holy Spirit will permeate the earth and darkness will turn to Light. Light will descend in a fresh outpouring of the Holy Spirit. My creation will be transfigured for My Glory.

Pray, little one, pray! Bid the Holy Spirit to come, come upon the earth and open wide the hearts of My people so the earth will know Love! My little lambs, do not lose heart, do not grow weary! Persevere in prayer. You are victims of Love sacrificing your lives in intercession for the lost sheep. I call you into the priestly ministry of intercession to pray for a new Pentecost! Come, enter and walk with Me, your Eternal Father, in My garden of heavenly grace and union. Be with Me! I, your God, will enrich your soul with Divine Love. Full of My Love, you shall draw many souls to Me. These souls may never have responded to My Grace without your intercession. I Am breathes upon earth to draw you back to Me. One man cannot be drawn to God without affecting all men. You are in relationship, a family. The Breath of God must be passed from one to another so that together, in a relationship of Love, you are drawn back to your Creator.

Persevere! The Kingdom of Divine Will, the new Jerusalem cannot be borne except through a painful transformation of the earth. You are feeling the labor pains now. The Holy Spirit is arousing many souls right now. His power to transfigure the earth will be made manifest soon. Be alert! Do not be discouraged. The evil that appears to be overcoming the earth will vanish in the Wind of the Holy Spirit. Preparation is underway on earth and the labor pains will be difficult. There will be a new Pentecost, a new heavenly Jerusalem. Do not fear. Let your hearts be open. I, your Eternal Father, bless you little one. Be at peace in My Love.

137. **5-16-96**
Jesus on Trust and the Spiritual Reality

Following Mass and Holy Hour before the Tabernacle, the Eternal Father drew me to the garden of heavenly grace and union again to teach me about the new Pentecost; the heavenly Jerusalem and intercession again. He directed my attention to the cross at the entrance of the garden and said with great tenderness: **My Own Son hung on that cross in the greatest intercession for all souls; in the most complete sacrifice of Love spanning all time.** I was enveloped with Divine Love and filled with Light in my soul in contemplation of Jesus on the Cross.

A stranger came up to talk to me and I was awakened from this prayer state. When I was alone again, I glanced at the Tabernacle. It was as if Jesus was physically standing before it. I saw this with my eyes open, yet, it was deeply interior. Jesus was extremely tangible both interiorly and exteriorly in this grace. It was natural to speak to Him and I poured my heart out. "My Jesus, my life seems out of control. Have mercy upon me and my family. I am a little afraid of what is happening. It is as if my hands are tied. I feel myself hanging on the cross and vultures tear at my flesh. You are permitting this, Lord. And the reality of my earthly life bears down and almost crushes me. Though my spiritual life is richly blessed, I am tempted that it is unreal, a fantasy. Jesus, please help me." Suddenly, I was overcome with the most profound peace of soul about my earthly life. I continued, "Jesus, I do not understand. There is so much I do not understand."

Jesus said: ***Soul, you do understand. You are on the cross and vultures are seemingly tearing at your flesh because there was too much flesh that weighed your spirit down! *Soul, you know that I have control of your family. You know that I have provided for you and always will. All things work for the good of those who love Me. Do you love Me, *Soul?**

I replied, "Yes, Lord. I love you so much that it hurts!" He said: **But it is sweet pain, isn't it, *Soul?** I replied, "Yes, Lord." He continued: ***Soul, I am doing a mighty work in your family. The strong current of the present tempest is pulling you every which way. Eventually, all will find the Rock that will hold you securely. All will come to know Me and you will be restored. Pray fervently! There is anger and lack of understanding. Great is the suffering. My grace is blocked now, but My Hand opens and closes doors according to My Will. My protection is great and My Love abiding. Is it difficult to trust Me, *Soul?** "My Jesus, you know that often it is extremely difficult to trust considering the behavior that I witness around me. Sometimes, I simply fear being deceived about what is real."

*Soul, your earthly pilgrimage is a concrete reality, but it is passing. Your spiritual journey is the everlasting reality. I am in both realities. But the greater one is your spiritual reality. Both realities are entertwined because it is the grace received in your

spiritual reality that enables you to walk upright in your earthly situation. *Soul, take My Peace. It is My gift to you. Live in it. Through your peace of soul, through your love, your family will be sustained throughout this tempest. My love sustains all. The cross becomes you. My eyes behold your beauty as a reflection of My Own. I love you tenderly, *Soul. Go in Peace. Your Jesus

138. **5-21-96** Rosary with Spiritual Director
Mother Mary's Army of Little Souls

I received an image of the Blessed Virgin Mary who took the form of a beautiful crystal vase. She placed flowers inside which represented souls. Waters of grace from the Holy Spirit fill her. The flowers were varied and many. The Son who shines through Mary, shines upon those placed inside her heart. The Son would shine on these souls anyway. But because they are placed inside the heart of Mary, there is a superabundance of God's Grace and empowerment, which comes from the love relationship of family. Mary is the Mother of the family of God and His greatest masterpiece. A soul has its own beauty, but it is embellished in the maternal beauty of Mary when placed in her Immaculate Heart where the life giving waters of the Holy Spirit flow.

Next, I received an image of an army of soldiers; a fleet of navy ships; and many Air Force planes in a V-flight formation going straight up. Our Lady spoke: *My dear children, my army of little souls is undergoing vigorous training in ways of spiritual warfare. You must be as well-formed as the army that defends a country. You will defend all God's children and intercede for the salvation of the world. The battle is fierce; the battlefield is all the earth. You shall be called to defend the eternal life of souls. You shall fight for the little ones; children who cannot defend themselves. Some of you shall be placed in the trenches defending the Church. Some of you shall find yourselves surrounded by darkness in the midst of a great storm upon the ocean defending the Faith. Your cargo is the Truth and must be defended with all your strength. Some will soar to the heights like Air Force jets which survey and protect in defense of life and love.*

Your duties in my army are precise for your gifts and talents. Like any team, it will require united effort by all. No job is too small. Together we shall secure the very heart of the Church. Through the birthing of the Kingdom of the Divine Will, a new springtime will arrive for the Church and the earth shall be restored to Love.

My dear children, my army consists of the little souls chosen by God before all ages to live in these decisive times to battle against evil; to make a stand for God. You are the purest of hearts who live in a state of surrender to God's grace and abandonment to God's Will. You are my humble and obedient soldiers. My army places no confidence in itself putting all confidence in the grace of God. It is He who called you, formed you, and will lead you to the victory, which He has procured. You shall be tried in your faith when the Mystical Body is made into the image of Jesus crucified. My Son appeared to be defeated on Calvary. The Church will appear to be defeated in the division of itself. Until the time of restoration, its glory shall be obscured. The Light of the Holy Spirit piercing your heart will sustain you in faith, hope, and love.

Then, I was given the image of a priest holding up a large monstrance with the Blessed Sacrament radiating brilliant light out to all who gazed upon it and I saw other priests giving Holy Communion to the soldiers in the army. The Eucharist empowered the souls to Love, which is the weapon necessary to defeat evil.

Mary continued: *My little children, you are being formed in the ways of love and sacrifice. You are battling evil through your own immolation and prayer. Carry your crosses and grow in wisdom and knowledge. Persevere, little ones. The gifts of the Holy Spirit are your weapons against evil. Thank you for your fiat to love. Your sacrifice, prayers, and tears are precious to me. I use them to increase love on earth. Live and rest in my heart. Together we go to Jesus. I love you, tenderly. Your Mother*

When Father commented that it would be difficult for priests to know what to do if their Bishop was not with Rome, or in disobedience, Mother Mary responded immediately saying: *Tell my priest wherever there are little ones gathered in prayer from the heart, there will the Holy Spirit be in your midst to shed His Light and guide you. He shall overshadow the children of God in the most trying times with the Spirit of Truth and The Way shall be made evident to you. God's own shall not be orphaned! The Holy Spirit will descend upon you in a most powerful way when the need is there for the good of the faithful! He will provide for you. By the power of the Holy Spirit you shall know the way of Truth and understand at a depth that you cannot comprehend now. Trust. God will shelter and care for His own in wondrous ways. Peace.*

139. 5-22-96
Union Through the Eucharist

Upon arriving at church for morning Mass, I noticed a coldness within my heart and prayed, "My Lord, I beg of You, let the holiness of this Eucharist penetrate my being so as to enkindle great love and gratitude for Your Holy Sacrifice and True Presence. Please do not let this heart of mine remain in coldness. I do not ask for consolation, but that you would be glorified by my love and appreciation for this Holy Mass." Even after praying in this manner, I had to fight temptations of negativity.

Mass began, but it wasn't until Holy Communion that my prayer was answered. Upon receiving the Host, tears flowed spontaneously from the power of His Presence within me. Quite suddenly, a grace came upon me which caused the Host to penetrate my entirety at the deepest level and I was enveloped in Divine Love.

Jesus said: **Dear soul, you shall soar like an eagle to the Father. The Holy Spirit will be your wings. I, your Jesus, will be your heart. The Breath of the Father will draw you to Himself. Like an arrow flies to its target, you will fly. At His feet, you will commune with your Eternal Father. He will wrap you in His Paternal Love, receiving you as My Image shrouded in the veil of Our Holy Mother who prepares you for union. You are loved, *Soul! The Father draws you to Himself to love you; to give you Divine Love so that you can love Him that He may share with you the perfect love that exists between the Most Holy Trinity. He gives you participation in the unending Divine Love of Father, Son, and Holy Spirit.**

As Jesus spoke, I saw myself soaring as an eagle soars, upward and beyond the highest mountaintops. Then the Wind beneath my wings drew me in an instant, straight to the Father. I sat at His feet. I leaned on Him. He embraced my entirety and I knew that I was a child of God, His own! I knew His Son was in me and I was in Him and the Holy Spirit was in me and I was in Him. Jesus and the Holy Spirit took me to the Source of life, the Creator of all! United, the Three Persons of the Holy Trinity enveloped the person that I am, and inexpressible love filled my heart and soul. I cannot express the beautiful reality of this grace received at Holy Communion and suffer to describe such sublime realities in words, which do not suffice. My God, may my incapacity not offend You and may You alone be glorified in my nothingness. Amen.

140. 5-26-96
Perseverance Through the Holy Spirit

At prayer group, Our Lady said: *My little ones, the grace of the Holy Spirit has come to empower you to fulfill your mission of love. You have been blessed by the Holy Spirit to persevere in the way of Love. You have great need of the grace of perseverance, in your individual and collective journeys. The enemy is encamped around you. The Light within you attracts him. You must fight the temptations and attacks of the enemy. He seeks to oppress, discourage, distract, and deceive you, and cause you to feel unworthy and forgotten. Please do not accept his lies. Stand on the Truth. God chose you. You did not choose this way.*

My little ones, you are chosen by God for this time and ministry. It is a sacrifice to accept and answer the call. You give glory to God. He blesses you in abundance knowing you have chosen Him and it has cost you. You have sacrificed your human will! You have given up control. Now God is your Master! This is not an easy way. It is contrary to the ways of the world, but it is the only way to achieve the Eternal Goal; union with God. I know that you struggle. You are weary of the battle.

My little ones, it has just begun. You are witnessing more. In your hearts you bear the burden of a world that is rejecting God, rejecting Love and Truth. You will observe less faith in the world. You will question God's ways. But by the power of the Holy Spirit, you will come to know and trust that God is preparing the world for complete transformation to birth the Kingdom of the Divine Will.

Your prayers and sacrifices, your lives, will bear fruit. You shall become the saints you are created to be. Your eternity will be spent in peace beyond comprehension, in love unspeakable, and joy unending. Your earthly pilgrimage is passing quickly. Persevere to fight the battle for Good. Rejoice in the Most Holy Trinity who set you apart from the world to be His own warriors against evil. Bless God with your love. Your heart is what He seeks from you in totality! The Holy Spirit will empower you with His gifts so that you can grow in the ways of love and holiness to serve God's children. Receive the Holy Spirit and live in His Love. You are never alone. The Gentle Guest of your souls guides you. I am with you also. Be at peace. I love you. Your Mother

141. **5-26-96** Pentecost Sunday
The Father Grants a Special Helper: The Angel of Enduring Love

I was very tired from moving my oldest son home from college for summer break and came under attack from the oppressive spirits of blockage, depression, futility, aversion to prayer, and retaliation.

When Father prayed over me to bind and cast these evil spirits out, I sensed a void created by their leaving and immediately he prayed for an infilling of the Holy Spirit and I was filled. Spiritual warfare is truly led by the Holy Spirit. Though I was a skeptic about it, I cannot deny the reality that I am experiencing, as the attacks of the enemy grow more frequent and intense. I thank God for a spiritual director and prayer group that are knowledgeable in the area of spiritual warfare.

In the evening, during Mass, I came under attack again. In the midst of Mass, I became extremely agitated about the state of families and youth and was overcome with negativity and futility.

After Mass, I went to prayer group. My peace was gone! Immediately, I was overcome with an aversion for God, prayer, love, the prayer group and myself. As the group would share, I heard interiorly, the devils around me, saying, "How stupid, utterly stupid!" I agreed. I began to think, "How stupid all of this is! I hate praying the Rosary. I want out of here. I must get out of this house and never come back!" Then the devils would say, "That's right! Get out. This helps no one. This is not prayer. What is the good of it? Who cares? What a waste of time! Do you like these people? What are you doing here? You are not fit for this. Get out. It is useless!" I continued to hear this kind of negativity and mockery from many devils throughout all the decades of the Rosary.

Occasionally, the Holy Spirit would say to me, "**Persevere in prayer. Persevere.**"

I continued the Rosary. In my heart, it was beautiful to pray. The attack was in my mind. Our Lady dictated a message following the Rosary on perseverance through the Holy Spirit.

Driving back home, I shared with Father the evil attack I underwent during the Rosary. As I shared, I was overcome by a terrible and strong spirit of self-hatred. It was so powerful that I could feel the evil spirit come into my being to oppress me, as if to literally press me into the ground. I have never felt such hatred within me. And the object of this hatred was most of all, myself. It was unbearable!

Father prayed over me immediately, binding and casting the evil spirits of hatred, mockery, self-degradation, futility, aversion, murder (of the spiritual life), games, blockage, fatigue and others. Then he prayed for the infilling of the Holy Spirit, asking the spirit of Love to come and fill me. He prayed for God the Father to come and embrace His child.

Immediately, the Father honored his priestly request and it seemed to me that I was in an all-encompassing embrace of the Father's Love. The Father spoke these words. **My child, I, your Eternal Father, grant to you this night an angel which shall be with you always. This is an Angel of Enduring Love. This angel is assigned to you from this moment onward so that you are assisted in enduring all things in Love. Also, this angel shall assist you to know that I, your God, endure all your imperfec-**

tions, faults, and weaknesses, in My Enduring Love. I am your Eternal Father and My Love endures all things, remaining steadfast for all My Creatures unto eternity! Receive My gift and blessing. Be at peace now. You are loved. I am your Father in heaven and on earth.

This was a most powerful grace which has remained with me ever since and the Angel of Enduring Love has helped me to endure many difficult trials in the area of love. When I am tempted to close my heart to love due to pain, the Angel of Enduring Love assists me to always love, to keep my heart open wide and persevere in love.

142. 5-31-96 Conference, Rome, Italy
The Eternal Father Speaks for a Priest

Before the Tabernacle in the church, the Eternal Father spoke for a priest.

He is a shepherd like My Own Son. I draw him to Me through the Heart of Jesus by the power of the Divine Love in his soul. The power of Love shall purify so that he is shrouded in pure love.

My little son, My priest, you are a new creation. The love, the fire that you have longed for, have prayed for, is given unto you by your Eternal Father. The value of the gift of your vocation is incomprehensible! I shall continue to draw you ever deeper into the unfathomable mystery of Divine Love and Mercy.

My little son, give glory to Me, your Eternal Father, through the continual offering of yourself. Exist in constant surrender to My Divine Will. Your cries, every prayer uttered in the depths of your heart, resounds in the heavens and call forth grace for souls. You are setting souls free from the snare of the hunter.

Be vigilant, My son! The enemy never rests! The power within you is evident to him. You shall overcome all obstacles.

Prostrate yourself before Me and cry out, "Father," from your heart. In Love, I respond, "My son"! Our embrace is complete like an unending circle of love. I, your Eternal Father, move your heart to long for Me, to cry out for Me. I satisfy your longing only long enough to create an ever-deeper longing. The fire within grows. My little son, My priest, your Eternal Father answers your prayers. I love you. Persevere. You are not alone. I am your Father.

143. **5-31-96** Rome Conference. 10:30PM in prayer in hotel room
The Feast of the Visitation and the Dogma

I heard: *Blessed be God whose Love created all things! On this day of remembrance of my visitation to St. Elizabeth, I confer upon you my tender maternal blessing. I promise that you are fully alive and protected inside my Immaculate Heart. You exist there as a very special family of little souls. Together let us prostrate before the throne of Our Triune God. Let us cry out for the grace of the Holy Spirit to permeate the earth so that all of creation is transfigured into His holiness, calling forth the reign of His Divine Will on earth.*

Your efforts shall bear fruit because this mission is born of the Holy Spirit. It is entrusted to Him and through Him it shall be fulfilled. Trust in my Immaculate Heart, united to the Sacred Heart of Jesus. Let the virtues of my Maternal Heart permeate your own. Walk in humility, purity of heart and obedience to the Holy Spirit. He is your guide. His gifts are yours.

When I visited Elizabeth, I had given my fiat without full comprehension of all that would be required of me. My "yes," my "fiat" was born of grace. So is yours. You say "yes" without full comprehension of the scope of this great mission. This is a sacrifice, a labor of love. I shall grant to you, my own maternal courage that you may persevere in fulfillment of your role toward this proclamation. I never cease to pray for you. I embrace you all. I love you. Your Mother

144. **6-1-96** Conference, Rome, Italy. Before the Tabernacle.
Our Lady to Priests: I Will Make a Difference in Your Journey.

Our Lady said: *Blessed are the priests, the shepherds that embrace the words that Jesus spoke to the beloved apostle, John, "Behold your mother." These priests are privileged to enjoy the treasury of my maternal graces.*

Beloved and cherished sons, permit my heart to be yours. Then you will have the abundant graces, which come through my heart. I will make a difference in your journey. I can relieve your burdens. I will lighten your load. I will take you on the more direct road to holiness, leading you swiftly and joyfully to my Son, Jesus.

Pray fervently for the priesthood. Turn with faith and love toward my maternal intercession, so that I can become for you a wellspring of grace. The Most Holy Trinity has given me graces reserved for you, our beloved sons, consecrated by the Sacrament of Holy Orders. But few of you are accepting all that I have to give. You who refuse my maternal intercession are wounded because of your refusal and are denied grace ordained for the priestly ministry. So many lock me out of their heart. I weep for you, my sons, who tie my hands when I so desire to grant you every grace leading you in the way of Love.

Blessed are you, my priests, who permit me to live in your heart. I come to you to reveal the truth of God's Love for you. Oh, vessels of election, grace upholds you always and everywhere, but you must be open. I come to you and shelter you from harm and temptation, making my heart your safe refuge. I feed you maternal milk so that you thrive in grace. The more your fellow priests accept my maternal intercession, by means of consecration, the more renewed the priesthood shall be. The vocation of priesthood brings with it every challenge, requiring every virtue. In the near future, your priesthood will be challenged more than ever before! Much will come at you from the world; from Satan. If you are not securely grounded in profound intimacy with God who is Love, you will find your vocation to be severely racked and tried. You will suffer when you need not suffer, if only you had done as Jesus said to John, "Behold your mother!" This was a statement from the cross, directed to all of humanity! This statement is pure gift, not burden!

You are vital, dearly beloved priests; vital to the salvation of the world, vital to the Church, vital to Jesus' flock, the sheep, which you tend. Yours is a privileged call with a great responsibility to God. Therefore, He opens the storehouse of grace available to you in and through my Immaculate Heart.

Take my heart as your own. Make every request through my heart. Though some of you deny me the privilege of tending to you, I never cease to intercede for all of you. You need not suffer alone! Permit me to comfort and guide you. I shall renew your priestly vocation for the days to come. My mantle draped around you will be your protection. My heart shall be your strength, courage, and hope. My hands shall comfort you and dry your tears. My arms shall embrace you in love so that you walk in perseverance and holiness.

Yours is a ministry requiring dignity made evident for all! Just as Jesus was a sign of contradiction, so are you who are called to be "in" the world but not "of" the world! Be transfigured, dearly beloved priests, into the image of your founder, my Son and Lord, Jesus Christ. Consecrate yourselves to my Immaculate Heart so that by means of your consecration I can distribute all the graces God has ordained for you. Why would you refuse such a gift? Could it be that you are not little enough? I love you. Your Mother

145. **6-6-96** In my Prayer Room
The Spirit of Negativity

My lamb, please be instructed by your Lord and Savior.

I observe that in the name of truth, prudence, and discernment, you are struggling with much negativity. The spirit of negativity is toying with you. He sees your constant prayer for truth, prudence, and discernment. And into these true graces of the Holy Spirit, present already in your soul, he blows continuous smoke of negativity to block, choke off, or cloud these graces. He does this with a subtle touch, which masks itself while producing the same result as blatant attacks causing con-

fusion and doubt in your soul. Giving into this tactic of the enemy, you exist in a state of less receptivity to grace, to the movements within your soul, because you are poised in a defensive mode. The danger of this in your soul is that your faith can be weakened. You can move into a state of unbelief rather than belief.

Soul, your faith is being tried and tested very much now. Yet, you must trust! The truth you seek, the truth you thirst for is with you, in you. My Holy Spirit reveals the truth in your soul at every moment and His Light and Truth bring *only* peace in your soul. Negativity brings only lack of peace as it infiltrates every grace to cloud or diminish it. There is an important difference between awareness of possible deception and fear of possible deception! Awareness of possible deception is part of the gift of wisdom and is the beginning of discernment and prudence. But fear of deception is a negative movement in the soul brought on by lack of faith and trust or denial of truth perpetuated by the infiltration of the evil spirit of negativity, fear, and unbelief, all of which disturbs your peace of soul. The goal of the enemy is to block your receptivity to My grace. You aid him in achieving this goal when you lose your peace, become confused, and deny the graces in your soul. While the Holy Spirit lifts your soul towards the heavens, the enemy tries to press your soul down into the abyss. He oppresses. I uplift. He disturbs. I am peace.

Receive like a trusting child. The presence of My Holy Spirit brings the gift of discernment, a part of wisdom. Furthermore, these spiritual gifts in your soul are to be discerned by My representative, the priest, who is your spiritual director. The Church provides the guidance and application of these gifts. It is for you to simply receive them. You have received much. There is so much more for you to receive. These are gifts, blessings that are beyond your human comprehension. Do not let the enemy rob you of such graces. Many of these graces are deposited at such a level within the soul that the enemy cannot enter this core reserved for God alone. His playground is your mind. You are the one who empowers the evil spirits to disturb your peace of soul. You open the door for him. I call you to walk in truth, prudence and discernment. But these have nothing to do with fear or negativity!

There is too much fear and negativity in the world today. This blocks My grace in many souls. It has affected the whole climate of this age and effectively drawn many souls away from Me and away from the Church. Many priests have fallen prey to this tactic of the enemy. Many souls who start out on their spiritual journeys end up being attacked in this manner and never cease to overcome it.

How is the spirit of fear or negativity overcome? Fear is cast out by perfect love. Negativity is cast out by deep faith. Because there is too little love and faith in the world today, My own creation has become weak in fighting the evils that oppress this age. The enemy steals from souls that which I, the Lord and Savior of all, have given by way of grace. Walk in truth so that you may guide many in the ways of truth overcoming the great deceptions of this age.

My creation, you are handing yourselves over to the enemy. Fight the good fight! Persevere in your faith! Let the love in your soul be the fire that casts out all fear, negativity, and doubt. Know the truth of who you are, sons and daughters of the Most High God who has already won the victory for you. I have gone before you to prepare a place for you in My Father's House. Do not let the thief take what is yours by My Blood. I love you. Your Jesus

146. **6-13-96** Prayer Group, the Feast of the Sacred Heart
Console My Sacred Heart

My little lambs,

As I told St. Margaret Mary, My tender Heart of Love is wounded because My Love is spurned. I asked her to console My Sacred Heart with her love, devotion, and service. I required the gift of her life in totality in atonement for the many souls who refuse to accept My Love. And many entered eternal life because of her sacrifice.

Today more than ever, My Sacred Heart of Love is wounded by your refusal of My Love. You still deny your God. I love you with tenderness and mercy that you cannot comprehend. Oh My creation, I cry out for you! I am the Lamb led to the slaughter in silence so that you may be redeemed through My Blood. I offer this Heart of Mine as pure gift for you. Why refuse such a gift?

My lambs, you who have turned with love to My Heart, console Me for the entire world. You who accept My Love receive more. Grace overflows this Heart of Mine which must pour out Love. The fountain of My Love is eternally abundant, but the vessels are few. You receive graces that enable you to love for those who cannot love until their hearts are changed. You become a storehouse of My tender and merciful Love. When the time comes, many can draw from you as from My Own Sacred Heart. This is the depth of the union granted to you who accept My Divine Love and live in Me.

Oh, My little lambs, I caress you in My arms. I feed you My Blood that saves and My water that gives life. I bathe you in My Light. You become for Me, a great consolation that soothes this aching Heart that longs to be loved by every soul created by the Breath of Love. Thank you for accepting what others so easily spurn. Many blessings are yours because of your acceptance that requires surrender. To accept love is to accept responsibility.

On this day of remembrance of My Sacred Heart, I shower you with graces, which shall bear fruit that lasts. You will feed many. While others offend the Father by refusing the gift of His Son, you give glory to the Father by accepting the gift that He has given. I love you tenderly and mercifully. Ask and you shall receive. I bless you this night and always. Your Jesus

147. **6-17-96** Mass and Holy Hour before the Tabernacle
Jesus on Suffering and Union Through The Cross

After Holy Communion, I prayed: "My Beloved Jesus, I am at once full of love and full of pain. My God, My All, have mercy upon my poor soul. If you are purifying me, so be it and thank you. Please help me to understand the good of it. Jesus, You observe the cruelty of my situation. It seems, I cannot gain an inch that the devil doesn't come and set me back two inches. My soul is pounded to the ground repeatedly. I hope against all hope for conversion for this soul, but I observe evil increase and good seemingly lose ground. Grant me the grace to trust in You and to have faith that there will be conversion someday. O, Jesus, I am sorry for the times I have failed to trust; failed to believe and hope in the midst of suffering."

Jesus said: **My lamb, My altar, tenderly I love you. My wrath is not upon you. Punishment is not upon you. You are being purified by the fire of Divine Love. You are My victim of Love. I am giving you a gift, My beloved one, union with Me on the cross! Oh, cross, Oh Highest Love! You are the sacrifice; the victim lamb upon the altar; an offering for the sins of many for the glory of the Father. You are a precious gift; a soul willing to suffer to win souls for Me.**

You search the Scriptures to find one whose journey is like your own. (Jesus is referring to how I was reading Scripture to find a similar situation as mine.) **Look at My journey. There is your answer. You are in the Garden with Me, My beloved one. Moments of desolation torment your soul. In the agony, you ask the Father to remove the Cup, if possible. The next moment you say with Me, "Not Mine but Your Will be done, Father!" Your will wants to embrace suffering for conversion of souls, but your flesh agonizes over the sacrifice. Then you are scourged with Me. It hurts does it not, little lamb? But Love enables you to offer everything to the Father. I, your Savior, give you the Love through the power of the Holy Spirit.**

The weight you feel is from the heavy hand of the devil who seeks to crush your soul. He toils to make you his conquest; to thwart My divine plan for you. If he catches you, he claims the souls that you would have gained for My Kingdom as well. But you are My conquest! I overcome you by the power of Divine Love. He overcomes souls by the power of evil. Evil is the lesser power. But it easily overcomes a soul who does not know the greater power of Divine Love. You know the greater power of Divine Love. The devil has no power over you except to test you

as I permit for the good of your soul. The more you learn his tactics of warfare, the more you will be able to free other souls from his evil clutches. I will use you to free others.

My bride, I am your spouse. We are wedded by the way of the cross. The cross is the unifying way of love. I am taking you from Gethsemane to Calvary that you become another image of Me; a sign of the Father's Love for humanity. You are raised up with Me on the cross that you may draw souls to the Father. Become the bridge like the Groom that laid His Life down for you and formed the Bridge for all humanity.

Truth, you pray. This is Truth! Do not accept the lie that presents itself when others become the mouthpiece of the enemy. What spirit is within the one that persecutes you? My lamb, free this soul with Me. Only Love sets one free. The mercy I have granted you must be granted to others. Plead for those who are blind and captive to "feelings." It is in the emotions that Satan strikes.

My lamb, I am testing you and raising you up. How can faith and hope be increased? How can you be raised to battle the devil who seeks to devour souls like vultures devour a kill? How can you be transfigured into My Image so that you co-redeem with Me? How can I beautify wretchedness? Who will offer sacrifice for the conversion of souls? There is one way. I Am the way. The way is a journey from Gethsemane to Calvary. Also, the way is Resurrection and Eternal Life. My beloved bride, few travel the way. It requires selfless love. I am the Source of love that sacrifices. I grant souls the grace to walk the way of sacrificial love. Many refuse Me. The way of love is not easy, though it is simple. I have taught you. All has been revealed in and through Me. The Holy Spirit is with you. He reminds you of all that I have taught you.

You cannot serve two masters. Most choose the world then the world masters them. Accept My teaching and live My Way, Truth, and Life. *Accept no lies*! The liar is a thief of your peace. He robs you of the Truth of My Divine Love. He confuses and causes you to doubt in the Father's Divine Providence, which is perfect for all of creation. He sows fear so that you doubt, become negative, and ultimately deny Me. I am the Truth that he wants you to deny. To deny My Grace in your soul is to deny Me.

You have many angels to assist you in this difficult battle. Do not hesitate to call on the angels that guard you and fight for you in ways you cannot perceive. You have an abundance of heavenly aid surrounding you at all times. You know the many saints who assist you along the way. You have been aided by these Holy Ones who never cease to pray for you and for all humanity.

Your trial is a great suffering. But far greater is the good that will come of it. It serves many high purposes. One of which is to beautify you for your Groom. I behold in you, My beloved little one, a new, radiant light that reflects a soul that has passed the test of Love. Like gold tried in fire, the beauty of a soul tried in Love becomes a rare and precious gift to God and to all.

The Angel of Enduring Love is with you to empower you to endure this trial. And this angel will remind you that I endure all your weaknesses and transgressions with merciful Love. I am your God who is Love that forgives and forgets as you prostrate before Me in humility and purity of heart. You intercede for many souls who would fail to respond to My Love without your intercession.

My bride, the cross is heavy. But I have provided enough grace that it will not crush you. When you are attacked, I provide the grace that enables you to endure and forgive. Walk the way of Love with Me. I bless you, My bride, leaving the sign of the cross to mark you as Mine forever. Be still. Be silent. I am God. You are not. Persevere to love. This is all that I ask of you. My love. My peace. Jesus

148. **6-19-96** Rosary with spiritual director, my home.
Blessing of the Book

Glorious Mysteries.

As soon as Father began the Resurrection decade, I heard and saw the following:

I saw a book in Father's hand. Immediately an angel, which I understood to be the Angel of Enduring Love, came and took the book from Father's hands. The angel, which was magnificent in its power and light, ascended upward through the heavens. In an instant, it seemed the angel arrived at the throne of the Most Holy Trinity. The angel presented the book to Our Triune God laying the book on the ground before the throne of the Most Holy Trinity. Many angels (beings of pure light) and saints (taking their human form) gathered around to observe God blessing the book.

The book was transfigured into light as the Most Holy Trinity poured graces upon it. These are graces to be given to the reader. I could see graced light fall upon the pages, transfiguring the book into light rather than a material book. Somehow the angels and the saints blessed it also. At the end of the blessing, the Angel of Enduring Love carried the book back to Father's hands. The Angel of Enduring Love is an extra angel that God the Father granted my soul in 1996 to help me endure an extreme suffering, a great trial. This is an angel from the Choir of Virtues.

Then I heard Jesus say: **Oh, My Creation! May your Faith be increased!**

Then I heard the Holy Spirit say: **May your Hope be increased!**

Then I heard the Eternal Father say: **May your Love be increased!**

Oh, My Creation
You are walking in darkness.
Receive My Light.
I am your Triune God who Lives.
You are My people living like orphans.
Turn from evil. Live in My Light.
I am God. You are not.
Let Love reign again.

Be transfigured and live in Me.
My Covenant is everlasting!
Be Mine. I am Yours.
Who is like unto your Almighty and Eternal God?
Darkness has covered you,

But I shall wash you with Living Water.
Be cleansed that you may be One with The Light.
Open your hardened hearts.
Let My Fire of Divine Love enter you.

Love alone will transfigure My creation.
The darkness shall not overcome you.
You shall overcome the darkness
By the power of Divine Love.
No longer will I endure your indifference.
The time of decision has arrived.
Do not be afraid. But choose Me.
I have chosen you to be Mine forever.
Come. I will dry your tears.

No prayer has been in vain.
No sigh of Love goes unnoticed.
Likewise, no sin goes unnoticed.
But My Mercy is unfathomable.
Do not put off your decision.
There is one thing you have that is eternal.
It is your soul.

Reflect, My creation, and pray.
I, your Triune, Supreme, and Eternal God
Am with you. Turn to Me.
I am Love, Divine, and Unconditional.
All that you seek, all that you require,
I AM.
In all ages I AM.

Second Glorious Mystery.

When Father prayed "help us know the Divine Will of the Father," I saw the following:

I saw a powerful lightening storm in the heavens. When the lightening would strike, it lit up the globe of the world, which was in total darkness. Lightening bolts would then hit and pierce the darkness to illumine the earth. When bathed in the light, I could see on earth, people gathered together in small groups, praying and reading spiritual books. A type of resurrection was resulting as souls were enriched and brought back to life becoming bathed in the Light and receiving Love. I understood the darkness on earth to be of a spiritual nature. I was amazed at how utterly dark the whole of creation had become. I understood that God's Divine Providence would transfigure the darkness of the world through a variety of signs, miracles, messages, visitations, and sufferings. Grace upon grace will draw us back to the Light. Lord?

Jesus said: **The graces of this age are a sign of My Mercy revealing and reminding all of creation, "I am a Living God!" In every generation, My Covenant stands and I speak to My people in wondrous ways.**

Next, I saw the prologue of John's Gospel. It was all lit up. Later, I saw our Prayer Group praying the Rosary. This is a sign of their intercession. As I am writing this, I see a snake trying to crawl on the notebook of writings on my desk, but immediately Our Lady put the Rosary over the writings and the snake disappeared.

149. **6-23-96** My home, 5PM
Jesus Asks: Do You Love Me?

Dearest Jesus, I ache from the pain. The anguish is beyond expression. Jesus, you know this. You see everything. My God, help me to bear this cross that crushes me. My Jesus, must I observe such suffering inflicted upon the family, the innocent ones? Have mercy! Jesus, there is nothing in me that does not hurt. I want to run. But where would I go, Lord? Your grace is just enough to affix my will to yours, Lord. It takes all the resolve of my will to keep me fixed to you.

Everything is darkness. Minutes seem like hours. My eyes are swollen from the tears. My head aches from the pressure. My heart is shredded into pieces. My body is tense and aching from pain. The enemy constantly whispers in my ear the most degrading lies that plunge me into constant battle against despair. It is exhausting. How little rest I am afforded. Jesus, Oh my Jesus, be my strength! Jesus said: **My lamb, do you love Me?**

"Yes, Jesus, I love you so much it hurts, yet I cannot run from the pain of it. Yes, I love you, Lord."

My lamb, live My agony with Me. Love is with you. Endure the blows that come at you with the loving grace that I give to you.

"Jesus, I must need more. I am barely able to do as you ask, Lord."

My altar, I am doing everything. All is grace. Simply put your arms around My grace. I uphold you. Do not become paralyzed in the pain of your suffering. Ask for everything that you need. I will grant it. Seek my courage, My strength, My perseverance. I will give you the grace! Do as I ask and great will be your reward. Do not let the pain of the present moment defeat you. Take My courage and My Heart. Hide yourself in the shelter of My Love. I will keep you safe. It must be this way for now. Suffering passes, while the fruit of it endures forever. Cling to Me. I am with you. You will not falter. Take My peace. I love you. Your Jesus

150. **6-26-96** Rosary with Father, my home
Consolation after Reconciliation

I had asked Father to hear my confession before praying the Rosary. Once he began, the Holy Spirit infused my heart with much light regarding my sins and weaknesses. To be moved to profound contrition is a special grace and I received this.

At the end of confession, Jesus became present to me in a most tangible way. It was as if He bent over me and gave me a very firm embrace. His Love seemed to pass through me and my soul was filled with His tenderness and mercy. Then He said: **Soul of My Cross, I love you infinitely. I love you just the way you are. Do not be afraid. You will not fail Me. I am with you always! I have not forsaken you or your family. Be patient. I am patient with you. I forgive your offenses.**

Do not be overwhelmed. Be at peace. Be still. You fail to believe that you are My Bride. Believe. I have made you My Bride. You are a reflection of your Mystical Groom as you drink

the wedding cup of sacrificial love. Your Groom is with you. Everywhere you are, in joy and in suffering, I am. You toss restlessly, but all the while you are enveloped in My Arms. What you are enduring could only be done in Me, through Me, with Me. Allow Me to hold you. Be still. Hold onto Me. You are not alone. Trust in Me! Drink of My Love. Drink of My Blood and Water. Live, Soul of My Cross, live in Me. You need not be strong. I will be your strength. Mercy is yours. You have been purified in the Sacrament of Mercy. You are reconciled. Thank you for living in the truth and telling the truth. I bless you My dearly beloved lamb, victim for many, victim of love. I receive your offering. You are My delight and I take joy in you. Be joyful in Me. I have given you so very much. I do not withhold anything. I give everything. Imitate Me.

Pray with My priest and I shall instruct you along the way of the cross. Do not be afraid. Go in My peace. Light is upon you. You shall not falter. Do only My Will. Love and pray. Sacrifice and work in silence and peace. Many will be blessed by My work through you. Your family will receive many graces through your suffering.

I kiss you on the forehead leaving the sign of the cross to mark you as Mine forever. I love you. Your Jesus

151. 6-26-96
Pray for the People of Bosnia

During the Rosary, I saw a number of army tanks. I asked Our Lady, "Where are these?" She said: *Bosnia. Pray for the people of this area.* Then Our Lady exposed her pierced and Immaculate Heart and brilliant rays of grace flowed upon us.

152. 7-2-96
Attack of the Spirit of Hatred

At 1:30AM, I was spiritually attacked in the following manner.

I was exhausted physically with the extra demands of the family. When I went to bed, I began to think in a negative way about my life being seemingly out of control. The minute that I began to think like this, the devil wasted no time coming through the door which I had opened for him. There was a sudden intensification of my feelings. More negative thoughts began to flow consistently as if from the outside. All the problems in my family were held before my mind and exaggerated making me feel more out of control and vulnerable. I became more disturbed by the minute. Then an overwhelming thought came repeatedly, which was to run from the responsibility, that I deserved a rest. I entertained the thought about "running" for a long time. Then came an influx of more negative thoughts about family, friends, the Church, and then myself. The negative thoughts against myself were the strongest and quickly they moved into hatred of myself.

In an instant, I was overcome by the most oppressive evil spirit of hatred. This spirit of hatred became the only reality that I could perceive in my mind, heart, and will. It seemed that my very soul was overpowered by this intense hatred which tried to block out the truth of love. This spirit of hatred was attempting to kill the love in me. It increased its oppression and exerted more hatred so that I thought I would be crushed to death physically. Death seemed the appropriate answer because I hated myself to such a depth that I thought I deserved to be hated; that justice would have me go with the devil to be hated forever. The devil presented an image of myself in which I could not find even one tiny thread of goodness. Then he repeatedly said, "You have screwed everything up! You cannot do anything right!" As I heard these words, I was filled with more self-contempt and hatred of everything. I thought I was going to die of "hatred."

I called my spiritual director for prayer and as the phone rang I kept thinking, "I have never known hatred like this!" I was in agony, afraid, and crying. The minute that Father answered the phone I said, "Please pray for me. I am under attack. I hate myself. I hate, I hate." Father began immediately to pray, but first he commanded me to be absolutely silent. I became still. He called upon God the Father and when he did so, I repeatedly prayed, "Abba, Father, Abba, Father, hold me. I am your daughter. Father I am yours!" Peace came. Father was filled with the Holy Spirit who led his prayers.

Father understood that God wanted me to surrender to Him at a new depth. Under the deepest influence of the Holy Spirit, Father led the prayer, a new prayer of surrender and asked me to repeat after him. Both of us were now in a deep state of prayer as he led, I repeated these words.

"My God, I surrender to You, my life! I surrender every minute, every hour, every day, every month, every year to You! I surrender my heart. I surrender my mind, my thoughts. I surrender my will." (To surrender my will was an agony because I knew that God would take my soul, my surrender to a new level and it would cost everything.) But I continued, "I surrender my future. I surrender my family. Take me, my God. I am Yours. Do as You will. I surrender completely. I surrender everything. I will not resist. I give You my life. I give You my love. I surrender."

As I repeated these words I sensed a part of me dying and it hurt, but it was not oppressive. It was freeing and healing.

When I think about this terrible attack, I see how the devil was tempting me to take back control of my life, to run from God. He was oppressing my soul, crushing it with evil hatred to block out love.

But God entered this trial and made good of it causing me to give up more control, to surrender to Him and to die to self so that I can live more fully in Him. What the devil oppressed, God freed when I turned to Him and prayed. Once I did this, the trial ended. I fell asleep repeating the words, "I surrender, I surrender, I surrender." Each time that I said this, more peace came, more stillness, more love in my heart and more certitude of my union with God's Divine Will, more confidence in Divine Providence, more awareness of His Presence in me, more hope. I ended up with an awareness of my nothingness being thoroughly surrounded by His Love.

This terrible trial proved to be a gift. I learn so much through suffering. God, being all merciful, would only permit such a trial of my soul because I had the proper spiritual support in my spiritual director. He would not permit this otherwise. Praise be to God!

153. **7-3-96** Feast of St. Thomas, Rosary with Father,
    My home 2:30 PM

Mary on Spiritual Warfare, Deciding for God and the Urgency of Invoking the Holy Spirit

When Father began the Rosary, my heart was pierced and I entered contemplation. I did not hear anything during the Rosary. As soon as Father finished the Rosary, Our Lady spoke these words.

My dear little children,

The Father continues to permit my visitation in the world today. I come with many heavenly graces ordained by the Most Holy Trinity for this time, for this generation. You shall continue to witness Satan's blatant attacks on souls, families, societies, churches, and nations. Everywhere that you look, you will find signs of his evil presence. He has penetrated this generation in blatant ways. More dangerous, are the subtle ways by which he deceives many. He disguises himself as "good" so that he is embraced by good people.

As long as you continue to function from your human thinking, human rationale, operating from what your mind thinks instead of what the Holy Spirit is saying within your heart, you shall walk in darkness. Your mind is easily overcome by the enemy's lies, his utterly false way, which leads to nothingness, the nothingness that He exists in. Nothingness exists where God is absent through rejection. I observe that God is rejected everywhere today.

I observe many of God's children, lost in indecision. Many of you are trying to live lives that are neither for God or against God. Remember what Jesus taught you. If you are not for Him, you are not with Him, and in fact, you are against Him. My children, you live your daily life as if you will walk the earth forever. The devil tempts you, deceives you, to put off deciding for God, to put off everything important. Your soul will live into eternity and you do not take care of it. You are more concerned with things that perish.

Do you not realize your life could end at any moment? Do you believe that you will make an account of your life before the Author of Life, the Lord, our God? You are responsible, accountable for your life and every moment, every decision in it. How often I *have implored you, to decide for God **now**. Make God a priority in your life **now**. Your spiritual well-being must be the most important part of your existence now, not later! Do you really think that God would ordain all the visitations, messages, signs, everywhere on earth, if these were not truly critical times of decision?*

You assume that the Church, the sacraments, holy places of pilgrimage, will always be available for you. I come to tell you that you cannot take this for granted. You are about to pass through more difficulty in the very near future.

I am thankful to my children, those consecrated to My Immaculate Heart, because you are gaining grace for the salvation of the world. The great battle in the world is a spiritual one. The spiritual battle is being fought by my army of little souls. These are the true and powerful prayer warriors who have responded to the grace of conversion. You are living the messages and saving many souls. You are defending much more than you can comprehend through your commitment to prayer and fasting. I observe, however, many conversions have grown cold, weary and you have returned to former ways of living.

*My children, you must invoke the Holy Spirit to help you. You must live in the Holy Spirit. It is the Holy Spirit who penetrates your heart, causing conversion. The same Holy Spirit also resides within your heart to continue to convert you along the spiritual way of life and holiness. If you are living in the Holy Spirit, you are living like a little child, completely open to the movements of God's grace within your heart. You know the movement, the voice of God. You have true self-knowledge. And you know the enemy and his tactics. Your heart is the area of love within you. You must live your **lives in love and for love**.*

Love is the origin. Love is the motive. Love is the way. Love is the goal. It is the beginning, the middle and the end of your life on earth. Love is eternal life. God is Love. You simply cannot live without the Person of the Holy Spirit. He lives with you, in you, teaching you and guiding you to Love. You must embrace fully, always and everywhere, the Holy Spirit of God! Too few know the Third Person of the Holy Trinity!

There was a pause in the dictation. Our Lady seemed distressed that too few know the Person of the Holy Spirit. I asked Our Lady,

"How does one come to know the Third Person of the Holy Trinity, the Holy Spirit?"

Our Lady said: *My child,*

The Holy Spirit comes to you at Baptism. He comes to you through all the Sacraments, through the Church, through other souls, in which He reigns. To come to know Him, you must desire to know Him. It is through prayer from the heart that this is accomplished. It is accomplished simply, gently, thoroughly, through grace and prayer. A simple formula, which disposes your heart, is the prayer of the Holy Rosary. He will make Himself known through the Mysteries of the Rosary because the mysteries are the Gospel message. He will impart more of Himself the more docile your heart, the more obedient your will, the purer your intention, the deeper your commitment to follow God's way, the more faithful you are to prayer, the greater your thirst for holiness, the greater your aversion to evil and sin. Again, it is enough to desire to know Him and then to pray. He will make Himself known to a soul. He will move the soul by His grace.

You could pray according to a simple prayer that I will give you now, but it must be from the depths of your heart. Remember, God knows the level of your sincerity and the purity of your intentions.

(Our Lady gave this prayer.)

In the Name of the Father, Son and Holy Spirit.
My Triune God, I thirst for love.
With all my heart, I desire to know you.
Almighty Father, please send the Holy Spirit into my heart.
Come, Holy Spirit, Spirit of Divine Love, Come.
Enter my heart gently. Lead me by the power of your Love.
Cause my heart to be alive with Love.

As my gentle, loving guest, bear witness
to the Truth of Love. Teach me
the Way, the Truth, the Life.
Teach me of Jesus, the Son, the Word Incarnate.
Through the Son, through Your Love,
Lead me to My Eternal Father.
In knowing Father, Son and Holy Spirit

I shall have true life on earth in You.
I surrender my heart to you.

Please give to me the Heart of My Redeemer.
I thirst for Love. Come, Divine Love. Come, Holy Spirit.
Cause me to know you, cause me to live by Your Light.
I long to leave the darkness to come into Your Light.
Holy Spirit, permeate my heart and soul with your
constant Presence. Grant your grace and gifts
that my thirst may be alleviated.
Sanctify me that I may give You Glory.
I love You, My Triune God. Reign in me. Amen.

My little children,

Do not be afraid to desire God. Do not be afraid to seek Him. Do not be afraid to be Holy. Do not be afraid to change your godless ways of living to become a holy people. All souls seek Love. Therefore, seek God, He is Love. If you are open, He will come to you in an intimacy of love that is irresistible. None can love like Him! I pray that you will know the Truth about God. God exists. He loves you just the way you are. He created you and chose you to be beautiful, to be with Him on earth and in heaven.

The ugliness of life that you are made to see all around you is not from God. He is all Good. The ugliness that you see in the world, that you feel inside of your being is not from God. It is from the devil, the liar, the thief, and your enemy, who seeks only more ugliness, leading to ultimate death. Why? He wants to take from God what belongs to God.

You belong to God. But you have a free will to decide for Him or against Him. You can make this decision for God only in and through the Person of the Holy Spirit. Decide for God today. Ask the Holy Spirit to come into your soul. Open your heart to love. God's Love is pure, holy, Divine Love. Begin to live from this moment on, a life worthy of one who is a child of the King of Kings, the Lord of All. He will raise you up, by the power of the Holy Spirit, so that when you are presented to the Eternal Father you will embrace one another as intimate family, wrapped in everlasting love that is holy. Please do not delay.

I love you, my little children. As your Mother, I am simply try-ing to assist you to know you are loved by God. The entire heav-enly court and I are at your disposal that you will turn back to God. You are not hidden or distant from us. In God's Mercy we are permitted to aid you along the way. Please accept the graces avail-able to you today. I bless you. Your Mother

154. **7-7-96** My home, 8PM
More Attacks and Jesus Reminds Me to Focus on Him

I am taken to the precipice. There is a constant bombardment of temptations and trials, which are increasingly more evil. They are taking their toll in every part of my being. The most consistent areas of attack include the following.

Despair about my family and in general.
Doubt about the spiritual life.
Futility of it.
Futility of writing the messages and aversion to them.
Impatience.
Discouragement and depression.
Self-contempt and self-degradation.
Indulge in compensation to relieve the pain.
Distraction, various and many.
Retaliation, revenge.
Temptation of being abandoned by God, lost.
Fear of failure and reputation and rejection.
Vulnerability and loss of control.
Resentment.

At this time, I perceive only suffering in my life and am left with a deep sense of futility. I feel that I am dying repeatedly.

In the midst of so much interior and exterior suffering, I was pierced violently in my heart by Jesus. This sudden piercing brings tears because it feels as if a razor sharp, red hot arrow has penetrated my heart. Jesus repeatedly does this and I said to Him, "My Lord, would you add to my suffering?" Jesus said: **Come to Me.** I hesitated. Again, **Come to Me.** I left the kitchen and went to my prayer room. I sat down before my statues of Jesus and Mary and wept.

Jesus said: **My bride, focus on Me, only Me.** I said: "Jesus, I cannot take this anymore. Please help me." Jesus said: **Soul, Satan has caused you to look everywhere except at Me. Focus on Me.** I said: "Jesus, I am on the edge. My suffering increases when You pierce my heart with such force." He said: **Soul, My bride, I am opening up your heart. I wound you with Divine Love to give you the grace to endure more, to love more, and to suffer more for the sake of souls.** His word penetrated me and I wept more because I sensed more suffering in the future.

Suddenly, I stopped weeping. The power of the Holy Spirit began to fill me and lead me in the following prayer. Jesus said: **Write all of this down for Me, please.**

"My Jesus, please remind me of how much You love me. Grant that I would know more deeply how You suffered for me. Reveal to me how You died for me. Take me to Calvary so that I can examine more closely all of Your wounds, Your lacerations, Your contusions. Remind me Jesus! Reveal the price that You paid for my soul. Remind me how much You endured that I might be saved. Remind me of the blood You sweat in the Garden of Gethsemane. Show me Your stripes from the scourging; how they carved Your skin with a whip. Show me the crown of thorns piercing Your scalp, mocking Your Kingship, ridiculing Your Kingdom.

Oh, that I could know more fully all that You suffered for me! Cause me to endure more for You. The greater my knowledge of Your sacrificial love, the more empowered I will be to become like You; the more reciprocal my love for You. Show me how You were beaten, stripped of everything, esteemed by few, betrayed by Your closest friends, utterly vulnerable, silent, rejected, tempted, alone, as the weight of the world, my sins bore down on You, my God! Show me how Your innocence was violated for all of the guilty.

Oh my God, my Jesus, help me to be more generous, more charitable! I spend time counting the cost of discipleship! Help me to stop counting the cost. Help me to be like You, loving and embracing all that is necessary to save souls! Open my mouth that I may drink from Your pierced heart, becoming a new creation; transfigured by Your powerful love which bears all and gives endlessly."

Jesus said: **Soul, I would have died for you alone. You are dying now. I am with you in your agony. You are My image; My victim, so wounded. Exist in My Divine Will. Do you not realize that the plans I have for you are all for good? Not one moment of your suffering is useless. You are more radiantly beautiful to Me in your agony. We are drinking the wedding cup together. You are never alone.**

I have assigned more angels to aid you in this trial. The enemy may be permitted to toy with you one moment, but I make good of it the next. I pierce your heart to open you to love so that you may endure all things and persevere to fulfill My work. I am your Master. Do not resist. Resistance prolongs your transformation. Be docile. I pierced your heart to remind you that you are Mine. I am the Lord of your life. Your life is Mine. You surrendered it. I received you. Now I give to you My own life that is true, abundant, and everlasting.

I said: "Lord, I perceive only pain. Everything hurts."

Jesus said: **Soul, then you are looking to yourself, wallowing in self-pity. Look at Me. Always be focused on Me. Do not let your mind wander about yourself, the future, where I am leading, or your situation. Look at Me on the cross. Examine Me; My wounds, My suffering and death endured for you, for sinners who spurn My love across every generation. Your cross would not bear down so heavily upon you if you focused on Me and trusted. Your suffering increases when you lose your focus of the truth. I am the Truth!**

I said: "My Jesus, things are getting worse. Trusting is more difficult by the day. My Lord, all is grace. Look, I am a beggar seeking the grace to trust you."

Jesus said: **Soul, I give you the grace, but realize this. When you persevere to do My will without understanding, even without complete trust, you gain merit in My eyes. You gain more grace. If I permit you to struggle with doubt, do you not realize that it is for your good, for growth? You are strengthened by the struggles, which I permit and even ordain for you. The devil does not attack you except that I permit it. Whatever I permit is for the good of your soul. It sounds harsh, My bride, but it is merciful, not harsh. I alone know what is best for your soul.**

My Wisdom oversees every detail of your formation. What I have chosen for Myself, I form precisely, by My own hand, creating unspeakable beauty where wretchedness existed. The center of your existence, your soul, is My domain. Never have you been more beautiful in My sight. When you perceived you were beautiful, you were wretched. Now it is the opposite. We are one. Depend on Me for everything. I give to you all good things, holiness and virtues that did not exist in you before this suffering. Do you love Me, Soul of My Cross?

I said: "Jesus, I love You. Yes, Lord, I love You.

He said: Rejoice My bride and victim for many. We are one heart. When I wound yours, My own is wounded also. I open up for you and you open up for Me. I want you to receive more: more love, more holiness, and more goodness. Focus on Me. I am focused on you. Bless Me, soul, with your love, courage, perseverance and trust. Will you do this for Me?

I said: "Yes, Lord of my life. Please stay in my heart. I am dependent upon You. Remind me always of Your passion and death for me that I may carry the cross with great charity. Stretch me, Jesus! I love and thank You, my God. I am Yours. Please keep my heart open to love. Amen."

155. **7-8-96** My home, 9AM
Remain Open to Love in the Midst of Suffering

As I was making coffee in my kitchen, very suddenly, my soul was illumined and I received an image of my human heart being pierced by a scalpel which opened it wide.

I received understanding that God is keeping my heart from closing up in the midst of a great suffering. I tend to close up when I am hurt. But God wants me to remain open, wide open, to love, especially those who inflict the pain. God heals me by wounding me with this piercing arrow of Divine Love. I may bleed, but I live.

"My God, Your ways are mysterious and wondrous; too much to take in, too lofty for humanity. Your wisdom is beyond my understanding. May it be enough for me that You 'will it.' I love you."

156. 7-11-96
Attack of The Spirit of Murder of the Spiritual Life

My suffering is very intense and I am exhausted again. As I was trying to go to sleep for the night, I was assailed by negative and self-degrading thoughts. Suddenly, I became aware of an evil spirit and it made itself known. It was the spirit of murder of the spiritual life. It was trying to crush me. I did not readily resist. I entertained thoughts of cooperating and giving up the spiritual life because it might relieve suffering. Besides, I was a little upset with God. There was a sharp recurring thought, "Let us kill your spiritual life." The emphasis was on the words "let us."

This evil spirit sought my very active cooperation to offend God. I have never before experienced such blatant malice towards God. It seemed to me that its goal was to mock God. I was not being tempted to quit God as much as I was being tempted to sin against Him in horrible ways, so that God Himself would send Me away from Him. Then I would be free to do whatever I wanted in this world. A lie is always presented because He is a liar from the beginning.

This spirit exerted a lot of evil power and at some level, I must have cooperated with it for too long because, suddenly, I heard the voice of Jesus and He was very firm with me. Full of Divine Authority, His words penetrated to the core as He said: **Do not tempt the Lord your God again!** He commanded me and I was struck with profound holy fear throughout. His words broke the attack and the evil spirit fled immediately. I shall never forget the Authority of Jesus' warning to me. I realized that I was playing with fire by entertaining evil temptations and not rebuking them immediately.

Though His words admonished me, He was full of forgiveness and unconditional love. I received a strong infilling of peace which prevented me from being overwhelmed with guilt. Though I am guilty, Jesus does not want my soul to be swallowed up in it. He wants me to know the truth of guilt, but it cannot be separated from His boundless mercy and love. I accepted His mercy and He urged me to begin again, enriched by the lesson.

157. **7-17-96** Rosary with spiritual director, my home, 5 PM
Empty Houses

The first image I saw was a house. The house looked beautiful from the outside. Seemingly then, Jesus took me inside the house. The inside of the house had been pillaged. I observe with Jesus a "nothingness," a profound "emptiness." That was all that was left inside the house. I experienced a "chill," a "coldness" remaining in the emptiness. Jesus' heart was pierced with pain, even agony, over the way this house has been ravaged. He suffers this. I suffered this. I asked Jesus, "Is this Your house, Your Church?" He said: **Dear child, this is My creation. This is the state of many men.** I understood that each human being is his house. Then Jesus spoke.

My creation,
The love of the Most Holy Trinity created you for love, for beauty, goodness and life abundant. But the spirit of the world has ravaged you, leaving behind empty shells, houses that have been gutted. You know not the dignity of your being. You are My creation, each a house created for Me, to be a reflection of My own beauty, goodness and life, full of every virtue, adorned in love and holiness.

Instead, the spirit of the world has entered in the night, caught you unprepared and asleep, and took from you the beautiful and good things I had placed within you, robbing you of true life and true love. And in the night, because you slept without Light, without awareness, you gave up so easily all that was rich and everlasting. You awakened, hardly noticing that your everlasting riches had been replaced with trinkets, trinkets that you readily accepted instead of true riches. Now even the very trinkets that you settled for are being taken from you. I observe you as empty houses. I receive from your emptiness only cold indifference, because you have little or no love inside you. Yet from the outside, you look as you always looked and the world perceives that you are alive as always. But truly you are like walking dead men. Asleep to the truth, emptied of godliness. The void that you are walks the days and sleeps the nights of one orphaned, lost and without meaning.

Some of you are awakening now to begin to see what has happened to you. You will begin a search for new life. Some will begin to fill the house with trinkets of a different variety. Some will begin to fill the house with true and meaningful things because your search, your desire, has led you to Me, the Lord and Savior of your life. If you but seek Me, you will find. If you desire Me, you will have Me.

Oh, My Creation, you fail to understand that the God of the Universe loves you, individually and collectively! The Love of the Most Holy Trinity is the creative master architect of each living house. You are living temples. I am within you by the powerful unifying love of the Holy Spirit. If you are an empty house, a pillaged temple, I am with you still. I do not leave you. If you are a full and beautiful temple, I am with you, filling you all the more with every good and holy thing of God. Oh, My Creation, you fail to believe that I, your Lord and God, never leave you. I do not abandon My own. And each belongs to Me. Each one of you is My own house, My temple. Fitting or unfitting temples that you are, I am in your midst!

Do I, the Lord of the Universe, suffer because you suffer? Yes, I choose to be united to your every suffering, your every joy, your every thing! Why? Because I, your Lord and Savior love you with an everlasting, unconditionally merciful Love. Open your eyes that you may see Me with you! Do not be afraid! Take My hand. Allow Me to fill your house with My Love. Permit Me to restore your house to Goodness.

My Blood washes you clean and makes you acceptable to the Father, if you but desire it! How long will you turn from Me! Embrace the world and you embrace death. Your very life is at stake. You consider not that you are but dust. You gamble that time is on your side. You are walking a dangerous path. All the while you add to your suffering and to the demise of many. The enemy gives you moments of pleasure, false peace and security. You while away time on these, but when you try to rest at night, you sense an emptiness. Perhaps there is more than this? I say to you, Come. Follow Me. I am in your house already. Awaken. Let Me teach you to live as I intended for you to live. All that I have is yours. I alone can fill the void. One by

one I call you each by name. My temples, let Me restore you to love! Your Jesus

158. **7-24-96** My home, 3PM, Rosary with Father
Mary on the Pope, the War Over Souls, Intercession with St. Joseph, Graces Reserved for Priests

"Our Lady on Praying for the Pope."

Father offered the beginning of the Rosary for the Pope. When he mentioned his name, I immediately saw a set of scales held in the balance by Pope John Paul.

Then Our Lady said:

Dear children,
You do not comprehend all that is held in balance by this Pope (John Paul II). Please pray for him always. He bears the heaviest of crosses. The vicar of Jesus on earth today is the object of much love. But also, there is much hatred of him. Above all, he is targeted by Satan. My maternal heart of love surrounds him so as to sustain the delicate balance that is affected through this living saint today. The Mystical Body is called to pray for him. He is a victim for many. You are blessed by his continuous fiat to the Divine Will. He is gift for you. Receive him into your heart.

"Our Lady on the War over Souls."

Next, I saw a thick rope with a knot in the center. It was being pulled back and forth. I understood it represented a tug-of-war. I saw light on one side and darkness on the other.

Our Lady said:

There is a war over souls. Satan knows his allotted time is passing and quickly. The devils are in a frenzy. Their goal is the demise of as many souls as possible. Their reason is to steal what belongs to God. God's response is the granting of grace upon grace for your souls.

Your response should be to turn from all evil, decide for God, drink of His grace, especially in the Sacraments. Pray. Live to love. Put God in the center of your heart. Love one another. You are a family. Fight the battle against evil. Be willing to fight for souls caught in the snares of the enemy. Free them from his nets by your life of obedience to God's Will. By means of your consecration to my Immaculate Heart, you become partners in my maternal intercession to save souls who would otherwise perish. Gather in my heart, little ones, my army, and we will work together to combat the destruction that the enemy causes in every corner of the earth. Look around you. He attacks families in the home and workplace; all of society, every nation.

You are living at the dawn of a new springtime. Winter proceeds now that springtime can come. In the winter, much dies so that in spring there is new life. It may appear that Good is dormant in this winter of man. But Good is abundant though hidden in many ways. This will be revealed in due season. God's work is all good, beauty, and light. With God, it often happens, that goodness and beauty remain hidden for Him until the appointed time comes. Then all are made to marvel at His wondrous ways. Persevere in this winter of man. Battle evil with God's Love. Love is the power that is always victorious. Peace.

"St. Joseph and Mother Mary Interceded."

I saw a certain soul driving the nail into the hand of Jesus to fasten Him to the wooden cross. I could see most vividly, as this soul drew the hammer back and then with great strength, forced its weight upon the nail to drive it through Jesus' hand, attaching it to the wood. Jesus was being crucified again. Standing near by this scene was St. Joseph and Mother Mary. They watched this soul closely. It seemed like a long time passed, with many tears shed by St. Joseph and Mary. Then, suddenly, Mary, almost in desperation, grabbed this soul's arm as he readied to strike again. She put a halt to his hammering. Immediately, St. Joseph grabbed the hammer out of his hand.

Then I heard St. Joseph and Mary say: "It will stop that suddenly! We intercede. We weep with you."

Then Mother Mary revealed to me the proper order of our sorrow. *Weep first because God is offended, then because this soul is in grave danger. Then you may weep for yourself.*

"Our Lady: Special Graces reserved for Priests."

There was a break in Father's prayer of the Rosary. He seemed unable to continue. I asked Our Lady, "What is happening?" Our Lady said: *I am exposing my Immaculate Heart to his soul. I have drawn back the veil to expose my heart. My Spouse, the Holy Spirit, is pouring grace into his soul, powerful grace! I am directing the virtues of my heart into him. He is receiving much grace. Love is overcoming him. Love is free to do so because this priest desires it.*

These are special graces reserved for my priests. Priests require these graces of love from my maternal heart. Graces come from God, flow through my maternal heart and are delivered by the power of the Holy Spirit. The Father willed the Holy Spirit to be my spouse. He wills the order of all grace to flow from the Holy Spirit through my Heart. He is unifying, creative Love. Union magnifies all Good. Union strengthens and protects. God can do anything. But rarely does He work in the singular. Love begets relationship. God works most powerfully in and through union of two or more. My priest is united to my Immaculate Heart. He is receiving abundant graces of love to strengthen him. Blessed is your union of the spirit. Peace. I love you. Your Mother

159. **8-2-96** Prayer Group
Mary: Faithfulness Pleases Me Most.

Dear children,
This is preparation so that when the world is purified and other souls need help, you will be prepared and able to help many in the hour of great need. Your purification is taking place now. This is preparation for vital work in the Church. Already you have begun to work by the power of your prayer, intercession, and suffering for the good of the Mystical Body.

Call on St. Michael. Call on the saints. They are at your disposal. Often talk to them. Make them a part of your prayer life bringing them into your daily life. They are your family. They will help you to ward off the enemy attacks. You are learning very much and quickly. You are a joy to my heart, a true consolation! What pleases me the most is your faithfulness!

When you fall, get up quickly. Be faithful to prayer. Turn to one another because in a group there is power, tremendous power and safety that is necessary against the enemy attacks. You can count on being his target. He sees that you are chosen. He is furious at your faithfulness, at your resolve to persevere! This night I thank you for continuing to be my army of little souls, my spiritual warriors. You are learning to battle effectively and you will continue to learn for your own good, for the good of many souls.

The purification will intensify in the world over the next several years. It is necessary for the darkness to be eradicated. It is through cenacles like yours that darkness will be dispersed. Many will be saved because of your light. I promise that the fruit of your labor will be revealed to you. You will rejoice!

Little ones continue to pray for the peace and salvation of the world. If you could see the sin of the world, if you could see the offenses against the Most Holy Trinity, you would understand that your crosses are so small, but God does so much through them! You would be pleased to offer reparation for the sin of the world, to alleviate the wounds that daily pierce the Sacred Heart of Jesus. Your love serves to alleviate the lack of love in the world.

Mankind is in a very grave state of being at this time. One purification after another will befall mankind. Take courage. God is with you! I am with you and St. Michael is with you. Call on us! You have been given many angels to help you in this time of battle. Fight the enemy like a true army and win souls for God. You have been brought into a very spiritual existence. Live the spiritual reality. Persevere to stay in the Spirit of God. Do not let the world draw you away from Him causing you to lose your peace. Elevate yourselves above the ways of the world by the power of the Holy Spirit in you. You have been drawn out of the world to do this work. You are suffering very much. All are carrying a cross. Know that your families will be the first to receive the fruit of your prayer, sacrifice, and love.

You are living at a very critical time in history. You were chosen from the beginning of all ages to live in this age of purification. You are empowered by God to endure the difficulties of this time of transition from darkness to the light.

All of creation, the face of the earth, shall be transfigured. Give thanks to God for having chosen and empowered you. Few, very few, give thanks to God these days. God so loves and blesses a grateful heart. And grace too comes to those who give thanks to God. Please continue to pray. The world is in great turmoil and prayer is necessary for peace. I love you, my little ones. Pray with me. Your Mother

Note: Mary's disposition was extremely gentle, very serious with a confident calm and quiet joy. Words cannot express the love that she has for us. She is a patient teacher. She came to free us from the enemy's attack tonight. There were long pauses throughout the message because she simply enjoyed being in our midst and showering us with love. During these times of silence, she would look lovingly at each one of us, study our hearts and bless us according to our needs, imparting virtues of courage and endurance.

160. **8-5-96** The Feast of the Dedication of
    St. Mary Major Basilica, Rome
Jesus on Mary's Fidelity

Beloved ones,

On this day of remembrance of the dedication of St. Mary Major, in honor of My Holy Mother, it is fitting that I speak to you of fidelity. In Mary, you have the highest example of human fidelity. Let Mary, our Mother, be your model of faithfulness to the Divine Will of the Father.

I learned obedience by what I had to suffer for the salvation of the world. And I knew the consolation and support of My Most Holy Mother. You need her help. Your vision must be elevated to Wisdom that comes from the Holy Spirit and Mary is the one who can help you to expand your vision and elevate it to the heavens. Her Immaculate Heart will carry you to Me.

She will bring you to the depths of My Heart and the heights of holiness.

The Holy Spirit empowered her maternal fiat, the "yes" that changed the course of history, bringing My human heart into your midst so that all could be saved from eternal death. She, the spouse of the Holy Spirit, will help you to give your fiat of faithfulness and teach you how to surrender to love.

My creation, become like Mary, holy, pure, and faithful. Your infidelity is piercing My Sacred Heart. Your waywardness wounds Me. Become like My Mother who loves and serves faithfully. All will be most swiftly united on earth if you take hold of her hand and allow her to bring to fruition the restoration that is to come through her Immaculate Heart.

The Church has always counted on Mary, turned to Mary and honored Mary as the model of true fidelity. Behold My Mother and yours. Take her into your hearts and make her a part of your families. She will bless you in every way. You will know Me more fully through her maternal heart, the heart that nurtured My Own. Allow her to be your mother. I love you.
Your Jesus

161. **8-6-96** Feast of the Transfiguration. After Holy Communion
Jesus: Listen! You will be Transfigured.

My children,

I revealed My Glory on Mount Tabor to prepare My apostles Peter, James, and John for the scandal of the cross. The Father confirmed My identity, "This is My Beloved Son, with whom I am well-pleased; listen to Him." This was to teach and strengthen their faith in Me.

The Holy Spirit is doing the same for you today. My creation, you are being prepared for many scandals which will come to the Church and the world. You are being taught, strengthened and guided by the spirit of prophecy in these trying times. You are being prepared for the purification of My creation, which will bring about a transfiguration of the world.

Blessed are the eyes and ears and hearts that are open to see and hear and receive what the Holy Spirit is saying in these times. Blessed too are the hands and feet of those who prepare the way for Me. Your labor of love will bring a great reward.

I, your Lord and Savior, remind you, "Listen!" Receive My Holy Spirit so that all will be well with you. Become a victim of My Divine Love. Intercede for souls who are lost. Become victim lambs and many will be rescued through your offering.

The sin of the world is incomprehensible. The consequences of sin bring suffering into all lives. Sin offends Me and hurts you and ripples out to hurt other souls. Because you have not yet understood that you are One Body in Me, you think that your sin is personal, affecting only yourself. But sin affects the entire Mystical Body like a cancer. One sick organ of the human body affects and compromises the entire body. The healthy parts of the body must compensate for the unhealthy ones. The sins of mankind are mutilating My Mystical Body.

I have raised up many victim lambs to compensate for the diseased portions of the Body. These intercessors for the world are saving souls from eternal death.

When the justice of the Father is set upon the world, it is an act of Mercy and Love because it will cut out the cancer of sin, purify the body and make it whole. You will be transfigured into a healthy Body (of Christ) of holiness and goodness. Let the spirit of prayer prepare you for restoration. Peace. I am your Lord, Jesus. I love you.

162. **8-12-96** In Church
Run to the Silence of My Heart

After Holy Communion, Jesus said: **My little one, peace. In these days when you find yourself tried in the fire, assailed by temptations and in dryness that permeates your life; when turmoil surrounds the circumstances of your life and you are dying repeatedly; when the pain makes you numb; hide yourself in the deep recesses of My Sacred Heart of Love and rest in Me.**

Run to the silence of My Heart! Listen to the soothing rhythm of My Love for you. Receive My Peace. Learn to walk in the mysterious and sublime silence of My Love with full confidence that you are in My Heart, the Heart of the Redeemer. Take the most precious gift of all, My Heart.

Grace has drawn you to the Source of Love. To have My Life in you, you must be emptied of yourself. What is dying in you is lowly. I will raise up life that is sublime.

My little one, you suffer more because of impatience, the desire for perfection in your duties, and a pattern of control. Be patient with yourself, accept your imperfection and give up control. Put yourself aside.

You are being transfigured into My image. I want you to become holy for Me. You are a sacrificial lamb, saving souls through the suffering and little offering of yourself.

Please do not think that you are alone for even one moment. Not one single tear or sigh of pain escapes Me. You are always in My Presence. Nothing is hidden from Me. Hide yourself in My tender Heart and I will do the rest. I am purifying you. I drew you out of the world to draw you to Myself. You are My lowly one who has won My Heart forever. Thank you for your sacrifice. Peace. I love you. Your Jesus

163. **8-21-96** St. Ignatius Church, 2:30PM on the Feast of St. Pius.
The Earth Wrapped in Her Mantle

In the Blessed Sacrament Chapel of Mary, following Mass, Father and I prayed the Glorious Mysteries of the Rosary together.

During the Resurrection Decade, I saw the globe of the world. Then Our Lady, together with myriads of angelic spirits who accompanied and helped her, draped her maternal mantle all around the globe of the earth. Now it was completely wrapped in her mantle, hidden within. Because the earth was shrouded in this manner, there appeared to be darkness. In reality, a great light was present, but it was hidden and secret for awhile and very protected by Mother Mary and the angels.

Something was happening in secret and silence. It was as if the earth was placed within the spiritual womb of Our Lady. This was leading to a birthing process.

Then the scene changed to the Resurrection. I could see the tomb where Jesus was buried. Inside, it was dark but within the hidden and silent chamber, a beautiful mystery rested until the day of Resurrection when Jesus arose and appeared in His glorified body. Our Lady said: *Focus on the Light that cannot be extinguished; the Triumphant One reigns, even in apparent darkness. Pray and be patient.*

164. 8-23-96 Prayer Group
Love is Not Selfish: Sacrifice!

My dearly beloved children,
Bless you and thank you for gathering to pray according to the Divine Will of the Most Holy Trinity. Praise and thank our Triune God who has blessed you. Many graces have come through the prayer of the Rosary. Persevere in your journey and be faithful to prayer so that you bring many souls to the Sacred Heart of Jesus.

I share with you the longing of my maternal heart that all would come to know, love, and serve God. There are so many hearts hardened from lack of love. Many concentrate on the care of the body, while few concentrate on the care of the heart. Few understand the true reality of sacrificial love. True love sacrifices! That is why Jesus has asked you to lay down your life for others. Selfish love is not true love because love is not selfish. Selfish love causes so much suffering in families, and in the world. It is divisive. Sacrificial love unifies. Faithfulness is waning and people are abandoning one another for the sake of selfish infidelity.

You who have been called into the ministry of intercession must present to the world the true meaning of love. You are called to be the victim lambs upon the altar now. In silence and hiddenness, you are the offering in the image of the perfect Lamb of God. Do you find yourselves becoming targets of persecution, temptation, and rejection? All that Jesus underwent for the salvation of the world you will undergo now. His sacrifice brought forth life, so will yours.

Prepare beloved children. Prepare the way for many! People will come to seek your intercession. All of the followers of Jesus will be persecuted in the days ahead! There is a storm brewing. The enemy plots greater attacks against souls who are attempting to follow Jesus' way.

You are my children of Hope. God has asked you to work for His Kingdom. Only the power of sacrificial love will enable you to do the Father's Will. You will assist the Mystical Body of Christ and minister to the wounds. Know the promises given through My Son. Open His Word and claim His promises. They will sustain you and increase your faith, hope, and joy. Be aware and awake always! Persevere! Pray! Above all, love as Jesus has taught you to love. Through the cross, you shall draw many souls to Jesus. I love you, bless you, and thank you. Your Mother

165. **8-25-96** My Home, 3PM
From the Cross, Inside the Sacred Heart

I was reading a book when a grace came over me. I was suddenly placed on the cross with Jesus at the moment of His crucifixion. Our union was such that I could no longer perceive where I left off and He began. Deepest silence enveloped me. Everything was so still! Somehow, I could perceive every soul that ever was, is, or will be created by God, from the beginning to the end of time. It was as if all souls were present at Calvary. Suddenly, my heart was infused with love for every one of them.

In this grace it seemed my heart would burst from this deeper realization of God's Love for all souls. It seemed that Jesus gave His Own Heart to me revealing His Sacred Heart as an infinite ocean of love that carries every soul within it. I understood as never before, that every soul is inside His Sacred Heart. Every soul draws from His Infinite Love whether they are aware or not. I understood His Heart embraces all creation, all time, and all space, in an unconditional, sacrificial love that loves without distinction. He loves eternally, even those who hate Him.

I understood that His Heart can only bring great good out of all the darkness in the world. Every soul is granted grace, mercy, and opportunity to awaken to the Love that holds us in existence. We are in His Heart! It is our home, whether we realize it or not. This Sacred Heart of Love surrounds us, believer or unbeliever, whether we perceive or fail to perceive.

For weeks, I was tempted to a sense of futility, and made aware of more evil manifesting in attacks against families. Jesus pushes out this sense of futility and fills my heart with hope by giving me His Own Heart.

First, He puts me on the cross with Him so that I understand that Love sacrifices itself for others. By placing me on the cross, my vantage point becomes so elevated, that I can see as never before. I see that all souls exist for Him as one family; that in His Heart, He gathers all of creation to present us to His Father in heaven. The Heart of Jesus is our gathering place. But Mary's Immaculate Heart is the quickest means of arriving in Jesus' Heart.

Prayer: "My God, if I were to contemplate all the days of my life, the greatness, the riches contained in the abyss of Your Heart of Love, I would know only a portion of the mystery of Your Divine Love for creatures. Permit me to explore Your Heart forever. Resting in it, I find my hope and joy and confidence that all will be well with the world because You hold us in Your Love. You have conquered the world through the cross! Thank you, My God, for teaching "nothingness" about the wisdom of the cross, and the truth of Divine Love. What a glorious mystery! Though it is folly to the world, it is wisdom to those who know You. Keep me hidden in Your Holy Heart. Jesus, allow me to live for You, for souls. Bless me, My Jesus, and permit nothingness to glorify You. Amen."

166. **8-28-96** Feast of St. Augustine in doctor's waiting room
How Little You Understand of Suffering

Reading a secular magazine, I heard Jesus say, **My little one, please write.**

My beloved creation,
It grieves My Heart to observe how little you understand of suffering. Suffering is touching your lives, and throughout

the world it increases daily. Suffering in and of itself is an evil that touches humanity, and is permitted because of original sin. Yet through Grace, suffering is transformed into good.

First, let it be known that much of the current suffering you endure is precisely because you have turned from My commandment to love. For I have said, love God with all your heart, your soul, your mind, your strength. Love one another as yourself. If you fail to make love Himself the center of your existence, then you become the center of your existence, living a life that is not in balance. This brings forth suffering. It is the interior sufferings of the heart that manifest themselves in many various exterior sufferings.

For example, today the demise of the family is causing untold pain for many souls. Often men or women make a decision to pursue life outside of the family, satisfying their selfish and worldly desires at the cost of a family that becomes divided. Then there is untold suffering for many. It begins a chain reaction of pain. Only the greatest love and sacrifice can heal those deep wounds of rejection and division.

Let it be known that I, your God, have not ordained such suffering for you, but rather I permit you to walk in the freedom of your own will, never ceasing to offer you the grace to live My law of love. My law of love preserves unity and forsakes self for the good of others. Your very sins are perpetuating great suffering in the world. Sin always causes suffering. Suffering is a consequence of sin. You cannot escape the consequence of your decisions and actions.

In this age, many fail to even acknowledge sin. Therefore, all the more rampant and serious are the consequences of the sin of the world. All the more suffering exists today because of such blatant and rampant sin. One human heart that is out of balance touches another human heart and perpetuates that which is within them, so that the entire world becomes out of balance, one man at a time, because one affects the whole. Does not an infection in one part of the human body affect the entire body with fever? Indeed, this is the case in the world today. My creation, you are diseased due to selfish sinfulness!

Let it be known, My beloved creation, that I, your Savior, your Redeemer, enter into all your suffering, your disease, and with the help of My grace, pure gift of My Love for you, I turn your suffering into merit after merit, bringing great good out of it. Indeed, the more you continue to walk in the darkness of sin the greater your suffering, but in My endless Mercy, I pour more grace upon earth so that *never* is there more evil than Good!

You cannot perceive this truth if you do not have Me, your Lord and Savior, in the center of your existence, because evil darkens your ability to see the Truth, perpetuating the lie that Good is waning. Only in the Holy Spirit, in My good grace, can you see and know the Truth that I, who am all powerful and all good, shall prevail. Remember, My little ones, the enemy wants you to despair, to feel abandoned, to be deceived again and again so that you continue to lose hope, to despair in your suffering, and finally to come to the point of not believing in God at all!

Your suffering is in vain only if it is not offered up or endured in the spirit of faith, hope, and charity. If you wrap love around each and every one of your sufferings, you gain for yourself and the world, more grace, more merit, and indeed, you are perpetuating the Kingdom of God on earth. I who created you, I who took on your humanity, embracing your very lowliness, know all too well the pain that exists in your heart, your body, in your world. And still, I unite Myself to your pain and suffering today. Indeed, I suffer with you, but not in vain, not for the sake of death, but for the sake of Life - only Life - Life that is eternal, unlike you can even imagine.

Therefore, My little ones, do not be fooled by the suffering that exists in the world. Nor should you accept the lie that suffering is punishment from God, or that it is useless! Without My good grace that would be the case, but I, who am all Love and all Mercy, permit suffering to touch the world in order to bring great good out of it.

Those who accept My grace have the wisdom that comes from Wisdom Himself to know that often it is in and through your human suffering, often at moments of your greatest pain, that My grace can reach deepest into your heart and cause your very soul to draw closer to Me, your Lord and Savior. This awakening, these moments of conversion are worth far more than any suffering that leads to it.

Therefore, My little ones, be hopeful and confident in the security of My Divine Love. Your suffering will end in triumph when My grace leads you to a place that exists without evil or pain, only Love Eternal.

To those little ones who wrap love around every pain and suffering, who refuse to sin and try wholeheartedly to live My law of love, to you I say, you are the remedy for the world! Your sacrifice draws healing grace for the world, because you are in Me and I am in you as offering for all.

I so love you, My creation! Repent of your sin and cease to follow your selfish ways, so that the entire body can begin to heal in My great grace. Your suffering shall not be in vain! Be at peace. Abhor sin, that your suffering may be lessened. My goodness shall be made manifest in the world if you but turn from sin and walk in Love. Your Jesus

167. 8-30-96 Prayer Group
Dedicate Yourselves to Prayer, Penance, Silence, and Solitude

My beloved children,

Peace! Tonight, I remind you to dedicate yourselves to prayer, penance, silence, and solitude. Permit the Holy Spirit to be your personal teacher. He can do this only in the peaceful silence of your heart in prayer. If your heart is not peaceful and quiet, you will miss His teachings and inspirations, which often come in a whisper.

You must come apart from the world each day to be alone with God. Strive to be in communion with Him always. You are learning so much. Each is growing in the gifts of the Holy Spirit. You are blooming, my dearly beloved, to my delight and to the glory of our Heavenly Father. By means of the cross, each of you are beautified because the cross of suffering brings forth great purity of soul making you beautiful in the eyes of God.

Have a grateful heart rejoicing in God who has taken each one of you by the hand to lead you to the higher road of union with His

Sacred Heart of Love. Because you have the Heart of Jesus for your own, you experience all that His Heart is made to experience including the rejection and ridicule of the world. His Heart continues to love even as He bleeds for the continued salvation of the world. Though you find yourselves bleeding with Him, you must continue to love. Only love can save souls and transfigure the earth into the new and glorious Reign of Jesus.

Your suffering will bear fruit. You are meriting many graces for souls. Thank you for your faithfulness. Please persevere. Stand in the center of the four pillars of contemplative prayer. They will be a strong protection providing many graces for you. Always and everywhere, contemplate the deep mystery of God's Love for you so that you can be transfigured into another Jesus for all the world. What is pondered in your heart will form you. Therefore, behold good and holy things, things of God, so that your formation continues to give God glory. You are very little and this pleases Him. He gives everything to the littlest ones. I bless you and love you very much. Your Mother

168. **8-31-96** My home.
Padre Pio Says: Take Courage and Fight the Enemy.

While I was awaiting a ride to Mass, I glanced at a picture of Padre Pio on the wall. Suddenly, a great peace came over me and I heard these words.

"Dear child, abandon yourself into the arms of the One you love (Jesus) and do not worry about things on earth because all things begin and end in Him! Were not the heavens and the earth created by Him?

"Worry cannot change anything except to cause your soul to look away from Him who is your peace. Oh, that I could reveal to your little soul the glorious merit of your suffering! Oh, that you could love the Sweet Guest of your soul enough to endure all things very patiently and in the supernatural peace that has God as its source!

"God permits you to be tried in the fire because He wants your love to be strengthened for Him. The wretched enemy targets you because you belong to God and that makes you the object of his foul hatred. Oh, how the wretched snake and enemy of all souls plots and toils to take you from the present course which is in God. That wretched snake; that foul beast targets God's closest little ones that he may make a mockery of God's choices. But he does not stop at mockery. He seeks to annihilate souls to carry them off to eternal death.

"Take courage, dear child! God protects like a mother and a father. But he strengthens his little children by letting them fight a few battles. This exercises the virtues and keeps you a fit soldier. Fit you must be! For you are in the King's army and fight for the Eternal Kingdom!

"Therefore, little soldier, secure your armor and continue to defend that little territory in you which belongs to the King, your soul! Do you not realize you are God's little soldier sent out to save souls from the snares of the hunter who devours his prey and spits them out in the eternal dungeon of hell?

"Take courage again! And again, little soldier! Do not be downcast! Do not worry but take the utmost care to live in the peace that Jesus Christ gives to you freely. Nothing will cause that wretched serpent to flee faster than seeing you in a peace that is constant and impenetrable.

"Oh, what little faith God's little soldier has! But, thanks be to God, you are growing through your present trials! And, thanks be to Almighty God, you are afforded every protection from various saints and holy angels including the great Archangel Michael, so that you are made to battle only a portion of the war waged against your soul.

"It seems to me that the Heavenly Court itself is protecting and defending your little soul! I will pray for you. I will assist you to be strengthened that you may desire to wage courageous battle against the wretched thief of souls. Pray with me. Pray that you will grow in zeal for souls and love for our Thrice Holy God.

"I see that the sword of Divine Love has pierced your little heart. And you are left to walk wounded all of your allotted days. Only God will suffice for you! Merit grace for the world and gain souls for God while it is possible for you. Your earthly exile is but a blink of an eye!

"I rejoice and thank Almighty God for the crucifixion I see you undergoing now. Your persecutor does you a holy service. How? He provides the opportunity for you to co-redeem! He provides the cross that purifies your soul. He is the instrument of your death that is necessary to attain true life in God.

"Believe me, little one, the war in him and over him is beyond your comprehension. Therefore, be merciful and strive to suffer silently and lovingly so that you may co-redeem his tormented soul. Be forgetful of yourself because the King Himself upholds and defends you. Therefore, why worry? Is it not better to trust that He will do it? I urge you on and I bless you affectionately in the name of Our Thrice Holy God. I am Padre Pio."

169. **9-3-96**
St. Joseph Guides Me about Family

I knelt before the statue of St. Joseph in the church and he began to guide me in some personal family matters. With all due respect and because of the serious nature of his advice, I said, "Dear St. Joseph, how can I be sure that this is you, really you?"

I heard: "Dear child, you can know the Community of Saints only through the darkness of faith. You cannot know me as you know those walking on earth because you are communing with my spirit for I am already in the Presence of God. We, who are in the Presence of God, continue to assist souls on earth. It is our goal to assist you to reach the same home that we have reached so that you also may live face to face with our Triune God!

You are aided and loved by the saints because we exist in God's Divine Love and that love is coming to you in incomprehensible ways. Believe dear little one. Though faith is dark, God's Love is Light. I am a small part of that Light which will illumine the way for you if you walk in faith.

Continue to hope and believe. I am overseeing your family. Remember, dear child, you must become like a little child, very little. It will please God and make your journey easier for you. I bless you. I pray for you and your family. I love you. I am (St.) Joseph. Peace."

Note: Prior to kneeling down before the statue, I had a headache and was filled with confusion and discouragement. When I left this prayer time with him, the headache was gone and I was filled with peace and hope again. This is the good fruit of prayer!

170. **9-6-96** Prayer Group
Mary: Courage and Hope: No Fear.

My little ones,

The personal purification that you are undergoing is a part of the purification of these times. Suffering increases because sin continues to increase. The enemy continues to target mankind with every type of deception and oppression in these final days of his roaming the earth freely.

Tonight I grant you the grace to have courage in the face of such darkness. Courage is necessary and is a great gift from the Holy Spirit. The courage granted to you is to be imparted to all whom you meet daily. Too many of my children are afraid. You must be children of courage, strength and hope. Your courage, strength and hope will be contagious. You will lead many to give up fear because of your example.

Be strengthened for the journey. Do not be discouraged by the crosses you are carrying now. Carry these crosses in humility and obedience, which draws much grace for you, your families, and the world.

My children, you have entered the time of the climax of evil. But you are in the very protected shelter of my Immaculate Heart. Together we battle against the enemy to gather souls back to God. Stay close together in my maternal heart so that my Spouse, the Holy Spirit, can guide you through these most difficult times.

The more childlike you become, the easier your journey will be because a child's heart listens and obeys which brings peace. You cannot have peace unless you humbly follow the inspirations of the Holy Spirit without doubt, hesitation, or counting the cost.

If you feel many burdens in your heart through these days of purification, it is because I have given you my maternal heart. I carry the burden of all my children in my heart. And I carry the blows that are dealt to my Son, Jesus, in these days of apostasy from the Church, deviation from the Truth, disobedience and rebellion. It adds to our pain that this is coming from those who claim to know, love, and serve Him while serving themselves and leading others astray.

You are interceding for much more than you can comprehend. But you need not understand. It is necessary that you listen and obey like a child, then, you will have Wisdom from on High. God is with you. Be at peace and pray for the salvation of the world. I love you. Your Mother

171. **9-10-96** Rosary with spiritual director, my home
The Suffering Church

At the decade of the Scourging at the Pillar, I saw the Church being scourged. The deepest cuts were inflicted upon her from within. Then, I saw various monasteries and missions. I understood these would be places of refuge for many in the future. Somehow they are under a "special protection."

At the Third Sorrowful Mystery, the Crowning of Thorns, Father prayed about how the crown of thorns was pushed down upon the head of Jesus, piercing Him. I saw immediately the crown of thorns being pushed down upon the Church, the Roman Catholic Church. But then I saw a church that was in the United States. It was painted red, white, and blue on the outside. There was a crown of thorns around it. It was being pierced all over.

Jesus spoke: **Pray fervently, My little ones. Pray for My Mystical Body. She is wearing the crown of thorns, and it is being pushed upon her, causing her to be pierced. She has begun to bleed already, especially in the areas of the liturgy and the priesthood.** I saw the following, very rapidly.

First, I saw cardinals, bishops, and priests, together with some women religious, upon the altar of this American church with legal pads. They were re-writing the liturgy.

Second, I saw a priest being squeezed to death by a crown of thorns pressing and piercing him tighter and tighter. It seemed the "pressure" put upon him was squeezing the very life out of him.

There were women waiting to put on his priestly garments.

Thirdly, I saw a person holding and manipulating a puppet on a string. The puppet on a string was an unknown pope. Most definitely it was not Pope John Paul but another man unknown to me. The person manipulating the strings of the puppet wore a hat labeled "Freemason." I remained in prayer and silence.

At the Fourth Sorrowful Mystery, the Carrying of the Cross, I saw an image of Jesus carrying the cross to Calvary. Then Jesus transfigured into a group of people bonded together to carry the cross.

Jesus said: **These are My little ones, My remnant, prepared by the Holy Spirit and the Virgin Mary, to preserve the Faith, the true deposit of Faith, in these times of rebellion, disobedience and apostasy. These are My chosen ones, My littlest and holy ones, who will be empowered by the Holy Spirit so that nothing shall prevail against them. There will be persecution, ridicule, mockery, and suffering, but together they shall persevere under the power of the Holy Spirit, who is in them and with them.**

Note, dear child, each of these wears a Rosary around their neck to signify they are part of the army of little souls who exist in the maternal Heart of Mary, who came down from heaven to prepare them for these critical times, this noble work. Each of these is open to her maternal graces, this being absolutely necessary for this little army, because it is the Woman Clothed in the Sun and crowned with twelve stars that will crush the head of the serpent, who has entered My Holy House to trample the Truth, to confuse My people and lead them out into the darkness to perish forever. Her foot will crush the head of the serpent who leads this rebellion, and her heart shall release this little army into My Sanctuary, to make of it a Holy House of Prayer once again! And these little ones who carried My Cross in these days of tribulation shall hand over a glorified Church to a holy generation, who will live in peace doing the Father's Will on earth.

Blessed are you, My little ones, who are now coming into the battle for which you have been so diligently prepared. By suffering and persevering in your spiritual journey, you have become prayer warriors under the power of the Holy Spirit. I bless you continually with My Love and My Peace. Your Jesus

172. **9-17-96** My home
Birth, Suffering, and Transformation: Individual and Ecclesial

The Birth: The Nativity

While resting because of the onset of a migraine headache, I began to enter a state of prayer and was seemingly taken to the scene of the Nativity in Bethlehem. It seemed I was in the cave of the Nativity with St. Joseph and Mother Mary. Jesus was there already. Jesus directed my attention to the sky to point out the brilliant Star of Bethlehem. It seemed He wanted me to truly observe and ponder it. I gazed upon the star for a long time. Its brilliance was indescribable, lighting up that Holy Night. The night received its radiance, and beauty seemed to touch wherever its light fell. Its purpose? To direct attention to the Word made Flesh, Salvation for the World, God's unspeakable, incomprehensible Love made manifest.

Then Jesus directed my attention to the Wise Men coming toward the cave of His Birth. The Radiant Star directed their path. They saw, they recognized, they went forth. I seemed to be lost in the beauty of that Silent and Holy Night.

After a while, I wondered what Jesus was teaching me. There were no words, but He continued to point to the star. Then some understanding entered my soul. The brilliant light in the sky, showing the way to Jesus, is a representation of the brilliant Light of the Holy Spirit. This Light shall increase and shine for all the earth to point the way *back* to Jesus. And wise men will see it, recognize it and go forth in it. The Nativity represented the birthing of a new era, the era of peace, the Kingdom of the Divine Will, and the birth of the glorified Church. Then it ended. All this happened very quickly.

The Suffering: The Crown of Thorns

I rested for a while, then I began to feel pressure all around my head on the outside and the inside. Inside, it felt as if my brain was swelling and causing tremendous pressure against my skull. I could feel every blood vessel inside my head throbbing, pulsating with pain. I tried to be perfectly still, because movement increased the pain. I began to feel pressure all around my head, on the outside as well. At certain points around my head I was being pierced with sharp thorns that penetrated deeply. Especially in my forehead, I felt as if it was swelling from the violence of the piercing.

Very suddenly, it seemed I was taken to the scene of Jesus' Crowning of Thorns. I had a most profound union, a oneness with Jesus that I cannot describe in words. I felt the purple robe drape around me, its weight adding to my pain. I already had the crown of thorns on, but someone kept pushing it down upon my head, causing excruciating bursts of pain that penetrated my entire being. I could hardly see for all the blood that was dripping into my eyes. I felt the blood fall down my face and neck. Then I was ushered out to the waiting crowd. I stood there, silent, hands tied together, crossed over one another and head bent downward. And I heard the words, "Ecce Homo." I heard them yell, "King of the Jews." They mocked me. They ridiculed me. They spat upon me. And I stood there silently, writhing in pain unspeakable. It seemed my head would literally burst from the pain of the crown of thorns. I was weak physically, very weak. The very sound of the crowd penetrated my being. Their laughter and hatred resounded in my heart. It seemed they were loud enough to be heard all over the heavens and the earth.

And in that moment of suffering, I felt my heart swell with an immense love for them, love so deep, that I willed to endure everything for the salvation of all. Love seemed to increase to cover all the hatred. This lasted perhaps a half-hour. Nothing that I write comes close to describing the experience.

I came to understand that I would witness mockery and ridicule of the Body of Christ, His faithful remnant in the days to come. I cannot find words to describe the pain of experiencing mockery and ridicule for something that I believe and love deeply. The very core of my being felt as if it was torn apart in understanding the pain of the mockery of Jesus, the King of Kings. And I understood that all His disciples would know this in the days to come. We must beg the Holy Spirit to come and fill us with His Love. Love alone can empower us for the days ahead!

Transformation in the Father's Gaze.

After the above ended I rested. Then, suddenly, it seemed that God the Father picked me up in His almighty Hand and brought me under His loving gaze. He observed His little one for some time. I felt so loved and protected under His Paternal Gaze. Then, I was permitted to view myself from His Eyes. I saw myself in His hand and I took on the form of a diamond, a diamond in the rough. But something was happening to me under His Loving Gaze. I was being transformed into a beautiful and clear-cut diamond that radiated light, His Light. The more He and I looked at one another, the greater clarity there was in the jewel that was me, His very little one.

I prayed: "Oh, my Heavenly Father, how I love You! In all Your Majesty, Sovereignty and Glory, You deign to gaze upon the dust that I am, and Your Paternal Love transforms me into Your very own beauty. How unspeakable Your ways! You are my heart's desire, my beginning and end, my Eternity! Never cease to hold me in Your Almighty Hand. Please keep me under Your fatherly gaze of Love and Mercy! Amen and Amen."

173. **9-23-96** Tabernacle following 8:30 AM Mass
The Marriage of the Holy Spirit and the Blessed Virgin Mary

Yesterday, during the Rosary with Father, at the Fifth Glorious Mystery, he prayed for the proclamation of the Fifth Marian Dogma, Mary, Co-Redemptrix, Mediatrix and Advocate. He received a very strong "confirmation in the Spirit" for this intention. Immediately, I began to see the most magnificent Dove of the Holy Spirit, Uncreated Being of Divine Love. I observed this for awhile, lost in His beauty, majesty, and radiance.

Then I noticed on the breast area of the Dove, an image of the Blessed Virgin Mary. The concentrated, powerful rays of light issued forth through Our Lady. I had not noticed her immediately, because she was practically lost in the brilliant light rays of the Holy Spirit. I saw that while the Dove of the Holy Spirit Himself was a Being of brilliant Light, His rays of grace issued forth toward earth through the being of Our Blessed Mother.

I heard the voice that I have come to know as the Father's Voice and He said: **Observe the Marriage of the Holy Spirit and the Blessed Virgin Mary.**

The Holy Spirit, infinite uncreated Being, is espoused to the Blessed Virgin Mary, a sinless created being, because the salvation of all created beings was made manifest in her virginal womb; the Word became Flesh in and through her by the power of the Holy Spirit.

The graces of the Most Holy Trinity are poured through her immaculate being. Her "fiat" continues for the salvation, ongoing redemption of all created beings until the end of time. The Blessed Virgin Mary was immaculately conceived, perpetual virgin, Mother of God, assumed into heaven, and she is, always and today, Mother of All, suffering, pleading, nurturing.

The marriage of the Holy Spirit and the Blessed Virgin Mary is the most important factor in her mediation of all Divine Grace, as well as her co-redemption, and advocacy. Let it be known that because of the Espousal of the Holy Spirit to the Blessed Virgin Mary, the crowning of Mary as Co-Redemptrix, Mediatrix and Advocate is also a crowning for the Holy Spirit. It is His Action, His Presence permeating her entire being that makes the Fifth Marian Dogma the truth about Mary. When this truth is proclaimed for all the world, the Holy Spirit Himself will embrace the entire globe of the earth in His infinite grace and love.

Many unimaginable graces shall be granted to the Church, albeit the remnant, in and through this proclamation. Let the voice of the people cry out for it! Let the hand of the Vicar of Christ bring it about! My Paternal blessing. Your Father

I observed the image again. But now I observed the wings of The Holy Spirit embrace the entire globe of the earth and press it into the area of His Breast, where Our Lady was. The wings of the Holy Spirit brought the world back to Himself (Love) through the Immaculate Heart of Mother Mary, His Spouse. Mary paled in size compared to the immensity of the Dove of the Holy Spirit, yet, through her "littleness," God chooses to pour all grace to bring the world back to the bosom of the Father.

Today, Jesus brought this image and message to mind again. He said, **Two very important truths are revealed in the image and message. First, the very humility of God is held before you. This is a stumbling block for many.**

Second, the very dignity of Mary, representing the dignity of all created beings, is held before you. This also is a stumbling block for many. All created beings are called to union with God by grace. The one sinless created being (Mary) is the Immaculate Vessel of Grace for all creatures. The perfect design of the Most Holy Trinity presents to all souls, the one immaculate created being, as model, as Mother of all ages and all nations, to be a sign of the Infinite Love and Mercy of God, creating a family of mankind.

Can you not recognize your own dignity before God in granting the espousal of the Blessed Virgin Mary to the Holy Spirit, Third Person of the Holy Trinity? Through the one immaculate created being, through the Immaculate Heart, you are called into union with God because the Savior of the world came into the world through her immaculate being, espoused to the Holy Spirit. Be filled with hope and gratitude. My peace. Your Jesus

174. **9-25-96** Tabernacle. In prayer after Holy Mass,
I saw these images.
Jesus' Image in the Pope, the Church, and as the Good Shepherd

First, I saw an image of Pope John Paul, on what appeared to be, an operating table. He appeared to be asleep. On top of him was perched a black beast on all fours. Underneath and all around him were black evil spirits. They were trying to tempt and crush him. And I heard the voice of Jesus.

Pray fervently, My lamb, for My Vicar on earth, My Peter of today. He undergoes yet another assault on his being, which is weak from fighting the good fight. His spirit, however, is stronger than ever. For it is My Holy Spirit within him that gives him My own strength and courage to continue to lead the Church in the battle against all evil.

The black beast is the evil of *Freemasonry, seeking to blaspheme My Holy Name. He targets My chosen Vicar to crush

---

* Footnote by Spiritual Director. — Freemasonry's virulent attacks on the Catholic Church in Europe for the past four hundred years are well-documented.

him, because he is My Presence upholding My Name, keeping it holy for all the world. Pray unceasingly for My Vicar and for the Church. It is urgent. The salvation of many is at stake.

Then I saw an image of the Good Shepherd, bathed in brilliant light, dressed in all white, carrying a little white lamb in His one arm and a staff in the other.

Jesus said: **My lamb and My victim,**

I am carrying you in My arms, pressing you close to My Heart. Listen. Hear. The beating of this Heart of Mine should resound in your being. It is the sound of My unending, unconditional, merciful Love for you, victim for many, and for all souls. You receive Me, as few souls are willing. Therefore, you have My Heart for your own. I alone am your refuge. Walk with Me, the Good Shepherd. Together, let us tend to the flock. Let us pasture the flock, as many are hungry and thirsty. Let us give them to eat of the bread of love. Let us give them to drink of the living water, mixed with the blood of salvation and life. The green pastures shall be restored in My Church. The living water and the blood of salvation shall be in the Seven Sacraments received by the flock purified. My lamb, I love you.

Then I saw an image of a beautiful tabernacle, alive with brilliant light and opened wide to reveal the True Presence of Jesus within. I heard Jesus say: **In the tabernacle, there is a treasury of My riches. I await you. I await all.**

*The ongoing messages will be published
in Volume III as soon as possible.*

About Family

By Grace, the Messenger

Some people have asked the publisher regarding my family and how they feel about these graces. I wish that I could share that we are all practicing our faith and praying together. But that is not the case. We are undergoing purification and attack like so many families today. The hand of God is working in various ways in each of our lives.

Prior to my conversion, we were doing our own thing and were in control, content and comfortable. We probably appeared to be an ideal American family. My conversion was a change and change causes a reaction and each person had their own reaction. There is love and support, belief and a deep respect for these graces, but there is not understanding. For the most part, they remain a mystery for all of us.

Following my conversion and God's grace touching our family in this profound way, the cross entered immediately. For a while, all of us seemed to move along together in the conversion, but then there was upheaval. I believe it was grace that made us uncomfortable to cause us to change individually and as a family. We began to suffer individually and as a family. This was a real mystery to me and caused me to pray very much for understanding and acceptance of it. I think it must be this way not because God wills suffering, but because God wills salvation. That is what the change, upheaval and suffering is about. It is the result of resistance to give up control and die to self. This is a difficult thing to do and human nature recoils from it. No one seems to want to do it yet.

My sons are teenagers and typically question everything about life in general. They are delightful and challenging: bright and tender-hearted with natural openness. And together with my husband, they are busy doing "their own thing." It seems that we are going in different directions most of the time. Often I am met with an attitude of "that's great if it works for you." Other times there is openness to the spiritual life, prayer, and beautiful discussions (sometimes heated) about our Faith. Then I can see in them, awe and wonder. In their own right, they have received some very special graces.

One day in church, in prayer before a beautiful and realistic crucifix, I was praying about my family and said to Jesus, "My Lord, You are a God of order. Something must be wrong with my family. It is not in order. Are You really present? What is happening?" Jesus said to me: **Look up again at the crucifix. Observe Me, the Lord of the universe, nailed to the wood of the cross. Where is the order? It appears disordered does it not? The cross of salvation is a sign of contradiction! The upheaval in your family is a cross meant to purify it. My Presence will bring order out of disorder. Do not worry, but trust and persevere in faith.**

In another lesson about my family on 12-16-95 (message #73 "Angelic Conversation"), Jesus sent angels to assist me to give up control of my family. I was asked to surrender my husband and children to God and to allow His grace to work in them to bring about their salvation. It would be done according to His Divine plan, not mine; in His time, not mine.

This is one of the burdens of my heart that I carry at every moment. But I have come to surrender more each day. I love my husband and sons more deeply than words can express and love allows freedom and focuses on the higher good. I have learned that I cannot control anything. God is in control. I must trust in His Infinite Wisdom and Goodness through the many joys and the sufferings of the family life. We are living out the hours of our own painful immolation and fighting against the terrible attacks of the enemy who seeks to destroy families.

As wife and mother, I am called to serve, sacrifice, and prayerfully intercede for the salvation of my family. Often I have found consolation in the lives of the saints such as St. Monica and St. Augustine. But only through grace and prayer have I found patience, endurance, and perseverance in faith, hope, and love. I remind myself constantly of the Scripture in 1Corinthian13:7-8, "Love bears all things, believes all things, hopes all things, endures all things. Love never fails."

I trust in Our Triune God, Mother Mary, and St. Joseph to whom I have entrusted my husband and children. And I am so thankful for the gift of my family, including my parents and brothers, all of whom help me to carry the cross. Every day at Mass I put them in the chalice and cover them in the Blood of the Lamb, which brings us safely home to our Eternal Father. Even though the purifying action of Divine Love is a suffering for us now, the cross is not the end. It is the means to new life, the resurrection. Praise be to God!

March 25, 1998,
The Feast of the Annunciation of the Lord.

I Will Restore You

Recommended Books

1. *The Navarre Bible*, all volumes, Faculty of Theology of the University of Navarre. (Four Courts Press, 1991).
2. *The Catechism of the Catholic Church*. (United States Catholic Conference, Washington, D.C., 1994).
3. *The Imitation of Christ*, Thomas á Kempis. (Confraternity of the Precious Blood, Brooklyn, New York., 1954).
4. *Abandonment to Divine Providence*, The Rev. J.P. DeCaussade, S.J. (B. Herder Book Company, St. Louis, Mo., 1921) (This is a classic edition, newer editions available through other publishers).
5. *The Silence of Mary*, Ignacia Larranga, O.F.M., Cap. (St. Paul Books and Media, 1991).
6. *In Conversation with God*, Volumes 1-7, Francis Fernandez. (Scepter, New York, 1988).
7. *Divine Mercy In My Soul*, The Diary of Sister M. Faustina Kowalska. (Marian Press, Stockbridge, Mass. 01263, 1987).
8. *The Complete Spiritual Doctrine of St. Therese of Lisieux*, Rev. Francois Jamart, O.C.D. (Alba House, New York, 1961).
9. *The Collected Works of St. John of The Cross*, Translated by Kieran Kavanaugh, O.C.D. (ICS Publications, Institute of Carmelite Studies, Washington, D.C., 1991).
10. *The Collected Works of St. Teresa of Avila*, Volumes 1-3, Translated by Kieran Kavanaugh, O.C.D. (ICS Publications, Institute of Carmelite Studies, Washington, D.C., 1985).
11. *The Great Unknown, The Holy Ghost and His Gifts*, by Antonio Royo Marin, O.P. (Western Hemisphere Cultural Society, New York, 1991).
12. *The Fire Within*, by Thomas Dubay, S.M. (Ignatius Press, San Francisco, 1989).

13. *Spiritual Warfare, Attack Against the Woman*, by Rev. George W. Kosicki, C.S.B. (Faith Publishing Company, Milford, Ohio, 1990).
14. *The Spiritual Combat and a Treatise on Peace of Soul*, by Dom Lorenzo Scupoli. (Tan Publishers, Inc., Rockford, Illinois, 1990).
15. *Intercession, Moving Mountains by Living Eucharistically*, by Rev. George W. Kosicki, C.S.G. (Faith Publishing Company, Milford, Ohio, 1996).
16. *Thoughts and Sayings of Saint Margaret Mary*, compiled by the Sisters of the Visitation of Paray-le-Monial. (Tan Books and Publishers, Inc., Rockford, Illinois, 1986).
17. *Preparation for Total Consecration according to St. Louis Marie de Montfort*. (Montfort Publications, Bay Shore, New York, 1992).
18. *The Dogma and the Triumph*, Mark I. Miravalle, S.T.D. (Queenship Publishing Company, Santa Barbara, California, 1998).